The EVERYTHING® Home-Based Business Book
Second Edition

Dear Reader,

When we began our careers, we didn't expect to end up running our own home-based businesses—but for more than a decade now, that's exactly what we've been doing. We've experienced firsthand the freedom and exhilaration that come from charting an independent course through the world of business, and we love it.

Along the way, we've been inspired by and learned from so many other people who are running their own businesses—in many ways, this book is a chance for us to share much of that inspiration. If you're running your own business, or thinking of starting one, it's our hope that you'll find encouragement, practical advice, and perhaps even validation for your dreams within this book.

The best advice that we ever received in business was simply to believe in yourself—that it makes all things possible. Now we're turning that advice over to you, along with a piece that comes direct from us: have fun—because it makes it all worthwhile!

Yvonne Jeffery Sherri Linsenbach

The EVERYTHING® Series

Editorial

Publishing Director	Gary M. Krebs
Director of Product Development	Paula Munier
Associate Managing Editor	Laura M. Daly
Associate Copy Chief	Brett Palana-Shanahan
Acquisitions Editor	Gina Chaimanis
Development Editor	Jessica LaPointe
Associate Production Editor	Casey Ebert

Production

Director of Manufacturing	Susan Beale
Associate Director of Production	Michelle Roy Kelly
Cover Design	Paul Beatrice Matt LeBlanc Erick DaCosta
Design and Layout	Colleen Cunningham Sorae Lee Jennifer Oliveira
Series Cover Artist	Barry Littmann

THE EVERYTHING® HOME-BASED BUSINESS BOOK

SECOND EDITION

Start and run your own money-making venture

Yvonne Jeffery and Sherri Linsenbach

Adams Media
Avon, Massachusetts

To Nanny, and in memoriam to Grandpa, for everything
—Yvonne Jeffery

Published by Adams Media, an F+W Publications Company
57 Littlefield Street, Avon, MA 02322 U.S.A.

ISBN-13: 978-0-7394-7087-9
ISBN-10: 0-7394-7087-6

Printed in the United States of America.

Contents

Acknowledgments

One of the great joys in life is the company of family and friends.

This book owes much to Mum and Dad, as always, for their constant love, support, and encouragement, and to my sister, Lorraine Weyermann, for inspiring and supporting me in so many ways. To the Jefferys in England, much love and gratitude for being such an amazing part of my life.

I'd also like to thank Susan Yuzwak for a friendship full of strength, laughter, and understanding. To my long-time friends and fellow writers—Judith Mulholland, Katharine Fletcher, Laura Byrne Paquet, and Linda Poitevin—a girl couldn't ask for better. I'm constantly in awe of all that you accomplish in your lives.

I'm also grateful to my agent, Barb Doyen, for a wonderful working relationship, and to the staff at Adams Media who have guided this book into existence with such care.

—Yvonne Jeffery

Top Ten Reasons to Run Your Own Home-Based Business

1. When you own a home-based business, you have the opportunity to make your living—fully or in part—by doing something that you love.
2. You may put in long hours as a home-based business owner, but the rewards for those hours will be yours—not someone else's.
3. From your clients and customers to your advisors and suppliers, you're able to choose the people with whom you work when you run a business.
4. The ability to set the hours for your own business can create a quality of life for you and your family that's difficult to achieve when you work for someone else.
5. From managing sales to producing your goods or services, running a business can help you achieve a level of self-fulfillment and self-confidence beyond that of a regular workplace.
6. The opportunity to make your own decisions can be exhilarating—you may have to live with a few mistakes along the way, but you'll learn from them . . . and your successful decisions will be your own.
7. No one limits your potential when you own your own business: If you have a dream, you can pursue it as far as you want.
8. Whether you're coming up with new products or new marketing campaigns, owning a business gives you the freedom to be as creative and innovative as you want.
9. A home-based business allows you to put your efforts toward whatever causes you believe are important.
10. As an entrepreneur—and that's exactly what a home-based business owner is—you'll be setting a great example for your kids about believing in, and achieving, your personal goals.

Introduction

▶ HOME-BASED BUSINESSES aren't a new idea at all. Working where you live and living where you work was the natural order of things until the 1700s, when machinery began to make factories and mass production possible. From that point forward, people increasingly left their homes to go to work each day.

Well, technology has now come full circle. You can now link up electronically with almost anywhere in the world directly from your home—and home can be a boat, the beach, or a mountain log cabin. No longer do you have to rely on local markets for your goods and services: The Internet gives you access to one of the most efficient and effective marketing channels ever created.

The opportunities for many home-based businesses have never been stronger, so it's not a surprise that more and more people are dreaming of creating their own business—and their own future. Surely, they think, working for yourself holds the answers: setting your own hours, working with people you respect, making your own decisions, and keeping all the after-tax profits. What a great deal!

Of course, the dreams don't usually include the fact that you'll be working just as hard, if not harder, than you already do at someone else's workplace, and that if something goes wrong, you have sole responsibility for it. But if that doesn't bother you—if you welcome the challenge—then owning your own home-based business could well be the answer for you.

This book is intended to guide you through the entire process of business ownership at home, from launch to closing. Along the way, it guides you through the process of figuring out whether a home-based business is actually the right answer for you. If the answer is "yes," then this book guides you through deciding what type of business to focus on, how to structure it, how to fund it, and when to launch it. You'll learn why a business plan is essential, and how to create one—and why it's a living document rather than a one-time effort.

Start-up might be the most adrenaline-packed phase, but it's only the beginning of the process—so this book also touches on every topic that you'll need to consider for your day-to-day operations. Staying on track financially gets plenty of attention, from the insurance coverage that you'll need to consider to the nuts and bolts of bookkeeping and tax filing.

But this book also goes a step further, letting you know how to reach your most important audience—your customers. It provides insight into the world of marketing and advertising, and even gives you a primer on networking and publicity. And once you've reached your customers, the book gives you tips and techniques for retaining them even while you're expanding your customer base.

You'll also find information on dealing with difficult people—from employees to customers—and difficult days. Let's face it: You're going to experience times when nothing seems to be going the way you'd envisioned it. Or maybe the isolation and independence suddenly seems too much of a good thing. You'll learn how to break through those tough times, how to keep yourself motivated, and even how to beat that all-star time waster, procrastination.

In short, *The Everything® Home-Based Business Book* provides you with the tools and the information that you need to create, launch, operate, and even sell or close your home-based business. By doing so, it makes a fundamental assumption: that with knowledge, commitment, hard work, and perhaps a little outside help, you can own your own successful business . . . that it's possible to turn ideas into livelihoods, and dreams into reality. The assumption is sound. Just look at the successful businesses around you that started at someone's kitchen table or in their garage. Then take another look at your dreams, with this book in hand.

chapter 1

Is a Home-Based Business Right for You?

If you're thinking that a home-based business is your ticket to financial success, quality family time, reduced stress, and greater satisfaction—you could be right. But before you start dreaming about how green the grass would be on the working-from-home side of the fence, carefully consider the challenges and changes that it's going to bring to your lifestyle. Then, if you—and your family—are ready for them, go for it.

Joining the Club

Home-based business owners are in excellent company. Across the United States and Canada, almost 15 million people describe themselves as being self-employed—as, essentially, the owners of their own businesses. And while self-employment figures tend to rise and fall depending on the economy (an economic downturn is often followed by a period of rising self-employment due to layoffs), the bottom line is that working from home is now seen as a viable and acceptable alternative to working for someone else.

FACT

The U.S. Census Bureau reports that 12.2 million Americans are self-employed—which works out to almost 10 percent of the labor force. The percentage is slightly higher in Canada, where the figure is 2.4 million self-employed, or about 14 percent of the labor force. The split between men and women home-based business owners in both countries is the same: two thirds of the self-employed are men; one-third are women.

Aside from economic factors, technology has played one of the biggest roles in boosting self-employment and home-based business figures. Thanks to the ever-improving capabilities of cell phones, e-mail, and the Internet, you can do business with people all over the world from virtually anywhere in the world. Setting up a home-based office has never looked so good.

Home-Based Business Advantages

If you feel trapped in an office cubicle or behind a store counter, it's easy to imagine the advantages of running your own business out of your own home: no more putting up with someone else's rules and regulations, no more commuting, and no more office politics. The same goes if you're already at home, perhaps with young children: Adding a few hours in the office to your day sounds like a quick way to earn extra money for the family. Well, you're right. While self-employment isn't for everyone, it does come with definite advantages.

Make Your Own Decisions

This is one of the biggest reasons that people cite for wanting to run their own businesses: the freedom to succeed or fail on their own merits. Too often, skilled and creative people feel stifled or limited in larger corporate environments: Stacks of rules and regulations tend to be designed for the company's good, not necessarily the individual's, and while some workplaces are a joy to arrive at every morning, many aren't. For those seeking greater control over their work life, self-employment can be the answer.

ESSENTIAL

> The most important factor to consider when you're thinking about a home-based business is whether or not it's going to make you happy—and specifically, whether it will make you happier than you are now. If self-employment also means self-fulfillment, you're on the right track.

Set Your Own Hours

When you work for yourself, you decide when you're going to arrive at work, how long you're going to spend there, what you're going to do in those hours, and who you're going to do it for. You don't have to justify your schedule to your boss, or ask for time off to take your child to the dentist. If you're faced with a sunny Wednesday afternoon or a mental block, you can go for a walk in the fresh air. Better yet, whether you're an early bird or a night owl, you can often adjust your hours so that you tackle the most difficult tasks when you're naturally at your best.

Choose the People You Work With

Playing office politics and dealing with difficult people can take a huge chunk of otherwise productive work time. It's emotionally draining to boot, reducing both motivation and efficiency. When you work for yourself, you choose your clients, your colleagues, and your employees. If one of these doesn't work out, you have the power to sever the relationship (tactfully and within any contractual or legal obligations, of course).

Improve Your Quality of Life

Long hours at work, combined with frustrating commutes, can create significant daily stresses. Work from home, and your commute is probably no longer than a set of stairs and a hallway (think of the money you'll save on gas). Your environment is likely to be more comfortable as well—no more dealing with crowded subway trains, harsh office lighting, or poor indoor air quality. The result is much-reduced stress, and a better quality of life.

Fulfill Your Potential

Despite pay equity legislation and an increasing understanding of human resources in the corporate world, many people still don't feel that they're achieving all that they could be in that environment. Maybe there's no room for advancement, no one's getting a pay raise this year, or the boss isn't as convinced of your skills as you are. Or maybe you're tired of feeling uncertain about the potential for layoffs when the economy hits a rough patch. Running your own business lets you aim as high as you want—and puts you in charge of achieving it.

Home-Based Business Disadvantages

It all sounds so good, doesn't it? But home-based businesses come with some unique disadvantages, too. If you're unprepared, they could not only give you a nasty shock, but could even bring down the business.

Financial Risk

No one leaves a paid job to start a home-based business intending to fail—but failure does happen. You need to ask yourself if you can handle the worst-case financial situation. Imagine a bad debt scenario, where your major client declares bankruptcy, and the check that you're expecting for work you've already done disappears. Can you handle the cash flow problem? If you can't, can you afford to lose the capital you've invested in the business? If the answer is still no, you need to think about a lower risk strategy.

ALERT!

It's estimated that up to 50 percent of small businesses will close within their first five years. The things that often trip them up? Insufficient financing, whether in the form of capital, credit, or sales; poor decision making on issues like managing inventory, accounts receivable and clients; and simply not realizing how tough business ownership can be.

Lack of Benefits

You also need to assess how much your current benefits plan at work (assuming that you have one) is worth to you. When you own your own business, many of those employer costs—health insurance, retirement plan contributions, paid vacation time, subsidized daycare, etc.—become yours. Can you handle those costs?

The Possibility of Burnout

You might think that your current boss expects a lot of overtime from you, but that will be nothing once you're facing half a dozen clients, all of whom want their project completed yesterday. Burnout is a very real possibility with those who are self-employed.

You become particularly vulnerable to burnout because most home-based business owners are wearing all kinds of hats at the same time. You're responsible for finding clients, selling them on the product or service, delivering what you've promised, billing them, collecting the check, and handling the accounting that comes with it. At various times, you'll be a computer technician, accountant, file clerk, debt chaser, and employee counselor. This isn't a problem, as long as you relish that kind of juggling act.

The Isolation Factor

If you're someone who needs people around you all the time in order to function most effectively, how will you handle being alone in the office all day, every day? Will client meetings, e-mail, and business association meetings fill the void for you, or will you find yourself inventing excuses to leave the office (thus putting yourself behind)?

Family Fallout

Even the most supportive of families can become frustrated if you're working so hard that you never leave the office, or if customer visits to the house begin to be intrusive. Similarly, if your spouse or children don't understand the boundaries of the home office, you may become frustrated when they seek you out even though you're trying to work.

Qualities of Successful Home-Based Businesspeople

There's nothing wrong with working for someone else. For the right person, at the right time, and for the right reasons, regular employment that comes with a regular paycheck might be the answer. Similarly, self employment might be the answer—for the right person, at the right time, and for the right reasons. So, how do you tell what's right for you?

Making the Grade

There are a number of qualities that you should possess—or at the very least, try to develop—in order to be as successful as possible in your home-based business. First, you need to be self-motivated and self-disciplined. The two go together, because there's no one around to tell you what to do next or even to criticize you for procrastinating on a big project. You need to be able to get yourself going every morning, embrace the day's tasks, and work until they're done.

You also need to be flexible, because during the course of the day, umpteen little brush fires will spring up to distract you from the main inferno. Some of these need to be addressed right away; others can be left until the major tasks are done. You need the judgment to figure out which is which. Looking at the bigger picture, you need the ability to change course completely when it's clear that something's not working.

It helps if you're organized, too, because it saves you time—and in a home-based business, time is always money. Being organized is closely related to successfully managing the juggling act that most home-based businesspeople perform every day: They're marketers, producers, accountants, and human resources professionals all at once. Throw in the extra roles of spouse and parent, and all those balls become progressively harder to keep in the air. Organization can make all the difference.

ESSENTIAL

If you're not sure whether you have the qualities that a home-based business needs, talk to someone who's already running one. Ask that person to be candid about where he or she came up with the qualities that are most important to success—because some can be learned as you go along.

A Quick Quiz

To help you gauge your natural suitability for running a business, take a look at the following statements, and rate your agreement with each of them on a scale of one to five, with one being the weakest agreement and five being the strongest agreement.

- Mistakes are good learning experiences.
- I like other people, but I'm happy to be by myself.
- Financial security is a goal, but I'm comfortable with risk.
- When I'm interested in a project, I work long hours to finish it.
- If I don't know something, I search out the answer.
- I like setting goals and accomplishing them.
- I like to solve problems—the more the better.
- I prefer to get my own way.
- I'd call myself a confident person.
- I have a clear idea of where I want to be in five or ten years.

How did you do? A score between 10 and 25 indicates that you might be happier keeping your day job or sticking to a hobby business. Boost the score to between 26 and 40, and you're a better bet for a home business. Look before you leap, but give yourself a chance. Between 41 and 50? Figure out what you want to do, pick the right time, and go for it!

Good Reasons to Start a Home-Based Business

It's easy to look at a home-based business for its potential to solve your current frustrations at work. But you need to be realistic: Will you truly be improving your situation or will you just be taking the problems with you to your home office? Home-based businesses that have the best chance for success start with a solid foundation and a positive motivation. The following reasons help to provide both.

You Have a Marketable Skill

Whether you're a great carpenter or a meticulous bookkeeper, you need to have a skill that will translate into a product or service that's in demand. You also need a reason for people to come to you for that skill: It may be enough if you believe that you can provide higher quality work than many of your competitors.

You Have a Good Idea in a Good Market

You don't need a new or even a brilliant idea—it just needs to match the needs of the market. For example, if three-quarters of the homes in your area have dogs, but there are no dog-walking services around, that's an idea that matches the market.

You're More Efficient

Again, your idea or skill doesn't need to be unique to you. But if you believe that you can deliver it more efficiently than the other people in the market, that gives you an edge when it comes to pricing, and therefore to competing.

You're Looking for a Lifestyle Change

If you are truly looking for an improved quality of life, and you're willing to take on the financial risks of a business, working from home could be for you. Just keep in mind that you may be working as hard, if not harder, for yourself than you would for someone else.

You're Determined to Be Successful

Your drive to succeed will provide the motivation to stick with it when things get tough or you face the obstacles that will inevitably crop up. Make sure that you have a clear idea of what you mean by "success," along with the will to make it happen.

You Believe in Your Own Abilities

It's natural to have doubts about your ability to handle an occasional task that you face, but you also need positive thinking to face those doubts and to tackle the task despite them. If you look forward to challenges and enjoy solving problems, a home-based business will give you plenty of opportunities to exercise those skills.

Bad Reasons to Start a Home-Based Business

Sometimes, self-employment can look appealing simply because you're so unhappy where you are. The solution may lie in addressing the reason behind your unhappiness. It might not be your job or your boss as much as finding yourself in an industry that doesn't fit your natural talents. Before you jump ship to a home-based business, look at your reasons. If they sound like the following, you might want to reconsider your strategy.

You Hate Your Boss

Almost everyone gets frustrated with the boss at some point. Try to take a step back from the situation: If you like your work, believe in the company you work for, and enjoy and respect your coworkers, then opening up your own business may not be the answer.

You Want to Get Rich

It's time for a reality check: Yes, sometimes, home-based businesses start small and grow big, and sometimes another company will come in and buy you out. But in the vast majority of cases, home-based businesses have the potential to earn a reasonable, but not millionaire-level income; getting rich quickly is not something you can rely on.

FACT

According to the U.S. Small Business Administration (SBA), only 3.5 percent of home-based businesses show gross receipts of more than $100,000 a year, and less than 1 percent have gross receipts of $500,000 or more. The vast majority—96 percent, in fact—report gross receipts of less than $50,000 a year, and 77 percent have gross receipts of less than $25,000 a year.

You Want to Cut Childcare Expenses

Dream on. Seriously. It's very, very difficult to combine taking care of children with running a successful full-time home-based business. Both children and businesses need your full attention; spending the day trying to satisfy both at the same time is a quick route to frustration. If you need to save on childcare, plan on working part-time hours or in shifts opposite your spouse.

You Have a Better Mousetrap

Leaving your day job because you have one idea for an invention is not the road to financial freedom. Sure, you have a better mousetrap—but what happens after everyone's bought it? Until you have a steady stream of products, it might be best to market that invention while you're still enjoying a steady paycheck.

You're Tired of Red Tape

You may reduce the bureaucracy with a home-based business, but you won't avoid it: There are still plenty of rules and regulations to follow. The biggest will be the tax issues that arrive courtesy of the Internal Revenue Service (IRS) or Canada Revenue Agency (CRA). Then there are local zoning regulations, professional standards, business licensing laws, and national legislation that deals with everything from employee relations to access for persons with disabilities.

ALERT!

Don't be tempted to try reducing red tape or taxes by going "underground"—accepting cash payments that can be hidden from the company's books, for example. Not only is it illegal to hide revenue this way, but it will void insurance coverage and leave you wide open for major liability suits if something goes wrong.

You Want More Leisure Time

A home-based business may give you more control over your time, but it won't necessarily give you more leisure time. In fact, self-employment often leads to serious burnout, because the office is always nearby, and there's always work that needs to be done.

chapter 2

Are You Right for a Home-Based Business?

For many people, home is a refuge from a very busy outside world, where four walls and a roof create a physical and emotional barrier from the pressures of work. For others, it's the center of family life, or perhaps a hub for entertaining friends and family—the place where neighbors are always dropping by, and weekends bring dinner parties and backyard barbecues. You need to carefully consider the changes that will result when you add a home-based business to the mix.

It's All in Your Attitude

A sense of determination and a drive to succeed are two factors often cited as the most important for home-based business success. It's absolutely true: Your potential really does lie in your attitude. If you approach the challenges of running a home-based business with a positive attitude, you'll find it easier to come up with solutions to your toughest problems, and to achieve your most ambitious goals. For your own good—and that of your family—however, there's another word you need to add to determination and drive: balance.

FACT

If you need a sense of separation between your personal life and your business life, a home-based business is going to present some unique challenges. Suddenly, the office is just a few steps away, and so is the phone. You might think you're your own boss, but in reality, each of your customers becomes a mini-boss.

If you're a tradesperson, such as a plumber or electrician, you'll likely be on call at all hours of the day or night. If you're marketing across the country, calls could be coming in when your customers are at work, several hours before or after you're in the office. Are you ready for this—and can you and your family adapt to the potential interruptions to the usual routine?

So—think about drive, determination, and balance. If your attitude includes all three, you'll be on the road to succeeding in your business, and more importantly, in life. Success in business is always better if it's a means to an end: greater self-fulfillment or a better family life, for example.

Hearth and Home

Since you're going to be working from home, there are few more important considerations than what your home looks like now, and how it will look once there's a home-based business in it. A kitchen table might be a place to start planning, but it's not going to be enough in the long term. You need to ensure that your home is a good fit for the business you're anticipating.

Location

If your business depends on customers coming to your home—such as an artist's studio—your home's location is key. Will your local regulations (see the section on Zoning, later on in this chapter) allow this in your neighborhood? Is your home centrally located and easy for customers to find? Is there adequate parking space?

Small business consultants often talk about the cost of a business location being equal to rent plus advertising. While locating your business in your home will save on rental costs, you need to factor in how much you'll need to spend on advertising in order to get people through your door. A $600-per-month rental location downtown with great walk-by or drive-by traffic may actually be cheaper than having to spend $1,200 a month on advertising your home-based location.

Available Space

Although many home-based businesses start with a desk in the corner of the master bedroom, this probably isn't a practical way to carry on. Most businesses need a dedicated space such as a den or spare bedroom. This not only gives you the space you need to work in, but also allows you to claim the business-use-of-home deduction on your income taxes.

ALERT!

Be security conscious. The computer equipment or business inventory associated with a home-based business can be a tempting target for thieves, who sometimes pose as customers in order to "case the joint." If possible, use a separate entrance for your business area, so that visitors can't see into private areas, and be sure to lock up business equipment and inventory.

If your business doesn't involve customers arriving at the door, then you don't need to worry about where it is in the house—as long as you feel comfortable working in the space, you'll be fine. Since you'll be spending a significant amount of time there, however, make sure it's conducive to work: natural light, electrical outlets for computers, and a door that can close are all important factors. Also consider safety: Many basements don't permit business use, because they don't have the necessary fire escape routes.

For businesses with lots of visitors, your space really needs to be right next to your home's main entrance: You don't want customers walking through your family's private space in order to get to your office. To create this space, consider converting a living room or a garage to an office, or using a walk-in basement area.

Available Storage

Will your home-based business require storage for inventory or parts? Even space for business records can be tough to find in the average home. Does your house provide enough space for your storage needs—and more important, is that space safe and protected? A basement that's vulnerable to moisture or to sewer back-ups is not appropriate, especially for key records such as accounting receipts.

QUESTION?

I don't have the space for storing records. What are my options?
Most communities have a variety of storage spaces that you can rent: everything from closets to garages to warehouses. You can also check telephone directories for record management firms: They often offer storage, and will even pick up your documents.

Phone Lines and Utilities

Your home also needs to have the infrastructure that your business will need. You may need an extra phone line or two to handle the business phone and fax lines, for example. Can your local phone company handle this, or would a cell phone work as a substitute for a landline if it's a problem?

Do you have high-speed Internet access in your area? This may be an issue if you're in a rural area or one in which demand for services is already high.

When it comes to utilities, ensure that your home's capacity matches your business's requirements. Can your home's wiring handle the extra electrical load for your computer set-up, for example? Will your business require extra water or heat or a conversion from an electric to a gas stove? If you're using an outbuilding rather than space within your home, does it have the utilities that you'll need? If not, do local building codes allow you to install them? How much will that cost?

Community Rules and Regulations

Of course, it's not enough to look only at your own home—you also need to consider your street, neighborhood, and community. Not all areas welcome home-based businesses, and some actually prohibit them. The latter is becoming rarer as self-employment grows in acceptance. Before you even think about a home-based business, you need to check your licensing and operating requirements. Launching a business that doesn't conform to these requirements is *not* an option.

FACT

Most community concerns over home-based businesses involve potential nuisance factors for neighbors: increased traffic, noise, unsightly equipment, and even environmental hazards. Be prepared to counter these with the advantages: home-based business owners can deter theft and vandalism simply by your being around when other people go off to work.

Zoning

Most communities are divided into a varying scale of uses, from residential to commercial and industrial. You need to know where your home falls on that scale and what your specific category allows you to do in your home: Zoning regulations often place limits on numbers of employees and signage, for example. Although that information is on file at your municipal or county office, you can increasingly find it on their Web sites, too. A quick Internet search or phone call may be enough to fill you in.

ESSENTIAL

> Don't forget to check home-based business rules with your co-op board and your condominium, community, or neighborhood association, as well. Some of these—particularly in planned developments such as mature living communities—will limit the business activities allowed in your home even more stringently than the local government does.

Even if your area isn't zoned to allow home-based businesses, you can request a variance, which would give you permission to proceed. A variance acknowledges that the rules don't always make sense in every situation, and that a low-impact home business (which has no noise, few or no in-person customers, and no environmental hazards) might be welcome despite the rules. The variance process can take extra time, and sometimes involves posting notices in local newspapers, so build that into your planning process.

Licenses

Even if your home-based business conforms to the zoning in your neighborhood, you may need a license to operate it. In some cases, this is as easy as applying for a permit to operate a home-based business: You'll probably just need to answer some brief questions about the planned business activities, and the number of employees or visitors who might be involved.

Some areas, however, require you to obtain a full license. This is especially true of self-employed building contractors, where you may need to prove liability, insurance, and workers' compensation coverage in order to be approved. Again, check with your local municipality or county office.

Advertising

Zoning regulations usually specify whether you can place a business sign outside your home (in many residential zones, you won't be allowed to), and how large the sign can be, where it can be placed, and whether it can be lighted. Make sure you know what's allowed, so that you can assess whether it meets your needs.

Some communities don't allow home-based businesses to advertise their street address in any way at all, even on a business card. You can get around that by renting a mailbox and using that as your business address—although keep in mind that courier companies will need a physical address for deliveries.

Parking

If your customers or employees will be coming to your home, you'll need to provide parking. Again, this is a zoning issue, which may require you to provide a minimum number of spaces or limit you to a maximum number. Remember that parking needs to be safe: well-lit, away from high-traffic areas, and with good visibility to protect both drivers and pedestrians.

Tax Issues

Income taxes are dealt with in Chapter 20, but the key issue for most people is that in order to claim a business-use-of-home deduction, the office space needs to be used exclusively for the business. There may be other consequences, too: In some cases, the business use of the space may trigger a tax liability when the home is sold—your accountant will be able to discuss these with you.

Your local municipality may also want its share of your profits, either in the form of property taxes (if your home office increases your home's value, your taxes may increase as well) or local business taxes. Do your research ahead of time to ensure that you're prepared for the expenses.

Family Matters

Unless you live alone, running a business out of your home will affect other household members. It's important to have their cooperation in order to make the business—and the family—run as successfully as possible. Your most important tool here is communication: As you research your home-based business plans, sit down with your spouse and your children and discuss those plans.

Communication

Obviously, your spouse is going to play a major role in your business success, whether he's involved in the day-to-day running of the business. You're going to need your spouse's support, whether it's providing a regular paycheck while you're getting started, or cheering you on when you hit a rough patch. Ideally, he'll welcome your initiative and your enthusiasm—in fact, your spouse might see that it's exactly the right solution for you.

ALERT!

A discussion about launching a home-based business can sometimes trigger or reveal other problem areas within a family relationship. If you need assistance to work these out, don't hesitate to seek local counseling services: Your current employer might even have a confidential employee assistance hotline that can help you work through the problem.

Some spouses will be less than enthusiastic, however, and some might be downright negative. Take the time to sit down, preferably in a neutral and pleasant space such as a restaurant, and talk honestly about why she feels this way. You need to listen to her concerns and also assess what she might not be saying out loud. Is she worried about finances or health insurance, for example? Does she wish she could leave her own job and start a home-based business? Is she concerned about the effects this might have on your family life?

Whether or not you agree with her concerns, at least agree that she has the right to voice them. Work together to come up with solutions that will keep the family unit operating smoothly. Be prepared to change your goals or your time frame for achieving them if you need to.

For your part, you need to be honest about the disruptions that a business in the home will create. You may need help answering phones or preparing customer orders, for example. Employees or customers coming to the house may mean more house cleaning and tidying. You may need peace and quiet during certain hours, especially if you'll be speaking on the phone to customers. Confidentiality might also be an issue: Family members need to know that they can't discuss your business outside the family unit.

Whatever the issues, be honest and up-front with your family. Discuss the home-based business with your kids in an age-appropriate manner. If you think it will help, involve your spouse and children in planning and running the business (make sure their roles and yours are very clear). Overall, make sure that they know what's happening and why.

Children

Some people start home-based businesses to take advantage of the down-time while children are napping or at school during the day. This can be a great way to ease into the business world and to balance the need to earn extra income with being available for your children. If you expect to replace your current regular paycheck with profits from a business, however, you'll need to give the business your full attention. Just as you would with a regular job, you need to find a childcare solution, whether it's a good daycare nearby or someone who comes into your home.

If your children are going to be at home when you're working, let them know what's expected of them and make sure that those expectations are reasonable for their age. They may need to find quiet activities, perhaps, or stay out of certain areas of the house while you're meeting with customers or use the home phone instead of your business phone. To be fair to them, children need to know all of this up-front.

FACT

If you don't have the funds for childcare, consider getting involved with a babysitting co-operative. Agree with a neighbor or with other local home-based businesses that you'll take turns to watch each other's children, giving you an opportunity to spend some quality time dealing with business issues.

Don't overlook the lessons that a home-based business can teach your children, however. People have been mixing trade and family life for centuries: Think about the traditional family farm. Kids can learn a lot about life from having a business right there in front of them—everything from trust and responsibility to work ethics and dealing with people. By getting your kids involved, they'll have a better appreciation for the time and effort you're spending on the business.

You might even find that your children are a source of great ideas and labor (and officially paying them to help can provide lessons on money management while giving you a tax deduction). And if they decide to launch their own businesses, from lemonade stands to landscape care, your children will have a great source of inspiration and advice: you!

Friends and Neighbors

Don't be surprised if you suddenly have more people dropping by the house or phoning to invite you out once they know that you're at home. Many of these people only hear the "home" part of what you're doing; they tend to ignore the "business." While you might appreciate the company every once in a while, you'll need to set some boundaries. Setting boundaries is especially important if you find people asking you to do things like watch their house, dog, or children. Sure, it's nice to be neighborly, but it's easy for one errand or favor to become many, and before long, you'll discover that you've accomplished very little that's work-related, despite being busy all day.

First, make sure that you answer your business phone in a professional, work-like way—that sends the message that you're at work. Let the home phone go to voice mail: You can always check the message to see if it's urgent; if it's not, you can deal with it at day's end. Tactfully but firmly, turn down invitations or requests that aren't work-related. If you're pressed for time, let the people know that you're working on a big project (you don't need to provide details), and simply can't get away from your desk right now. But remember: "No" is a full sentence, if it needs to be. Don't waste time by feeling that you need to justify your response.

If you find it challenging to turn people down, keep a list of your day's tasks in front of you when you answer the phone, and focus on them while you're talking. If it's more important to run your elderly neighbor to the doctor (and it may well be), then by all means, do so. But if you need to focus on your marketing strategy instead of the pooch next door, don't feel bad about saying no.

Assessing Your Financial Fitness

Since it can take months to bring a business to the point where it's earning a profit—or even breaking even—one of the most important factors to consider is money. You'll find tips on establishing start-up financing in Chapter 7; first, however, you need to figure out how much money you and your family need to live on. That will help you to set your business goals and financing requirements.

An honest evaluation of your own finances can do nothing but help you: You might find that you have funding sources, such as antique collections, that you didn't realize you had. Or, you might find that you're on shaky ground and that going without a steady paycheck could put you in earthquake territory. In the latter case, you don't necessarily have to give up your home-based business dream—but you might want to lengthen the time frame to give yourself some time to strengthen your foundation.

Family Finances

If you don't currently know how much money your family spends each month, and on what, you need to figure it out. The easiest way is to track all your spending in some kind of diary for a full month, separating it out into various expense categories, such as rent, car loan payments, and groceries. Include everything that you can think of, including children's allowances, and even payments such as vehicle registration that might come up only once a year (just divide the expense by twelve)—and then add it all up.

Now consider all your income sources, such as investment dividends, your pay, your spouse's pay, and pensions. What happens when you remove your paycheck from the equation? You need to make sure you account for this when deciding how much financing your business needs in its first few months and where that money's going to come from.

Risks

One of the biggest financial risks you face in starting a home-based business is bankruptcy, which—depending on your business structure and which state or province you live in—could take a large chunk of your family's personal assets, from vehicles to a portion of your family home. You need to be very clear on the level of financial risk that you're taking on.

ESSENTIAL

For help assessing your personal finances, especially if you need to reduce your debt, check out *www.debtonadiet.com*. It's based on the book of the same name and offers debt-reduction and money management tips, including how to check your credit report and your FICO (credit) score. If you're really in trouble, contact a nonprofit credit counseling agency.

One way to measure whether you're financially fit enough to take on a business is to look at your family's net worth. Total all of your assets (home, vehicles, furniture, savings accounts, retirement savings plans, investments, etc.) and compare this total to the total of all your liabilities (how much you owe on mortgages, vehicle loans, credit cards, etc.). If you owe more than you have in assets, you're in the red—you need to look at your own finances before you start managing those of a business.

Goals

Now that you know where you're starting from, assess where you want to go. Do you dream of a rich-and-famous lifestyle, or are your goals more modest—a comfortable living with reasonable provisions for future needs, such as kids' college educations and retirement? Maybe you've always wanted to retire early, or perhaps just need some extra income to add fun to the family agenda. Do you truly want a home-based business lifestyle, or do you see it as a springboard to something else? Answering these questions will help you to figure out what kind of income your home-based business needs to provide.

Lifestyle Changes

If money is an issue as you start your business (and it is for most people), look at your lifestyle. A regular salary can be a very comfortable concept, whether it's funding a large latte on the way to work or a new car every couple of years. To make launching a business more financially viable, examine where you could reduce your living expenses. This can be as complex as reducing your debt or as easy as renting a video instead of heading to the movie theater.

While you might feel pinched at first, thinking of this as "buying back your life" will make it easier—you're giving yourself the chance to be your own boss, and the satisfaction of building a business from the ground up. And you don't have to give up all treats; in fact, you shouldn't . . . that just leads to resentment and frustration. Consider scaling them down, instead (takeout instead of restaurant dining) or find treats that don't cost much (Shakespeare in the Park instead of the opera's opening night gala). Just make sure your family's involved in deciding which changes to make to ensure that you have their support.

Do You Need a Safety Net?

One last factor to think about is whether you need some kind of a safety net of benefits—the kind that regular employment often provides. If, for example, you have three kids who'll need braces over the next five years, take a look at how much a company dental plan will pay toward that expense and how much it's going to cost to replace it with a self-employment plan or no plan at all. The same goes if a member of your family needs extensive health care coverage. Sometimes, going it alone doesn't make financial sense.

Similarly, are you just a few years from retiring with a pension? Assess how much it's going to cost you to leave now (your company's human resources office can help you with this). It might be worth continuing your paid employment for a couple of years until retirement, so that you qualify for that pension—which will then make it financially easier to start your business.

chapter 3

Choosing the Business

The most successful home-based businesses start with a great idea. It might be a product or service that no one else is offering or a unique or otherwise competitive way to provide a product or service that plenty of people are offering. The key is to find an idea that's suited to both your skills and a home-based office—and, hopefully, an idea that makes your pulse beat just a bit quicker. Because if you're excited about the idea, there's every chance that your customers will be, too.

Inventory Your Skills and Knowledge

Your first step to developing a business idea that will work for you in both the short- and the long-term is to find something that you're good at doing, that you know a lot about, or that you'd be happy to learn about. You need to figure out where your skills and your knowledge lie—and you might need to think beyond your own perceptions. Try the following exercise to kick-start the process.

QUESTION?

What can I do if I don't have many skills or areas of knowledge?
People sometimes overlook their best attributes or even perceive these attributes as negative when they could be turned into something positive. Ask a trusted (and positive) friend to give you his perspective.

Put yourself into "brainstorming" mode. This means you're going to write down whatever comes into your mind, and you're not going to judge it—you're not even going to think about it at first. Then, ask yourself what you enjoy doing. This can be in any part of your life, whether it's an element of your current job (e.g., analyzing financial statements), a hobby (e.g., building dolls' houses), or a pastime (e.g., hiking). Fill pages of paper if you need to, but include everything that you can think of. These are the skills that you enjoy.

Stay in brainstorming mode, and ask yourself what you know about. Maybe you have detailed knowledge of the accounting rules for start-up businesses or maybe you can tell a car engine ping from a knock at ten paces. Think about the subjects that people come to you to ask questions about. Again, write everything down, without stopping to judge what you're writing.

Once you've finished brainstorming, take a look at your lists from a more analytical perspective. Your skills might reveal that you're highly organized, that you enjoy dealing with details, and that you love hosting Saturday-evening dinner parties. Maybe on the knowledge side, you've written down that people are constantly asking you for your recipes or for tips on how to create that great floral centerpiece. You might want to consider a home-based business that handles event planning, event set-up and decorating, or even catering.

ESSENTIAL

Although you can certainly brainstorm your way to your unique set of skills and knowledge, it can be illuminating to spend time with an expert. Check out career counseling services at your job or in your community: They'll use tools like the Myers-Briggs Type Indicator® to reveal your natural aptitudes and interests.

Keep in mind that whatever you choose for your business, it's important that you enjoy it. You're going to be spending a great deal of time doing it, and you'll need to be self-motivated and self-disciplined for much of that time to make the business a success. Starting with something that you're passionate about, or that you love doing, is a great way to get you on the right path.

Good Choices for Home-Based Businesses

Home businesses fall into three major categories. First, there's the service-oriented office in a home. You might be writing resumes or keeping accounting records for other businesses, but it's likely that walk-in customer traffic is minimal, especially since technology makes it increasingly easy to work by transferring computer files.

The second category is retail-oriented businesses, in which the product or service requires a customer visit. This might be a craft shop, hair salon, or daycare, for example. You'll need parking space for this business and an area either in the home or an outbuilding that's completely dedicated to the business.

The final category is contracting businesses such as plumbers, electricians, computer specialists, or landscapers. These businesspeople handle the business administration from home, but actually do the work off-site at the customer's home and business. It's very rare that a customer will visit the contractor at home, so the office might simply be a place to handle the bookkeeping and marketing functions of the business.

Service-Oriented Businesses

Many home-based office-type business owners meet with their clients at the client's office or perhaps over lunch or coffee at a restaurant, rather than having their clients come to their home. Therefore, you likely won't need to worry about issues such as parking and accessibility.

Business-to-Business Services

Many people create successful home-based operations by taking on the tasks that other business owners don't know how to do, don't have time for, or want to outsource rather than handle in-house. This can be everything from medical transcription to bookkeeping to taking care of employee payroll and benefits payments.

FACT

According to the SBA, some 60 percent of American home-based businesses are in service industries, such as bookkeeping, writing, or tax preparation. Another 16 percent are in construction; 14 percent are in retail trade, and the rest include a smattering of manufacturing, finance, transportation, communications, wholesale trade, and other industries.

Information Technology

Despite the bursting of the dot-com economic bubble, information technology remains a hot field for business in general and home-based business in particular. This area covers everything from software development to computer repair to network and Web site development and can often be marketed effectively to a range of both individuals and other businesses.

Consulting

If you can provide advice that other businesses or individuals will pay for, whether it's suggesting structural changes within an organization or putting together a marketing plan for a new product, then you could consider becoming a consultant in that field. A common offshoot of this is training: Once you've developed the initial training packages, you can often just tweak them to suit different clients or audiences. And since both consulting and training can easily take place at the client's site, or an off-site meeting space, you don't need a large office in your home.

Professional Services

Professionals in occupations such as legal and accounting services often work at home. As long as you're following the rules of your regulatory body (such as those governing trust account management or client confidentiality, for example), and have a space within your home that can be dedicated to meeting clients without fear of interruption, working at home can work well.

Retail

People have been "living over the store" for centuries, with a walk-in storefront on the ground floor and living quarters behind or above the store area. This is great for security, because it means you're close by, even when the store's not open. To accommodate the need for display and inventory storage space, this tends to work well in a larger building where you can seal off the store area from the living area or where you have an outbuilding that you can turn into a store.

Alternatively, you could set up your retail business to rely on direct mail, catalogs, or even trade shows or farmers' markets instead of physical floor space in your home. Retailers are increasingly setting up "virtual" storefronts on the Internet, either in addition to other methods of selling or as a complete replacement for them. And, of course, your store can be selling products that you make yourself or that you've purchased from other people.

Contracting

Since contractors (builders, renovators, and other tradespeople, for example) work almost exclusively at their client's site, they can often use a home-based business rather than increasing their overhead with a warehouse or display office. When they need to have clients make decisions about materials, the contractor often takes his clients directly to wholesale or retail building supply or décor stores—and he can stay in touch using a cell phone. Back at the home office, he needs some kind of administrative space—and it also helps to have a secure garage for vehicle, tool, and equipment storage.

Other Options for Home-Based Businesses

The home is often an excellent place for an artist to think and create. It can also be a convenient base from which to launch a business providing personal services to busy families and professionals. And don't forget about well-known products traditionally sold by home-based representatives, such as Tupperware.

Artists

A home-based business is a natural for an artist, whether you need a desk with a computer for writing or a room with good natural lighting for painting. The advantage for visual artists is that you can set up your own studio if you want, welcoming your customers into it either on a regular basis or for special "studio tour" events—but if you'd prefer to avoid this, you can. Simply sell your art through the Internet or through art or crafts galleries.

Personal Services

From housekeeping to dog walking to personal shopping, there's a huge array of services that today's busy families are willing to pay someone else to help them with. In fact, high-end concierge services that take care of all your errands—even your dry cleaning—have become options even for less-than-high-end homes. And, of course, traditional cosmetic and wellness services such as massage are still popular choices for home-based businesses, whether the service is provided at the client's home or at yours.

Brand-Name Marketing Organizations

Product lines such as Mary Kay and Avon have long offered people a chance to break into home-based businesses in a low-risk way and for a relatively small investment. They often provide coaching and sales tools and plenty of incentives to hit your sales goals. Just be sure that you're dealing with a reputable company, rather than a pyramid scheme that relies on people's initial investment in the business instead of focusing on ongoing sales.

Challenging Choices for Home-Based Businesses

Aside from certain illegal or dangerous practices that are controlled by many states and provinces—manufacturing fireworks, for example—there are few things that you can't do from home. You will, however, be limited by your local zoning regulations: Many municipalities refuse to allow home-based businesses that could create noise, traffic, or odor problems in the neighborhood. And there are some business choices that make it challenging to be successful, even when they're permitted.

Manufacturing

Anything that requires major manufacturing or chemical processes might be an issue. This is a factor of the limited space that many people have in their homes, and the environmental safeguards that are in place to protect communities against hazardous waste or inadvertent chemical leaks. If you have a rural property, however, where space and neighbors aren't issues, and you're able to comply with environmental and safety regulations, you may be able to get around these challenges.

ALERT!

As you research your business idea, you might find ads on the Internet or in newspapers that promise big bucks for people working at home. These claims are at least over-inflated and often completely misleading. As with most other things in life, exercise caution: If it sounds too good to be true, it probably is.

Food Services

Although many food companies might have begun over the kitchen stove at home, food preparation services can be challenging as well, unless you have a very well-equipped kitchen. Because it deals with so many health and safety issues, food preparation is highly regulated. You'll have to pass various inspections (both scheduled and surprise), and your appliances will need to be in great shape. If you're happy to follow the regulatory and licensing rules, you can still do well—but you need to be prepared.

Part-Time Versus Full-Time

Some home-based businesses function as a replacement for regular full-time paid employment: They go beyond covering all their own expenses to producing profits that support their owner's family, contribute to college and retirement savings, and do all of the things that a full salary and benefits package would normally do. Other business owners are happy with part-time businesses that are an offshoot of a well-loved hobby, perhaps, or simply add extra income to either paid employment or to retirement.

Hobby Businesses

These businesses often grow naturally out of something that you enjoy doing, whether it's knitting, woodworking, photography, or gardening. You might find that there's a growing demand for your products or services as people find out about your talents. At that point, you can decide to turn the hobby into a part- or full-time occupation.

FACT

If you expect to deduct your expenses when tax time comes around, both the IRS and the CRA emphasize that you must be in business with the intention of earning a profit, whether you're part- or full-time. These agencies will generally allow you two to three years of losses, but may disallow your deductions if there continues to be no sign of profit or progress.

The advantage is that you're already known for your work, and you likely own all the tools or equipment you need to do the job. Plus, you know you enjoy the work. Some people do find, however, that when they add profit pressures to a pleasant hobby, it takes away much of their enjoyment, becoming too much like work.

Retirement Businesses

Your motivation for operating a retirement business—which is often part time—could be financial need or simply your enthusiasm for an activity that keeps you active, alert, and engaged. It can also help you remain a part of the larger community, which many retirees say that they miss once they no longer head off to a job every day.

E ALERT!

If you want to operate a home-based business during retirement, be sure to check whether it will affect your government benefits. In the United States, if you're below the full retirement age of sixty-five (or sixty-seven for those born in 1938 or later), earning money over a specified amount could reduce some of your benefits. In Canada, it could reduce your benefits at any age.

Going into Partnership

A partnership combines the talents and resources of more than one person: Where one might fail, two might succeed. And with two or more people, the business benefits from more time, money, and expertise. Unfortunately, partnerships can also lead to conflicts.

You need to consider whether you're launching a home-based business because you prefer to work alone. If that's the case, then you might not be the best candidate for a partnership, especially if that partner is a friend or family member. All too often, when the partnership fails, the relationship does, too—the stress and the negative emotions can stay with you for a long time and cause all kinds of fallout within your family circle. On the other hand, if you enjoy working closely with other people, and you put a clear partnership agreement into place (see Chapter 8), a partnership can be a great choice. It allows you to reduce your individual risk and share the load of running the business.

Buying a Business

There are four good reasons to consider buying a business to operate out of your home: location, time, money, and competition or market share. If an ongoing business has an ideal location, can save you time or money, eliminate competition, or provide market share, it might be worth paying for. The basics are listed below, but for more information on buying a business, check out Chapter 6.

Buying an Independent Business

It's entirely possible that someone in your area already has a home-based business that does exactly what you want to do—or close enough to make it worthwhile. Think about it carefully: If they have a good reputation, they'll have an extensive customer base and a lot of goodwill. If they're looking to sell, stepping into their shoes might give you a great shortcut.

Other benefits may include an inventory that's ready to go, ongoing contracts for services or the equipment that's needed to provide the business's products or services. One thing to watch for, however, is whether you can transfer the business's location into your home or whether the business's current home is part of the deal. In the latter case, you—and your family—need to decide whether it's worth the move from your house.

Buying Into a Franchise

A franchise is a business structure in which the owner of the overall company relies on individual investors to open their own branches of the business. The use of the company name, the products or services provided, and the marketing activities are all fairly centrally controlled in order to protect the reputation of the company and its other franchisees. You often have to prove to the franchise company that you have the skills, knowledge, and financing to make a success out of your branch: It's not as easy as plunking down your money and opening up the store.

ESSENTIAL

If you are considering one of the work-at-home franchises offered by any number of companies across the country, have your own lawyer review all the contracts and paperwork—and be prepared to step away from the franchise agreement if your lawyer suggests that the terms are too stringent.

Once you're in, you should expect to receive a fair degree of assistance, but this is something you need to check on before you sign up: Some companies are better than others. Many have "operating manuals" for you to follow, so that you're not wasting your time when it comes to developing processes, and they'll often conduct national marketing campaigns that will help to drive customers your way. Of course, this all comes at a cost: Fees vary from a few hundred to thousands of dollars, which might pay for everything from the exclusive right to use the franchise name, an exclusive territory in which to use it, a client list, or even a storefront.

chapter 4

Researching the Market

Choosing the business that's right for you is only part of the formula for home-based business success. You also need to choose a business that's right for the market: After all, if you don't attract enough customers, it's hard to earn enough revenue to keep the business going. The first steps include researching your customers and your competitors, which will also lead you toward writing your all-important business plan (Chapter 5).

What You Need to Know

So, what exactly do you need to know about your market? The short answer is as much as possible, because the better you understand the marketplace—your customers and competitors—the better business decisions you're likely to make. If you know, for example, that most residents in your neighborhood have jobs that take them downtown during the day, and that home burglary is a problem during those hours, you're probably safe in assuming that there's a market for a home-based business that specializes in security consulting—helping people to make their homes less vulnerable.

ESSENTIAL

> When you speak to information sources such as librarians, suppliers, local business officials, or business owners, remember that any of these people could be potential customers or sources of referrals. Some might even be in a position to offer valuable advice or mentoring. Always present yourself as professionally as possible.

It's essential to continue to monitor the marketplace, however—it's not enough to do your research once. Hopefully, you've chosen a business in a subject area that you're already passionate about or at least interested in. That means that you're likely researching all the time—reading trade association magazines, for example, or keeping an eye on statistics. All this will help you to target the right customers at the right time with the right product or service.

The Market

You need to know which people could potentially do business with you. What are they looking for from your product or service, how do they shop for it, when do they shop for it, and what prices are they willing to pay for it? Just as important are the businesses where your customers are currently shopping. Who would be your competitors, what range of products and services do they offer, and how are they pricing everything?

The Business Environment

Looking at your specific market would be considered a "micro" approach. It's also important to take a look at the bigger picture—the "macro" approach. How is your local economy performing? Are there major new corporations arriving to increase local employment and thus buoy up people's willingness to spend or is a factory on the verge of closing, thus putting people into "save" mode?

You also want to look at local governments and business organizations. How business-friendly is the area in which you live? Are there miles of municipal red tape or is everything fairly streamlined? Are there small business development resources in place that you can take advantage of? Do you have a variety of lending institutions from which to choose?

Sources of Information

It might be challenging to figure out where to start researching, but once you take the plunge, you'll find that the real problem is an overwhelming quantity of information—and a baffling number of places to look for it. If the market research process seems intimidating, just tackle it gradually. Start by making a list of the information that you want to know about your customers, competitors, and local economy. You'll find that one source of good information often leads directly to another and that keeping it organized by subject area (in different file folders or binders, perhaps) will help it all make sense.

The Internet

You can find a huge amount of information simply by entering a few well-chosen keywords into an Internet search engine. If you're being overwhelmed by results that don't really apply to you, try making your search more specific. Adding a location to your keywords will usually make the results more helpful.

Local Experts

While the Internet has certainly made research easier, don't overlook the experts down at your local library. They're often able to pinpoint excellent sources of local information and can also order books or other resources through interlibrary loan systems.

FACT

Also turn to the people who are part of your daily life: friends, neighbors, colleagues, medical professionals, or business owners. They might have insights into the marketplace that bare statistics wouldn't reveal, especially when it comes to the psychology involved in purchasing decisions. A cup of coffee with one of these people could be a great investment in money and time.

Local small business development corporations or resource centers or municipal or county economic development offices usually have all kinds of information about the local economy and the business sectors already in it.

Government Offices

Federal and state or provincial governments are also excellent sources of business information. The U.S. Census Bureau (*www.census.gov*) and Statistics Canada (*www.statscan.ca*) have a wealth of demographic information that's available to you, much of it completely free of charge and easily searchable on their Web sites. You can break the data down into specific geographic areas to identify key customer characteristics that are important to you such as average household size, composition (how many children or single parents, for example) and income.

Research Tools

You can also conduct your own research using a variety of tools, including test marketing (handing out free samples, perhaps), focus groups, and surveys. For example, you might be planning to launch a lawn-care business. You can find demographic information through your national census organization to identify areas near you that have an upper-middle-class demographic—the population segment that you feel will be most likely to hire your services. You could send out a direct mail survey to the zip codes or postal codes that are included in that area, and then follow it up by selecting one or two specific streets for a door-to-door survey. Surveys could take a variety of forms—phone, e-mail, direct mail, or in-person—but they all achieve the same aim: They assess the needs and expectations of your customers. For example, if you were considering setting up a gift basket service in your area, you could ask people the following questions:

1. **Have you ever given a gift basket to anyone for any reason? If not, why not?**
   a. Not available
   b. Too expensive
   c. Never thought of it
   d. Not appropriate

2. **If you do send gift baskets, how many times a year?**
   a. 1–2
   b. 3–5
   c. More than 5

3. **What occasions are most appropriate for gift baskets?**
   a. Birthday
   b. Thank-you gift
   c. Get-well gift
   d. Mother's Day
   e. Valentine's Day
   f. Christmas
   g. Other ______________

4. **To whom do you give gifts or gift baskets?**
   a. Female family member
   b. Male family member
   c. Female friend
   d. Male friend
   e. Female coworker or employee
   f. Male coworker or employee
   g. Other ______________

5. **What items do you think are most appropriate for gift baskets?**
   a. Baked goods
   b. Fresh fruit
   c. Flowers
   d. Magazines or books
   e. Nuts and candies
   f. Herbs and spices
   g. Small gifts
   h. Other ______________

6. **How much do you typically spend for a gift or gift basket?**
   a. $5–$10
   b. $11–$25
   c. $26–$50
   d. $51–$100
   e. More than $100

7. **On what do you base the contents of the basket?**
   a. Price
   b. Contents
   c. Attractiveness
   d. Other ______________

8. **When you purchase a gift basket, do you want it to be delivered to the recipient?**
   a. All the time
   b. Sometimes
   c. Never

9. **If gift baskets were available in your area, would you purchase them as gifts?**
   a. Yes
   b. Maybe
   c. No

10. How would you prefer to shop for gift baskets?

a. On the Internet
b. In person at a store
c. Printed catalog
d. Phone call

Keep in mind that fewer than 10 percent of people traditionally respond to questionnaires, so if your response rate seems low, don't worry. The respondents might be the people who care most about your business, so there's still a good chance that your survey results will be accurate. To increase your response rates, keep the surveys as short and as quick to complete as possible.

ALERT!

Don't ask potentially sensitive questions in surveys or questionnaires. Even if the survey is confidential, people don't like to reveal information about age, income, family size, or other personal characteristics. Instead, focus on how they might use your specific business product or service.

Before you launch any research tool, check whether you require any special permits or licensing, and be sure to obtain them. You don't want to run afoul of local authorities and your neighbors before you've even launched the business.

Finding Your Customers

Once you've done all that market research, you'll have a good idea about where to look for your potential customers. If you're looking for individual consumers, then the census data, as mentioned above, can help you identify the people who have the income and family structure that you're looking for. You can also buy mailing lists that are tailored specifically to various geographic, demographic, or business areas.

If you're looking at selling to other businesses (often known as B2B or "business-to-business"), then phone directories, trade associations, chambers of commerce, and business development centers can help you identify potential users of your product or service. Also consider nonprofit organizations and schools in this category.

A third type of customer is government offices, from local to regional, state or provincial, and national. They all have clear contracting-out guidelines and processes, often requiring you to submit bid packages in response to "requests for proposals." Government Web sites have, in many cases, become the easiest and most effective way to investigate the contracting processes required and to find out about various bid opportunities.

Scoping Out Your Competitors

Now that you know who your customers are, you need to find out if they're currently buying the product or service that you'll be trying to sell them and where they're finding it. That means figuring out who your competitors will be and analyzing whether they're targeting the customers that you want to target. You want to assess what your competitors are offering, how they're offering it, and what they're charging for it. How are they differentiating themselves from their competitors? (They might be advertising the lowest price, for example, or the finest service.) If many of your customers will be in your local geographic area, you can check your phone directories to look for listings of businesses that might be similar to yours.

ESSENTIAL

Even if your customers aren't in your local area, the local phone directories could be a mine of information: Many display ads will list Web sites that you can then study to find out how various companies are structured, what they're offering, and even their pricing structure.

Of course, the Internet is one of the best sources for competitor information. Figure out which keywords best describe your product and service and type them into a search engine. First, check out the businesses that come up in either your geographic or business area; then look at some that might not seem applicable at first—you might find great ideas for your local customers by adapting an idea that a small business might be using on the other side of the country or even the other side of the world.

It may also be worth speaking discreetly to your contacts around the marketplace; they can often provide insight into why certain companies are successful and why others are stumbling. Choose your conversations carefully, however. It may not be to your advantage to reveal too much about the business that you want to launch before you're ready to reach out to your customers.

Differentiating Your Product

Once you've established who your customers and competitors are, you can figure out what will set you apart from the competition in the minds of your customers. If there are five other businesses in your town that offer office administration services such as transcription, for example, how are you going to get the attention of your potential customers—what can you offer that no one else is offering? Maybe no one else handles overnight service on rush jobs, but you think that you can deal with the pressure.

Whatever it is that sets you apart is often referred to as your "unique selling proposition" or USP. Perhaps your chocolate truffles use only natural ingredients; perhaps all your daycare staff has early-childhood-education certifications—whatever it is, your USP will help your customers recognize why they should be buying from you and not from the other businesses. Remember: If you can't tell your product or service apart from the others out there in the marketplace, your customers won't be able to either.

Pricing Strategies

Part of your market research involves pricing your products or services and the different methods that you can use to accomplish this. If you offer a product, it's relatively straightforward: you estimate what it will cost to produce or purchase the product, add in a share of your overall expenses, plus a reasonable profit margin. You will be limited, however, to the price that the market will bear—which is what customers are willing to pay for the product. You also need to factor in the effect that reducing or increasing the price will have on sales: you might find, for example, that reducing the price slightly will result in enough additional sales that you're actually making more profit than you were when the price was higher.

In terms of market research, you need to know what your competitors are charging for similar or comparable products or services. This may be as easy as checking their Web sites, reviewing their catalogs, visiting their stores, or phoning and asking for a quote. You should be respectful of their time and privacy, however, and never cross the line into what might be considered corporate espionage. Just remember how you'd feel if someone invaded your business privacy in that way.

ALERT!

Beware of setting your prices too high or too low. If prices are too high, they'll reduce your customers' ability or desire to purchase the product or service. If your prices are too low, people will assume that the quality is also low—this is especially true when it comes to services. Don't undervalue yourself just because you're starting out.

Pricing a service is slightly more complicated, and, in many cases, depends largely on what other businesses are charging for similar services or what typical labor charges are in your industry. You could base your price on a flat fee (e.g., a three-page resume would cost $300 to write and edit), or you could base it on an hourly or daily rate. Keep in mind, though, that you can lose money on a flat-fee project if the job turns out to take a lot longer than you expected and you don't have a contingency factor built into your contract.

To figure out where to set your rates, think about the annual income you want to earn and work backwards. How many hours a week will you be working and how many of those will be income-earning time (as opposed to marketing and administration, for example)? How much time off will you need? Work out how many hours a year you'll actually work, and then divide that into your income goal.

FACT

Say you want to earn $60,000 a year before taxes and other expenses, and you're willing to work forty hours a week, thirty of which you think will be productive (earning) time. You factor in two weeks of sick days and three weeks of vacation. That means that you'll need to charge $42.55 per hour.

Forecasting Costs

Since costs are a major part of determining pricing strategies, it helps to know what kinds of costs (expenses) you're looking at. These include direct and indirect costs.

Direct costs are often referred to as your "cost of goods sold." These are the costs that went directly into the product or service that you're providing. If you have a landscaping business, your direct costs might include materials such as rocks, bricks, or sod that you purchased for a specific job. If you're producing wooden planters, the wood pieces, screws, and paint that went into each planter would be the cost of goods sold.

You'll often hear indirect costs called "overhead." These include the expenses that aren't related to a specific job or product, but are nonetheless necessary to keep the business running. This is everything from vehicle maintenance for your landscaping truck to advertising for the finished wooden planters. Businesspeople often underestimate indirect costs, so think about everything that you'll have to pay out of your business earnings, from office expenses to marketing to health plan costs.

You can research the costs involved in your business, whether direct or indirect, by checking the prices of supplies through stores, wholesalers, or catalogs and by checking through your own records (to find out, for example, how much you spent on vehicle maintenance last year).

Forecasting Sales

As part of your pricing strategy, you'll also need to research what expectations might be reasonable in terms of weekly, monthly, or annual sales. You can base this on talking to potential customers, suppliers, or local business experts, or by looking for industry statistics: the U.S. Department of Labor, U.S. Department of Commerce, Industry Canada, and local economic development offices may be able to help.

Trade or professional associations often conduct surveys of their members to produce a snapshot of annual earnings; these are usually broken down by an identifying factor such as company size. Local, regional, and national business magazines also run annual surveys of the most profitable or successful companies, while trade magazines and newspaper business sections are also good sources of information.

chapter 5

Writing Your Business Plan

It's not wise to begin a road journey to a new destination without a road map: You might get there in the end, but you open yourself up to wrong turns, false starts, and serious delays. It's just the same for a business, except that your road map is a business plan. It sets out your destination, how you plan to get there, and what you'll need along the way. Not only will it keep you on the right path, but it becomes your key sales tool for obtaining financing.

Elements of the Plan

A business plan typically includes a written overview of the business with a description of the product or service provided, the market served, the competition faced, and the people involved in the business. It might also show financial projections going out three to five years, with revenue and expenses detailed monthly for one year. If your business is in operation already, your plan would also include past financial documents such as income statements and balance sheets.

Your business plan could include some or all of the following:

- Title Page
- Statement of Purpose
- Table of Contents
- Business Description or Executive Summary, including:
  - *Product or service*
  - *Location and competition*
  - *Management and organization*
- Marketing Plan, including:
  - *Description of the overall market*
  - *Target market for the business*
  - *Customer needs and characteristics*
  - *Analysis of the competition*
  - *Overall sales plan*
- Financial Data, including:
  - *Capital equipment needs or assets*
  - *Funding sources*
  - *Cash flow projections*
  - *Income projections*
  - *Balance sheet*
- Supporting Documents:
  - *Resumes of management and partners, letters of recommendation*
  - *Personal financial statements and cost-of-living budget (for a sole proprietor)*
  - *Past financial history (business financial statements for the previous three years, if available)*

- *Relevant contracts and legal documents*
- *Documentation of market research, if any*

While it's true that plenty of businesses launch and survive without a business plan—and that having a plan doesn't necessarily guarantee success—taking the time to write one gives you a chance to clarify exactly what you want to achieve with the business. It also provides hard numbers that will either back up what your instinct is telling you about the marketplace or let you know that you need to rethink elements of the business. And as any coach will tell you, writing down your goals and the steps you plan to take to achieve them gives you a competitive edge even before you start.

Which Elements Do You Need?

A business plan can be a lot of work, but you might be able to scale it down, too. The depth of detail that your plan requires depends on the complexity of your business, the level of risk involved, the nature of the competition, and the margin or room for error. If yours is a part-time service business without inventory in a strong market with few competitors, you can get away with the basics: just pick and choose the elements of the plan that apply to you.

If you're investing your life savings in a highly competitive business with razor-thin margins, however, you need to plan every step carefully and constantly review your progress. This will enable you to make the critical decisions that will determine your success and failure, so you need a strong, detailed business plan. Similarly, you'll need a detailed plan if you're planning to quit your job to launch the business.

ESSENTIAL

If creating a business plan seems overwhelming, break it down into basic elements and tackle it one piece at a time. Start with expense projections, taking it month by month, or work on your business description first—whatever you're most comfortable with. For more help, check out the forms available in business planning books, software, and Web sites.

Of course, you'll also need a business plan if you need outside financing. Banks and other small business loan organizations all require a business plan when you apply for loans or lines of credit. But even if you don't need funding, the plan will help you forecast revenues and expenses, track your progress, and make decisions. It's the process of creating the plan and referring to it later that's most valuable to home-based businesses.

You may also need a full business plan if you're submitting tenders for large contracts (for government work, for example), you want to form a cooperative or strategic relationship with another business, or you've been approached to sell or merge the business.

Description of the Business

This statement would include several paragraphs that tell the reader what kind of business yours is going to be and what your overall goals are. Basically, you'll describe your product or service, how you'll differentiate it from your competition, whom you're going to sell it to, and how you're going to sell it.

You'll also touch on where you're located and what structure you'll be operating under (e.g., sole proprietorship). This section should also provide a brief context for the business, including an overview of the market, the competition, and the primary customers. It's a good place to include your mission statement, too.

If this is the only part of the plan that someone reads, you want the person to understand all of the key points that the plan contains. However, what you really want to do is hook the reader and make her enthusiastic about turning the page and discovering all of the details behind how you're going to achieve your goals. The business description doesn't need to be "cute," but it does need to convey a sense of your passion.

Marketing Plan

A marketing plan should answer questions about who will buy your product or service and how you expect to reach those customers. You want to describe what your customers will expect and need from you and how you plan to meet those expectations and needs. In short, you should cover the four "Ps": Product; Pricing; Placement (or how you're going to provide your product to the customer); and Promotion.

Just like the overall business plan, a marketing plan can be long and complex or short and simple: it just depends on what your business needs. But it should indicate how you're going to reach and retain your customers, whom your competition will be, and how you plan to make the customers come to you instead of the competition. You'll also be looking at how big the market is overall, and what portion of it you can expect to capture.

Elements of a marketing plan can include:

- Overall Market Analysis
- Goals
- Target Market Analysis
- Competitive Analysis
- Strengths, Weaknesses, Opportunities, and Threats (SWOT) Analysis
- Marketing Strategies

Just pick and choose the elements that you feel make sense for your business. And be sure to refer to your plan frequently, checking off each step of your plan as it's accomplished and reviewing your assumptions and projections.

Overall Market Analysis

In this section, you'll describe your surrounding economic marketplace. Which sectors are doing well, and which are in an economic downturn or perhaps threatening to fail? Which part of the overall market will you be targeting, and what is the regulatory framework involved—which licenses and permits do you need, which regulations do you need to comply with, and will you be collecting sales tax?

Goals

It's essential to write down clear and concise descriptions of your business goals. Depending on your situation, you might want to describe them in terms of annual sales, market share (or the number of customers you want in your database at certain points in time), or the annual salary that you want to draw from the business. Simply choose a reference point that makes sense for your business and for the reasons that you're launching a home-based business. You can also add less tangible goals that are important to you such as giving a certain percentage of your net profits (after expenses) to a nonprofit or charitable organization.

Target Market Analysis

This section comes from the market information you collected about your customers in Chapter 4. It will describe who your customers are; where they are located; and which characteristics define them. This could include demographic information for individual consumers (such as age, income, family size, and education), or it could cover defining characteristics for businesses or government clients (business or office size, location, customers, and services provided).

ALERT!

> Customers tend to be moving targets—their interests and needs change over time, sometimes very quickly. The key is to constantly refine your knowledge of the market and become more accurate over time about how the business will grow. That way, you'll recognize market changes and can adapt quickly to new customer demands.

The target market analysis also includes factors such as the number of customers in your area, and their purchasing decisions—how often they'll buy the product or service that you're offering, for example. Your intention here is to clearly describe what your customers will expect from your product or service, and how you'll deliver on those expectations.

Competitive Analysis

This is also where you'll use the research described in Chapter 4. You'll list who your competitors are; where they're located; how they're structured;

how successful they are; and how long they've been in business. Also assess what you like or dislike about their operation—what seems to be working for them and what doesn't?

You also need to describe who their customers are, where they're drawing those customers from, and why the customers are choosing them (their USPs, for example). What's their pricing structure? Are they offering benefits or services to their customers that go beyond good prices? This analysis gives you a chance to establish what your USP will be in comparison to your competition and how your business will compare in terms of pricing and structure.

SWOT Analysis

In this section, you'll assess your business's strengths, weaknesses, opportunities, and threats (SWOT). This will help you to quickly take advantage of opportunities for growth, and should help you prepare for problems, thus reducing their impact on the business.

When you look at your strengths, consider what you have going for you. How do your products or services meet your clients' needs? It could be that you deal well with other people, making your customers feel comfortable in your store and thus bringing them back again and again.

Conversely, what are your weaknesses? For a sole proprietor, this often involves personal limits—there's a finite number of hours that you can work each week before your family life suffers and your stress level rises. In addition, assess your products or services: Are they fully meeting your customers' needs and if not, why?

You may not be ready to take advantage of the opportunities that you identify in this analysis, but knowing that they're there always gives you options. Are there ways that you can establish new client bases for example, or add a related service or product area to build on existing ones?

You also need to consider the threats to your business. Many will come from your competition—undercutting your prices, perhaps, or expanding into your geographical area. But threats also come from inside the business: Not keeping current with the marketplace, a lack of time to follow up with clients, or a failure to protect your ideas (your intellectual property) can cost you money or clients. Do you have a contingency plan that will handle equipment failure and even weather-related problems?

Marketing Strategies

Based on your USP and the customers you're trying to reach, you need to determine how you're going to reach them. This might include strategies such as purchasing advertising in various media (from newspapers to television), and generating media interest in your business to achieve free, positive publicity.

FACT

If you want to increase your market share, you could list all of the local media outlets that reach the people you've identified as part of your target market. Include how much each outlet charges for its advertising and when spending that money would be most effective.

Once people know that you exist, how are you going to get your product to them? If you're going to be distributing your product through other salespeople, perhaps through consignment stores, for example, this is the place in the business plan to show how you'll do it.

Essentially, you're going to take each of your goals for placement and promotion and list the strategies that you're going to employ to achieve them. Maybe you could obtain testimonials from customers that you can use in your advertising, for example. Remember the Internet, too. Although not every business benefits from a Web site, an increasing number of customers are expecting to at least check you out online, if not actually make the purchase over the Internet.

ALERT!

Don't forget that you need to review your plan and evaluate your progress and performance. How often should you review the plan to check reality against your predictions? (Weekly or monthly, perhaps.) Are you achieving your goals? If not, what are the problems that you're encountering? Do you need to change your strategies?

Listing your marketing goals and strategies isn't enough to make them happen. Depending on how complex your plan is, you may want to break out the steps involved into an implementation plan, where you list individual tasks and when you're going to do them. This provides a very clear road map, which might help if you're feeling unfocused because there's just so much to do at once.

Financial Plan

Your financial plan deals with risk and reality. It lets you establish how much money will be at risk as you launch the business and operate it, and it translates numbers such as sales forecasts and expense breakdowns into the reality of whether you'll be making a profit, and when.

First, establish the administration side of financial matters. Who will look after your day-to-day bookkeeping and how? Accounting software now makes this much easier than the steam-powered days of huge account ledger books, but you still need to keep up with entering in your receipts and creating your invoices. At the end of the year, who will use the bookkeeping records to create your financial statements, and who will prepare your income tax returns? You can certainly do some or even all of these tasks, especially if you're a sole proprietor. More complex business structures, however, will usually need expert assistance.

ESSENTIAL

Much of the information in your financial plan can take the form of financial statements: sales and expense predictions, cash flow statements, income statements, and balance sheets, for example. For a small operation, you might just need to look at income, expenses, and cash flow. If you're looking for outside funding, however, you need the full package.

Your financial plan needs to explain how much money the business needs, how much money you have now, your predictions for revenue and expenses, and the assumptions that you've made to arrive at those assumptions. You'll be looking specifically for your break-even point (where revenues begin to cover expenses). Along the way, there are key ratios that financial investors will use to assess the financial health of your business, including turnover, debt-to-equity, and assets-to-liabilities calculations.

FACT

It's okay to be wrong when you're making estimates and educated guesses within your business plan. That's why businesspeople often create three projections: one best case scenario, one worst case scenario, and one scenario that's in the middle—they'll be prepared, no matter what happens.

Funding Needs

Assessing your financial needs in three different areas—capital, operating, and reserve—will establish how much funding your business will need to launch and then to operate. Although it can be difficult to estimate figures before you begin running the business, this will at least provide you with a start point: You can always go back and revise your figures later if you find that your estimates weren't accurate.

Capital Costs

"Capital" refers to items such as real estate, furniture, equipment, and vehicles. These items are sometimes called "nonconsumables" because their lifetime is generally more than a year, and these materials are not "used up" quickly the way that other items are, such as office supplies. Will you need to invest in any equipment to get your business up and running? If you want to open a catering business, for example, will you need new refrigerators or a delivery van? You can estimate costs by calling equipment vendors, checking trade catalogs, or calling in a contractor (to quote on renovations).

Operating Costs

Make a list of your operating expenses: payroll (you and for any employees); insurance (business and health); taxes; utilities (electric, telephone, water, Internet access), cost of goods (inventory for resale, supplies for making a product); transportation (cost of a vehicle, gas, maintenance), and anything else that comes to mind. You need your list of expenses to be as complete as possible here, so include one-time or annual operating expenses (such as licenses) in your first month of operation.

ESSENTIAL

It's best to estimate higher rather than lower, so that you won't be taken by surprise if your costs are higher than you anticipate (and this isn't unusual in a start-up). Once you total up your expenses, you'll have an idea of the funds you'll need each month to cover your operating costs during your start-up phase.

Cash Reserve

You've estimated your foreseeable expenses; now you need to estimate how much might be reasonable to cover unforeseeable costs. You should have insurance to cover catastrophic problems (the theft of all your equipment), but what if it takes you twice as long as you expect to build your revenue base? What if your vehicle breaks down? Having at least a modest cash reserve can give you great peace of mind. If a cash reserve isn't possible, try to have a source of reasonably priced credit available, such as a line of credit.

Financial Statements

The easiest way to show all of the figures that you're working with is to break them down into the financial statements that will provide you—and your lending institutions—with clear, easy-to-read information. First, an Income Statement shows your revenue and your expenses for a particular time period (often a month or a year), and it is also known as a profit and loss statement or an operating statement. It can be helpful to show several time periods along with a total for the entire time: You can use a column for each of twelve months, for example, and a final column that reflects the annual totals.

Sample Income Statement: Gift Baskets Galore Year 1	
Item	**Total**
Sales	
Baskets	15,500
Total Sales	15,500
Cost of Goods Sold	
Materials Cost	6,540
Freight	327
Delivery Cost	981
Total Cost of Goods Sold	7,848
Gross Profit	7,652
Operating Expenses	
Advertising	1,000
Utilities	600
Office Supplies	300
Insurance	900
Accounting	600
Depreciation	800
Misc.	300
Total Operating Expenses	4,500
Net Profit (Loss)	3,152

A Cash Flow Projection is very similar to a budget: it takes a particular time period (say, a year) and breaks it down into manageable parts (months, for example) so that you can see when the revenue is coming in and when the expenses are flowing out. This is important, because it shows you exactly when you might be short of funds.

Sample Cash Flow Projection: Gift Baskets Galore First Quarter				
Summary	**Jan.**	**Feb.**	**Mar.**	**Total**
Opening Balance	3,000	2,110	1,675	
Receipts				
Cash Revenues	500	500	600	1,600
Accounts Receivable	0	250	400	650
Loans				
Other				
Total Receipts	500	750	1,000	2,250
Disbursements				
Material	600	600	400	1,600
Freight	60	60	40	160
Vehicle	30	250	40	320
Advertising	500	100	100	700
Utilities	50	50	50	150
Office Supplies	25	25	25	75
Insurance	75	75	75	225
Accounting				
Misc.	50	25	10	85
Loan Payments				
Total Disbursements	1,390	1,185	740	3,315
Total Cash Flow	(890)	(435)	260	(1,065)
Ending Balance	2,110	1,675	1,935	

Balance Sheets show how much your business is worth at one point in time, and are often used by lending institutions. The entire sheet is designed around this equation: assets = liabilities + equity. Your total assets on the left-hand side must equal the sum of your liabilities and equity on the right-hand side—hence the "balance."

Sample Balance Sheet: Gift Baskets Galore March 31

Assets		**Liabilities and Equity**	
Current Assets		***Liabilities***	
Cash	1,935	Accounts Payable	85
Accounts Receivable	200	Debt	3,000
Inventory	950	TOTAL LIABILITIES	3,085
TOTAL CURRENT ASSETS	3,085	***Equity***	
Fixed Assets		Start-up Funding	5,000
Vehicle & Furniture	5,000	Retained Earnings	0
Total Fixed Assets	5,000	Total Equity	5,000
TOTAL ASSETS	8,085	TOTAL LIABILITIES AND EQUITY	8,085

Financial Analysis

Many lending institutions will analyze your financial statements using key financial ratios or other calculations to determine your business's fiscal fitness. These figures, including break-even point, turnover, debt-to-equity, and debt-to-assets can also provide you with a guide to how you're progressing.

Break-Even Point

You can calculate how many items you need to sell in order to break even (cover your costs) if you know some key figures, including the item's selling price, its cost of goods sold, and your other expenses during the sales period.

First, subtract the item's cost of goods sold from its selling price. This gives you what's known as the contribution margin. Then divide your other expenses (operating costs) over the specific period of time by the contribution margin.

In this case, the calculation is the year's operating costs ($4,500) divided by the contribution margin (which is the unit selling price [assume an average of $60] minus the cost of goods sold [51% or $30.60]). This gives you how many units you need to sell to reach the break-even point (153.1 units).

Turnover

This is important to any inventory-based business, whether you're producing the product that you're selling or you're buying it for resale. The greater the turnover, the better, because it indicates that the business is more efficient—that it's generating greater sales. To calculate turnover, divide your total sales for a period of time (say, a year) by your average inventory during that time (this is one reason why retail stores conduct periodic inventory counts).

ALERT!

Be sure that you're using the same valuation method for each part of the turnover calculation. Value both the inventory and the sales at cost, for example, or at what they're worth at your selling price. If you use inventory at cost and sales at retail price, you'll throw the calculation off completely.

Debt-to-Equity

This looks at how much financing you're using to fund the company compared to how much you've put in yourself (or how much your shareholders have put in). Divide your total debt (the total, not the monthly payments) by your total equity. If the ratio decreases over time, it means that you're successfully reducing your reliance on debt financing. If the ratio is greater than one, it means that you're financing the business more through debt than you are through equity, which can indicate a riskier venture.

Debt-to-Assets

This ratio indicates the relative health of your business when it comes to your debt. To figure it out, divide your total debt (the total, not the monthly payments) by your total assets (from cash in the bank to accounts receivable to furniture and tools). Generally, you want to see the ratio decreasing over time: Whenever it's less than one, it indicates that your assets are greater than your debt (which is a good thing).

Funding Sources

You may have savings on hand that you're planning to invest in the business. This is the place to list money that you already have and also sources of outside funding that you need. For outside funding, itemize how much you need and whether it's for capital, operating, or cash reserve needs. (You'll usually receive a better interest rate on loans for capital expenses, because the loan can be secured by the asset that it's paying for, such as a vehicle.)

Then list your potential sources for that money, being as specific as possible. Perhaps you believe that your bank, with which you've had a long and positive relationship, is your best source of funds. Look at their financial products and decide which one best fits your situation. If your home needs renovations to accommodate your office, for example, a home improvement loan or line of credit that's based on the equity in your home might be the best option. If you don't believe that local financial institutions are the answer for your needs, identify other sources, such as the SBA or Industry Canada small business programs (see Chapter 7).

Management Plan

A management plan might seem pretty simple for a sole proprietorship. After all, you'll be the owner and the manager, and the buck will always stop with you. Even so, you should give some attention to the management plan portion of your business plan—and if you're looking at a more complex structure, you definitely need to consider how the business will be managed.

The management plan will detail who is going to run the business. This could be you, you in conjunction with one or more partners, a corporate board of directors, or your employees. For all of these people, you need to spell out exactly what their roles and responsibilities will be (job descriptions can be very helpful here).

Then you need to compare that to their qualifications, experience, skills, and education, so that you can demonstrate how each person will fulfill their duties. What are their strengths and weaknesses, for example? (This can be an interesting question to ask and answer for yourself, too.) If there are skills or knowledge that will be needed within the business, do you (or your management team) have them? If not, how will you acquire them?

FACT

> Identifying potential shortfalls on the management side isn't a problem as long as you offer solutions, too. For example, if handling busy periods or projects that are too large or complex for your business alone is a problem, suggest working with associates, virtual teams, contractors, or casual employees.

Finally, you should give some thought to wages or salaries and benefits packages for the management team. This is equally important in a sole proprietorship that's providing your sole source of income—you need a sense of how much your personal living expenses and insurance coverages will be so that you can ensure the business is providing you with sufficient funds.

chapter 6

Buying a Business

In many ways, a home-based business is just like any other small business: a service or product is provided to customers in exchange for payment. And, just like other businesses, a home-based business will need a positive reputation (goodwill), a customer base, and possibly, inventory. Sometimes, it's easier, faster, or more economical to buy those aspects of a business rather than building them from scratch. When it does make sense, buying a business can be a quick way to get yourself up and running.

Advantages to Buying a Business

There's no doubt that launching your own business is a risky plan. You can run into all kinds of challenges—some that you'll expect, and some that you won't—and it can become tiring to come up with solutions to all of them. So, in some cases, buying a business can provide distinct advantages. As briefly mentioned in Chapter 3, the four key reasons to go the purchase instead of start-up route are location, time, money, and competition (market share).

Location

Since many areas restrict the business activities that you can conduct in residential-zoned areas, you might have to consider moving in order to open the business that you've decided on, especially if it's retail-based. And, as long as you're moving, you might want to look for a good location that has not only the right building, housing, road access, parking, and so on, but also has just the kind of business that you want to run. If the owner is selling, and the price and other considerations are right, buying the entire business might be advantageous.

FACT

If you want to run a kennel, for example, but you know your neighbors will object, consider buying an existing home-based kennel business. An established kennel is likely either located within an appropriate zone, or "grandfathered" into a zoning variance. If the location, reputation, and customer base are all sound, it could be worth buying both the property and the business.

Time

No matter what kind of business you want to start, it will take you some time to establish it and to create a customer base. If an established business of the same type already has 250 loyal customers, how long do you think it would take you to reach that same level? One year? Five years?

Money

Will you be profitable when your business is initially growing? If the answer is "no," how much would you have to invest in order to stay in business? Would it cost more or less to buy the already established business? In this case, buying a business might yield a profitable operation virtually overnight for no more than it would cost to invest in your own start-up business.

Competition (Market Share)

North American business is based on the concept of competition. If you can beat the other business's quality, customer service, or price, you can earn your share of available customers. But sometimes a competing business is so well established and the size of the market so fixed that there might not be room for more than one business to provide a specific product or services.

For example, if you have your heart set on running an automotive detailing home-based business, but the area you live in is small, and there are already two automotive detailers who've been operating for years, then you'll be facing stiff competition. But you might find it possible to buy out one of those two existing businesses. If the price (among other things) is right, then buying can eliminate the competition problem.

Disadvantages to Buying a Business

Of course, one distinct disadvantage to buying a business is that you need to come up with the purchase cost upfront. When you're starting up on your own, you may be able to spread the expenses over a period of time; with a purchase, you need the lump sum right away, which means that you'll likely need to find financing. (The good news is that the business will probably have three years of sound financial statements, so obtaining financing might be easier than for your unproven start-up situation.)

You also need to do a significant amount of research to ensure that you're buying a profitable, reputable, and worthwhile operation. This includes taking a look at the accounts receivable, for example: Are the accounts in fact collectible or are they bad debts that are unfairly inflating the value of the business's assets? Checking the business's references and making inquiries wherever it makes sense to do so, from the Better Business Bureau to the neighbors, all takes time.

ALERT!

Ensure that your purchase agreement includes a "noncompete" clause, which prevents the current business owner from operating a similar business in the same market for a specific period of time, often several years. Otherwise, you could find yourself competing with the former owner in a market where he's much better known than you are.

What You Can Buy

In an ideal world, once you pay your money for an ongoing business, you'd start running things the next day and enjoying the profits, which would be high enough to pay off your investment in a reasonable time. Of course, it's rarely that easy, especially because the existing owner may not want to sell every piece of the business.

Generally, you can buy the entire business—what's referred to as a "turnkey" operation—or you can buy elements of it. Business buyers will often purchase only the business's assets, for example, such as buildings and equipment; they won't also purchase the accounts receivable or take on responsibility for the accounts payable.

Real Estate and Equipment

For some home-based businesses, you may be buying a home that includes a business. A country store, bed-and-breakfast inn, or kennel might include a location and buildings that are specifically geared toward the business.

Along with real estate—or separate from it—you may be buying certain capital equipment involved in the business. Freezers and display cases, tools, cash registers, and computers are all items that can be included in the purchase price. However, you don't have to buy the real estate associated with the business. Take a newsletter production company, for example. You can buy their client list, ongoing contracts, business phone number, computer equipment; and newsletter archives, but you don't need their location in order to function successfully.

Inventory and Customer Lists

In addition, inventory that's on hand—items that the business owner has purchased or manufactured but not yet sold—can also be part of the agreement. For both product- and service-oriented businesses, buying a customer database or client list is possible, along with existing contracts (which might be particularly important in the case of service businesses, as long as the contract is transferable between owners).

Goodwill

A good reputation may be priceless, but when you're buying a business, you might have to put a value on the company's positive standing in the community. It's known as goodwill, and because of its intangible nature, it's difficult to price. The business owner will likely have an idea how much it's worth; whether you agree with the person may be a negotiating point.

If that dog kennel that you want to purchase has been established for years, for example, is well regarded by local pet owners, has good credit among its suppliers, and generally has an excellent reputation for cleanliness, reliability, and fine service, then that business has built up considerable goodwill. That reputation is worth something. After all, how long would it take you to build that same reputation if you were just starting out?

How to Find Businesses for Sale

One of the best sources for local businesses for sale is your newspaper. Ignore the ads that have overwrought claims about how you can make thousands of dollars a week from your own home and the ones that promise to give you everything you need to get started in a particular business. These often turn out to be scams—remember, if it sounds too good to be true, it probably is.

Instead, focus on the ads for businesses that match your needs: small, home-based businesses that have been operating for some time. Assuming that these businesses are offering a product or service that you want to offer, one of them could be the opportunity you're looking for.

ESSENTIAL

If you're looking for a franchise, contact the franchise headquarters of the company that you're interested in to find out more. Or, check out the International Franchise Association. You'll want to review what's called the Uniform Franchise Offering Circular (UFOC) as a starting point: It lists key information about the company, including initial costs, ongoing fees, training, and support.

You can also talk to commercial real estate agents or lawyers who specialize in business acquisitions—look for them in phone directories, on the Internet, or in local business associations. They often hear about businesses that aren't necessarily being advertised for sale, but are on the block nonetheless. (Owners may be reluctant to advertise that they're selling in case this discourages customers.)

Of course, there's no reason why you can't simply introduce yourself to the owner of a home-based business that you'd like to buy and ask if she's thought about selling. Even if she hasn't, your question might prompt her to consider your request, especially if it comes with a ballpark offer that she likes.

How to Research a Potential Business

Before you invest a significant amount of money you'll need to perform what's known as "due diligence." This entails going over every element of the business to ensure that everything is as it should be. That's why you need an accountant who's familiar with this kind of business to review the books and why you'll want to inspect all inventory and capital equipment that's part of the sale. You also need to get a sense of customer loyalty. As long as you conduct your due diligence properly and completely, you'll be able to reduce the risks of buying a business that you might not be familiar with. Of course, if you already know the business, the risks may be lower anyway—but do your reviews regardless to avoid any nasty surprises later on.

The Professionals

This is not a time to go it alone: call in a lawyer who specializes in business acquisitions and an accountant who can examine the books of the business. You can ask other businesspeople for recommendations or check with local chambers of commerce or small business development centers.

ALERT!

Legal and financial experts cost money, which can be difficult to swallow if you end up backing away from the potential business purchase. Think of their bills as your insurance, however: don't skimp on professional advice when it comes to buying a business. Your future financial health may depend on following their advice.

The Paperwork

Your lawyer should help you draft a "letter of intent," in which you basically offer to buy the business. It should be nonbinding at this stage, however, meaning that either you or the business owner can walk away from the purchase process at any time. It will likely include a price for the business, what you expect to receive in return for that price, and any conditions that you want to place on the sale. Generally, you'll need the letter of intent for the business owner to release proprietary information such as financial statements.

In return, the business owner will probably ask you to sign a confidentiality agreement. When you sign this (after your lawyer has reviewed it), you're prevented from revealing any of the business's proprietary information to people outside the purchase process, and you can't use the information for any purpose other than the purchase.

Existing Contracts and Legal Obligations

If the business currently holds a lease or is a party to any kind of contract, whether it's for supplies, sales, or an alarm monitoring system, you (and your team of professionals) need to review the written paperwork (deeds, contracts, etc.) to ensure that you know the extent and conditions of the obligations you're taking on. And when it comes to a lease, be aware that you may have to renegotiate it or apply for a new one: Leases don't always survive a change in business ownership.

While you're at it, review every document that the business holds, from customer, supplier, vendor, and employee lists to its marketing materials, business structure, and job descriptions. If it has certifications or licensing from specific professional, governmental, or educational institutions, check with the institution to make sure that all is in order.

Financial Statements

Your accountant will need to review the tax returns and business financial statements for the previous three to five years as part of the due diligence process. As part of the sale preparation, the business owner should have had a qualified accountant audit the statements: If this hasn't been done, you can insist on it or pay for it to be done. Check that any taxes that are shown as due annually have been paid up.

Red Flags to Watch For

While you need to conduct your due diligence reviews in all aspects of the business, there are a few areas that are known as places to hide negative information or other items. Of course, the existing business owner would prefer that you not know about them. While you don't want to approach the review in a way that alienates the owner (you may need their goodwill to help you get off the ground later), you do need to be thorough, and it's fair to question anything that you don't understand or aren't happy with.

Hidden Debts

If the purchase price includes inventory or equipment, is it all paid for? Make sure that liens are listed and bills are paid (or outstanding balances due are noted) as you finalize the price. You don't want to pay $1,000 for existing pet supplies only to find out that the previous owner hadn't yet paid for them.

Overstated Earnings

Your accountant needs to review the income statements for the business to ensure that the previous owner really is generating the revenue and profits that are on the books. Accounting rules and procedures have been significantly tightened in recent years, due to financial scandals at several large multinational firms. If it can happen there, it can certainly happen down the road from you.

A craft business, for example, might have any number of items out on consignment, in which other retailers have taken on the inventory but will pay for it only when it sells. These need to be listed as part of the business's inventory, not sales, because if the items don't sell, the retailer can simply return them.

Receivables

Accounts receivable—money that customers owe the business—can be a tricky area. If you purchase the receivables, it can create an immediate cash flow for your business as the receivables become due and are paid. However, it's hard to dispute the amount or the payment terms with the customer if they disagree with these terms. First, you weren't privy to the conversation they may have had with the previous owner about discounts or extensions, and, second, you want to retain the customer's business.

If you don't purchase the receivables, the previous customers will pay their bills to the previous owner, and you're out of the loop. That means you're essentially asking longtime customers to go to the trouble of opening a new account with you, the new owner. This might be just the interruption the customer needs to start looking around at other sources of the products or services that you're offering.

ESSENTIAL

If you discover issues with the receivables during your due diligence process, consider backing away from the purchase completely. Although it's possible that the owner has just made a mistake, it could well be a sign that all is not straightforward in other parts of the business either.

Financing the Purchase

If you don't have the money already in the bank to buy the business, financing the purchase may be easier than financing a start-up. If you've done all of your research well, you'll be offering your lending institution an established business with a proven track record of revenues and profits.

FACT

There are some other, more creative ways to finance the business purchase. These often involve the existing owner holding the note with an agreement to repay it over time depending on how the business performs—or there could be a sliding scale of ownership over time, with you gaining more ownership the more you put toward the sale price.

However you choose to finance the purchase, you'll need to ensure that the business is able to carry the debt. For example, a small home-based service business might be for sale for $50,000. You need to finance $40,000 of that figure. For the past three years, the owner has netted $30,000 after expenses and before taxes. The bank is willing to lend you the $40,000 on a five-year note at 10 percent interest. That means that your monthly loan payments will be around $850 or $10,200 annually. This leaves you with a net of just under $20,000 before taxes.

Think about it: If you have personal expenses (including taxes) that total more than $20,000, and you don't believe you can increase the revenues of the business to the point where they'll cover those expenses, you're looking at a loss. The business doesn't have high enough revenues to service that debt, so you shouldn't take on the loan.

It should go without saying that although financing a business purchase sounds like a good solution, your lawyer and your accountant should have the last word on whether it's a good idea in your specific situation.

chapter 7

Finding Start-Up Funding

You can have a great idea and plenty of drive and determination, but for many businesses, if you don't have the dollars it takes to turn the idea into cash flow, you'll be going nowhere fast. Yes, you can absolutely start a business on a shoestring, and, in fact, that's a good strategy if you're concerned about risk or debt. But if you need cash to get started, there are a variety of ways to come up with it.

Assessing How Much You Need

Part of the business planning process is to determine how much money it will take to start and operate the business until it can generate the revenue to support itself. Your business plan (from Chapter 5) involved drafting a financial plan that included identifying your funding needs (capital, operating, and reserve) and forecasting your cash flow. Your business plan also allowed you to set goals for the times when you'll break even and then start to earn a profit.

ESSENTIAL

It's good planning to work with three financial scenarios, especially when it comes to cash flow: your best-case predictions; your worst-case predictions; and one set of predictions that's pretty much in the middle. That way, you'll be mentally (and financially) prepared whatever happens.

By adding up how much (1) you'll need to invest in your assets to start the business (your initial capital); (2) you'll need to operate it on an ongoing basis, (operating expenses); and (3) you'll be bringing in (cash flow), you'll clearly see how much you'll need in start-up funding. Assess in detail at least the first six to twelve months of your needs this way.

Ensuring that you have adequate financing to take you and your family through the start-up phase of your home-based business is critical. You need to be completely honest with yourself about your personal income and expenses, and you need to be realistic when it comes to forecasting your business's needs. A strong foundation that's based on solid facts and figures will give you the edge you need when it comes to assessing where and how to seek financing.

Minimizing Funding Needs

You're looking at either using personal savings to finance the business or borrowing the money. When it comes to borrowing, the sources of money range from your own home (a second mortgage, for example) to a small business loan from your local bank, to venture capital. But there's a middle ground, too, often referred to as "bootstrapping."

Bootstrapping Techniques

Bootstrapping means starting small, cutting corners, continually reinvesting money into the business to foster growth, and finding every creative way possible to make your business work without starting with a big pot of money. The advantage is that by keeping your debt low, you're also reducing risks and maximizing profits. Consider whether some of the following bootstrapping techniques might work for you.

- **Liquidating assets.** This is a fancy way of saying that you're selling something of value that you own—whether it's a car, a coin collection, or a piece of antique furniture. If you don't require a lot of start-up cash, and you're not overly attached to the item, the sacrifice might be worth it. Just make sure that your family agrees with you.
- **No-cost promotion.** This involves leveraging every available free way to promote your business. Constantly ask for recommendations from your current customers. Call the local newspapers and find a story angle to get yourself in the paper (see Chapter 18).
- **Vendor credit.** Use your personal reputation to establish credit with other vendors and suppliers wherever you can. Always pay these bills on time, but certainly use the payment grace periods that these businesses are prepared to offer, such as thirty days from the invoice date.
- **Additional revenue sources**. Look into part-time jobs, renting out a room in your house to a student, or doing anything legal that will earn some extra cash to invest in the business.
- **Buying used.** Bargains are available on all kinds of used equipment, from office desks to vehicles. Auctions, liquidators, and used furniture stores are all good options.

When buying used items, do your research so that you'll know when you're really getting a bargain, and make sure that the item you're buying is a sound investment. Your tools and equipment are essential to your success; don't go for a bargain if the quality is questionable.

Bartering Services

Consider your talents and your labor among your assets. If you don't have cash, you might be able to swap services with someone who has what you need—especially if that person is in a similar situation. Alternatively, check the Internet or phone directories to see if there's a local or national bartering organization that you can join. These organizations often work on a points or credit system, where you can build up the credits to "buy" something by "selling" your goods or labor.

ESSENTIAL

> Just because cash hasn't changed hands doesn't mean the IRS or CRA isn't interested in the bartering transaction. You need to keep a record of the value of the exchanges for tax purposes and enter them into your accounts as either income or expenses, as applicable.

Be a Cash Flow Hawk

Monitor your cash flow so that you know exactly what you have to pay out and exactly which client checks are due at any given time. Ensure that you collect your receivables on a timely basis and make full use of any terms offered by others on payables that are due. It's all about staying solvent while making your available cash and credit work for you.

Personal Savings

If you have a nest egg sitting in investments or a bank account, that's great: maybe it's a good source of business funding. First, however, ask yourself what you've been saving for. If it's sitting in a retirement savings account, you may be exposing yourself to tax penalties by withdrawing it early. In addition, contributing to retirement savings accounts can be tough during the first few years of a home-based business: That money may be worth more to you in terms of securing your retirement than it would help in launching your business. Also, take a look at how much your investment is worth. If, for example, it's in stocks that have lost value since you bought them, you'll be making that loss very real if you withdraw the money now.

FACT

> If an investment that you're considering cashing out has lost value and isn't likely to ever recover it, then taking the money right now makes sense. If it could recover, however, you might want to hold onto it to recoup your principal. This is really tough to predict, but a financial planner might be able to offer good advice.

You can also consider using the equity that you've built up in your home (that is, the difference between what your house is worth and how much is left to pay on your mortgage) as a source of funding—it's possible to take out a loan or second mortgage based on that equity figure. However, you have to understand the risks involved. If the business fails, and you can't come up with the money to repay the loan, you may be forced to sell your home in order to pay it back—or even worse, the bank could repossess your home.

Credit Cards

It's so tempting to max out the credit cards—and even apply for new ones—to provide the funding you need. And, yes, credit cards can be extremely helpful when you're starting or operating your business. But there's a cost to all of this easy credit, and it's called interest.

Interest rates range from about 8 to 21 percent, so if you're not paying off your monthly balance due, you're paying a lot for the use of that money. High-interest loans like these can eat away profit margin in a big hurry, and if your business is in a delicate cash flow stage, those credit card payments can mean the difference between success and failure.

Given that caveat, it's not a bad idea to have credit cards available in case you need them for occasional cash flow management or for emergency purchases such as computers that stop working in the middle of a key project.

ESSENTIAL

> If you need to borrow a small amount of money (say, $1,000) for a short time (less than thirty days), in order to squeak by until a client pays his bill, credit cards can certainly help, either through purchases or cash advances. Pay the credit card off as soon as the client pays his bill, to limit interest charges.

Credit cards can also help to establish a better credit rating for your home-based business. Obtaining a credit card in the name of your business, using it regularly, and paying it off as soon as the bills become due, shows good financial management. Ultimately, however, you must be wary about credit cards. They can be helpful tools, but it's very easy to get in over your head with credit card debt.

Lines of Credit

Many financial institutions offer lines of credit, which cost you significantly less than credit cards when it comes to interest rates. A line of credit is often tied to the prime interest rate (at a given percentage above prime, for example). Essentially, this option can provide a maximum amount of money that you can draw on (often $10,000 for an unsecured line of credit), allowing you to access the funds whenever needed, and then pay the money back when you can.

There's usually a minimum monthly payment involved, but again, it's often less than a credit card company would require given the same amount of debt. And although life insurance is often a requirement too, you can reduce the cost by linking the life insurance to the amount that you've actually borrowed, rather than the maximum you could potentially borrow.

The flexibility and convenience of lines of credit make them the funding source of choice for many home-based businesses. A line of credit is also a great way to pay off higher-interest credit card debts—just don't rack up the credit card bills again, especially until the line of credit is paid off. As always, while a line of credit is a good money management tool when wisely used, it's not a replacement for careful spending.

Friends and Family

Although borrowing from family and friends is always a possibility, think it through carefully. Can the family member making the offer really afford to lend it to you? If the business fails, can they afford to lose the money? And what would happen to your relationship in that case? Businesses come and go, but family ties are forever.

ALERT!

> This source of start-up funding can be a major financial and emotional minefield. If you do decide to go this route, at least take it seriously. Draw up formal paperwork showing the amount lent, the interest rate, the timing and amount of payments, and what happens if you default on the loan. And, above all, honor the commitment you've made to protect not only your own integrity, but also your relationships with those closest to you.

Consider, too, whether the loan comes with strings attached. Will you be expected to visit every weekend to show your gratitude? Or report regularly on the health and status of the business? Will your judgment be questioned, and will the source of the loan want decision-making power over certain spending or other business choices?

Financial Institutions

It's rare that an entrepreneur with little more than a good idea and a willingness to work can walk out of a traditional bank with an unsecured business loan. If yours is a start-up business, without a track record of revenue and a solid customer base, you'll need to prove—usually through your business plan—that you're worth taking a risk on. And you'll often need to put up some kind of security or collateral, which the bank can repossess if you stop making payments on the loan.

Government Programs

The Small Business Administration (SBA) might be one way to access start-up funding. In most cases, the SBA doesn't lend money directly—rather, it works with banks and Small Business Investment Companies (SBICs) to guarantee loans for small businesses that otherwise wouldn't be able to qualify for a traditional commercial bank loan. Most home-based business start-ups would find the Microloan program one of the most useful SBA funding options.

These Microloans, which are available in amounts up to $35,000, are provided through intermediary lenders, each of which has its own loan requirements (typically, these will be similar to a bank's requirements). It will likely be easier to obtain a loan to purchase an asset (such as a vehicle) that can stand as collateral, and your personal guarantee is still required (if the business fails, you still owe the money). The loan cannot be used for existing debts or for real estate: It's designed for inventory, supplies, furniture, fixtures, machinery, or equipment.

Canada has a similar federal program—the Canada Small Business Financing Act—which provides loans for small businesses through banks, credit unions, and many other lending institutions to a maximum of $250,000 to help finance the purchase or improvement of property or equipment.

QUESTION?

Where Can I Find Lenders Who Work With Government Lenders?
For a list of intermediary lenders with the SBA's Microloan program, go to SBA's Web site at *www.sba.gov*, and then click on the link that says "Financing Your Business." In Canada, go to Industry Canada's site at *www.ic.gc.ca*, and click on the "Small Business" link.

In both the United States and Canada, various levels of government offer many other small business financing programs. Check phone directories and the Internet for state and provincial listings and for regional or municipal programs. Useful search words include business or economic development, opportunity funds, economic diversification, and small business financing.

Local Financial Institutions

Even if you don't qualify for a business loan, you can still apply for personal loans, home equity loans, or vehicle and equipment loans—assuming that your personal credit is good. For example, if you're planning to open a catering business, and you need a vehicle, your bank might be willing to give you an auto loan for the van that you need: The van itself becomes the collateral that reassures the bank that it won't lose its money. Financing the van then allows you to spend the capital that you do have on other items.

Venture Capitalists and Angels

Venture capitalists won't usually be investing in the average home-based business. While they're willing to take risks on new businesses, they're typically looking for a high rate of return that would come from relatively fast and significant revenue growth. If you fit that bill, however, you might be able to make a good case for yourself.

Even if venture capital firms aren't the answer, you may be able to find a patron who is willing to back you, commonly referred to as an "angel" investor. For example, have you impressed a successful local businessperson who has money looking for a good use? Get your business plan on paper, make an appointment, and go have a chat. The worst that can happen is that you'll get turned down. But you might also get an introduction to someone else who can help, an offer of help in some form other than cash (mentoring can be a powerful tool), or a reference to help you establish credit in the business community.

Boosting Your Chances

No matter who your lender is, the lender will be concerned about one overriding factor: the risk that he's taking on by giving you the loan, compared to the return he'll gain by charging you interest. Your entire approach needs to focus on convincing him that you're worth the risk. As a start-up business owner, that's a challenge: Banks, for example, often want to see three years of business financial statements in order to make a decision about how credit-worthy you are.

FACT

Lenders often judge you by the five "Cs" of credit: your Capacity to repay the debt; the Capital that you're personally investing in the business; any Collateral that can secure the debt; the Conditions of the loan, such as what you're going to use the money for; and your personal Character.

There are some things that you can do to improve your chances of success, however. And even if you're turned down, don't give up. Learn what you can do to improve your chances, and try again.

The Paperwork

Lenders want to know that you've done your homework and that you have a detailed, practical, and achievable plan in place. That's where your business plan comes in: It should provide all of the information they need to assess your chances of success. This includes the type of business you want to launch, the services or products you'll provide, your competition, your customers, and your financial forecasts. You also need to provide detailed information about how you came up with your start-up funding requirements and where the money will be spent.

As a start-up, you'll also need to provide details about your personal finances including your net worth (your assets minus your liabilities), your current debt loads, and the amount of credit that you have available. (If you have a wallet full of credit cards, for example, a lender will consider you a risky bet even if you're not using them all. The lender will be worried about your ability to repay your debt in case you max out all available credit.)

The Preparation

Rehearse your presentation to the lender so that you're completely comfortable with the information that you'll be presenting and with the way that you'll be presenting it. No doubt you know your numbers by heart by now, but don't rely on memory. Remember that, in large part, you're selling yourself to the lender. The lender has little to go on but your numbers and the way that you come across. If you're unsure of yourself, she'll be unsure of you too. Present yourself as confident and knowledgeable, however, and you'll add credibility to your business plan.

ALERT!

Before you apply for financing, check your personal credit reports. A credit report is available free of charge annually through the major credit bureaus: Equifax, Experian, and TransUnion in the United States, and Equifax and TransUnion in Canada. If the reports show any inaccuracies or problems, you need to know about them before approaching your lender.

The Answer

If you're approved, that's fantastic—but before you celebrate, make sure that you go over all of the terms of the loan. The repayment schedule, interest rates, loan payments, and the situations under which the lender can force you to repay the loan in full immediately need to be reasonable and practical given your financial forecasts.

If you're not approved, take a deep breath and swallow your disappointment. Ask your lender—without being defensive—why the loan was refused and ask if the lender could provide any advice or suggestions about improving your business plan or presentation. The lender might be able to suggest local business development resources and other sources of funding for you. A professional approach at a tough time will impress the lender—and might even be enough to let the company come through for you next time.

chapter 8

Start-up Steps

There's no shortage of tasks to complete as you work up to launching your business. Taking your time to work through all of the start-up steps, however, will give you the best possible chance for success. There's nothing worse than having to scramble to address a name or a tax issue while you're also trying to deal with your first customers. Do yourself a favor: Plan and prepare. Then enjoy your first sale!

Choosing Your Timing

If you're planning to give up regular paid employment in order to start a home-based business, then your resignation date is a key decision. All of the business and financial planning that you've done so far will help you arrive at the right answer. You need to choose a time that makes sense for the business (launching a landscaping business in the fall could guarantee you a very tough winter) and for your finances (if you're not yet ready for life without a paycheck, stick it out for a while at the job).

ALERT!

Be discreet at work about your plans: If your employer hears that you're planning to leave, they could escort you out the door sooner than you expected. Even if you need to give a certain amount of notice, be prepared for a quick exit—some companies would rather pay out your notice than risk your potentially sabotaging the company.

Even if you decide to keep the paycheck for a few more months, establish a clear timeline for when you feel the business will be ready to launch. For each week or month—whichever makes sense—assign specific tasks (and savings, if that's applicable) to ensure that when the timing's right, you'll be ready.

A word to the wise: Check your existing employment contract, to make sure that your business doesn't fall into the category of a noncompete clause that limits your ability to join or run a business that might compete with your employer. And, of course, using your employer's resources (from pens and paper to client lists) to help you launch your home-based business would be entirely unethical and probably illegal. Don't do it.

Choosing a Business Structure

Your home-based business will take one of three basic forms: a sole proprietorship, a partnership, or a corporation. Each of these forms has its pros and cons, and you'll need to decide which is best for your situation.

Sole Proprietorship

This is the easiest structure to adopt for a business. You're the owner—the sole owner—of the business, and from a legal and tax perspective, there's no difference between you and the business. As the sole owner, you get to make all the decisions and keep all the profits.

The good news is that starting and operating a sole proprietorship—and ending it—is relatively straightforward. The bad news is that if your business fails, all of your personal assets are on the line: You have what's referred to as unlimited liability. Creditors are free to come after your house, car, antique furniture, and savings accounts, for example. And because you're self-employed, you don't qualify for unemployment insurance or worker's compensation.

Although this can be a sobering thought, it's still a logical choice for many businesses, especially when you *are* the business. In fact, if your home is the business's address, and if you're borrowing money using personal assets such as your home as collateral, trying to separate yourself from the business for liability purposes (by incorporating, for example) might not even be possible.

FACT

According to the SBA, more than 90 percent of all home-based businesses in the United States report that they are sole proprietorships—they're run by one person, and have no paid employees. The statistics aren't as clear in Canada, but at least 50 percent are likely sole proprietorships.

Partnership

When you combine forces with another person (or people) in business, you've created a partnership—essentially, a multiparty or dual proprietorship in which each party is self-employed. This tends to be the choice of many husband-and-wife teams.

A partnership is easy to organize, much like a sole proprietorship, and has the same drawback in terms of unlimited liability for each partner. This is important, because it means you can be held responsible for the business's debts based on a mistake that one of your partners has made.

You can also create a limited partnership, in which one partner (the general partner) has unlimited liability, and the others have limited liability (often the same amount that they've invested in the partnership). Essentially, a limited partner is an investor, while the general partner operates the business.

It's critical to outline the partnership agreement ahead of time, when everyone is in a positive frame of mind. Agree on paper each person's responsibilities, duties, investments, and profit shares—and on an exit strategy, to handle the process if one partner wants out, or if the entire business is going to be dissolved. If things get ugly later, at least the contract will be clear.

ALERT!

If you're considering a partnership—even with a family member—you should sit down with a lawyer to formalize the partnership agreement once you've decided on the basics of how the business is going to operate. Consider the legal fees an investment in your future.

Incorporation

Corporations are legal entities that are separate from their owners. On the plus side, this means that shareholders have limited liability in the case of business losses or failures (although if the business can't be separated legally from an individual who owns the corporation, this can be challenged in court). Corporations are taxed on their own income, while shareholders pay tax on their salaries and dividends.

Forming a corporation—incorporating—is more complex than a sole proprietorship or partnership, and it's more expensive to create and maintain. But, if you foresee considerable growth, extensive outside investment, and significant risk for the business, forming a corporation might be worthwhile.

Limited Liability

For home-based businesses in the United States, Chapter S Corporations might be a better choice if you want to incorporate. Geared for small businesses, an S Corp doesn't pay tax on its income: Instead, income and expenses are divided among the shareholders, who then report them on their own income tax returns. Unlike a partnership, however, liability is limited. In a way, this business structure provides you with the best of both worlds.

However, there are stringent record-keeping and reporting standards for S Corps (that translates into bookkeeping expenses), so for most home-based businesses, an S Corp might be unnecessary. It's possible, though, to convert a sole proprietorship or partnership to an S Corp in the future.

Choosing a Business Name

Your business name is going to be around for a long time, so you need to carefully consider your options. It should be straightforward enough to let prospective customers know what product or service you provide. Being clever can help customers remember your name, but it means little if they don't have a clue what you do. And, of course, you need to stay away from names that are already registered or trademarked: otherwise, you can be sued and forced to change the name or even pay damages.

Using the name of your town, street, or a feature of the surrounding landscape can be particularly advantageous if your location is key to what you're offering. It also works if you're in a small- to medium-sized community where you might be the only business of that type and the population is large enough to serve as your entire market. If the geography won't matter to your customers, however, or you need to cast a wider net for customers than the local area, it might be better to avoid that reference.

You could consider using a "power word" in your name, to suggest how well you do your job. Precision, momentum, and quality are all examples of power words. This is part of creating an image for the business: Consider how you want a potential customer to view you. Think, for example, of how you'd feel dropping your child off at a daycare named Merri-time Child Care or Country Sunshine Daycare. You'd feel reassured, and that's exactly the image they want to project.

Using your own name can also work, especially if your service is closely tied to your personal reputation for quality work (this is one reason why lawyers and accountants so often use their own names). First names create an image of a smaller business that's folksy and warm; last names give the impression that you're a larger firm with extensive resources and plenty of professionalism. If you plan on selling the business at some future date, however, think carefully before naming it after yourself: a less personal name could be more attractive for buyers—and do you really want your name associated with someone else's business?

ESSENTIAL

As a home-based business, you're not likely to have a multimillion-dollar advertising and promotion budget to help you build your brand. Do yourself a favor and decide on a name that tells your story, leaves a positive impression, and is easily pronounced and remembered.

Registering Your Business Name

The process of registering a business name will differ from state to state and province to province, so check with your appropriate government office to find out how to go about it. Local chambers of commerce or small business resource centers can also help. Typically, you'll need to pay for a name search first to ensure that no one else has registered that name.

If you're a sole proprietorship and you're not using your own legal name, you need to register your "doing business as" (often abbreviated to "dba") name. This is usually straightforward, with a quick form and an application fee, although some areas require you to advertise a notice of your business name in the newspaper.

If you're a legal partnership, you may need to file a partnership formation notice with your state or province. The formal name doesn't have to be the same as your trade name—just file a "dba" form with the appropriate authority.

If you decide to incorporate, you'll automatically register your name in your state when you file for incorporation with the secretary of state's office. In Canada, that will be done either provincially or nationally, depending on which jurisdiction you want to be incorporated under.

Even after you register a business name, it's possible that another business out of state or in a different industry will also register and use that same name. But your registration will give you some rights, especially in the face of a potential competitor using your business name or one that's similar.

ALERT!

Check with the registration office to find out how long the name will be valid and whether the registration needs to be renewed at any point. You don't want to build all that name recognition with your customers only to lose the name to someone else because you didn't realize that you had to renew your registration.

Obtaining an Employer Identification Number

You'll need to contact the IRS to obtain an Employer Identification Number (EIN) in several cases including if you (1) plan to hire any employees; (2) have a Keogh Plan; or (3) plan to withhold income tax. An EIN, is filed for on Form SS-4 and identifies your business for tax purposes in much the same way that a Social Security number identifies you as an individual. If you have several sole proprietorships and you need an EIN, you'll use the same EIN for all of them.

If you're a sole proprietorship without employees, however, and you don't fall into the other categories above, you can simply use your Social Security number—remember that you're not an employee of the business in this case and that the business's income and expenses are actually your income and expenses. If you change your sole proprietorship to a partnership or corporation, however, or you fall into the categories above (hiring employees, etc.), you'll need to file for an EIN.

In Canada, you may need to contact the CRA to obtain a business number. If the business will be earning a gross annual income of $30,000 (Canadian) or more, you have no choice: the business number becomes your identification for the federal Goods and Services Tax (GST) that you then have to charge your Canada-based clients and remit back to the federal government.

Dealing with Sales Tax Collection

If you're operating a home-based retail business in a state or province that has a sales tax, you'll likely be required to collect the sales tax from your customers at the time of the sale and remit it back to the state or provincial government. You'll need to apply for a state or provincial tax number and set up your bookkeeping so that you track taxable sales clearly. Check how often you need to remit the sales tax to the government: i.e., weekly, monthly, or annually.

FACT

If you travel out of state or province to consumer shows, you might need to collect and pay sales tax to the host state: Check to see which rules apply. You may also need to collect and remit the sales tax that's applicable in the state or province of your customer for mail- or Internet-based sales.

Dealing with sales taxes can be a cumbersome and time-consuming process, but researching it with government offices well ahead of time will save you many headaches later on.

Obtaining Business Licenses

Certain kinds of businesses require not just registration of the business name but also licensing. These businesses may include accountants, auctioneers, chiropractors, lawyers, optometrists, architects, land surveyors, dentists, funeral directors, psychologists, veterinarians, electricians, plumbers, restaurants or food preparation services, insurance sales, daycare providers, financial planners, and many other service providers and retail shops.

Check with your local municipality or county, with your state or province, and with applicable professional organizations to find out whether you or your business needs to be licensed in your area. Your place of business may need to be inspected as well, so leave plenty of time before your planned opening date to get the appropriate licensing in order.

Opening Business Checking Accounts

Once you've registered your business name, you can head to your financial institution of choice to open a business checking account (you don't want to order your business checks until you're sure of your name). First, however, identify which kind of account to open.

Most home-based businesses can get along fine with a conventional personal checking account, which often has cheaper fees than a business account. If you're a sole proprietor, the bank considers you and the business as the same financial entity anyway. The business accounts often have more detailed record keeping, but unless you need that level of detail, using a personal checking account should be more than adequate.

ESSENTIAL

Open your business account as soon as it's practical after you start spending money on business expenses. Every legitimate expense is an investment on your part, so tally them up and make sure they're part of your bookkeeping system, because you might be able to claim them as tax deductions later.

The important thing is to have an account for your business that's separate from your personal account. The IRS and CRA both recommend keeping all personal and business finances separate. This can be a bookkeeping challenge for many home-based businesses, but the painstaking record keeping will be worth it if the government ever calls on you to justify your business deductions.

The other advantage is that a separate business account may be seen as more professional when you're dealing with vendors or suppliers. Home-based businesses may not be taken as seriously as conventional businesses, so by showing that you're running the business professionally, you're boosting your credibility.

Picking a Financial Institution

Begin by sitting down with the customer service representative at your current financial institution. Ask about the various accounts that are available, including escrow or trust accounts if your business will be required to deal with these. When making your choice, think about how many checks or electronic payments you're likely to make in a month and how many deposits you might have. Is there a limit on either? ATM cards can be helpful for making check deposits (night deposits for cash are available, too) and for withdrawing petty cash.

FACT

> You may have chosen your current financial institution when you had your paycheck direct-deposited—as a home-based businessperson, you're likely to be driving there to make deposits on a daily or weekly basis, so consider whether the location is still as convenient to your office as it was.

Using your current financial institution can save you time—you can make one trip for both personal and business purposes. But be sure to comparison shop, since other institutions may offer a better deal for small business customers.

If you envision needing a business loan in the future, establish an account with the financial institution that seems most open to that possibility. Even in today's world of corporate banking giants, personal relationships do matter.

Credit Cards

If you're planning a retail business, then you'll need to seriously consider accepting credit cards for purchases. Credit card companies will tell you that credit card customers spend more per visit on average, and it certainly does provide an important convenience factor. But from your point of view, it's not free, and you'll want to shop around for the best merchant account for your needs. Start with your financial institution—they likely work with a reputable credit card processing company, and you'll be able to enlist the help of the institution if you ever have problems.

ESSENTIAL

You should consider obtaining a credit card in the name of your business. Again, this looks more professional and also helps you to keep personal and business expenses separate. If you use a personal credit card for a business expense, be sure to pay that amount directly out of your business checking account when the bill comes.

Find out not only how much the card companies charge, but which cards they allow you to process and what the fees are for each. Fees and percentages for merchant accounts will vary from company to company. If you sell via direct mail, phone, and the Internet exclusively, expect to pay more than for face-to-face sales in which you're able to process the customer's card in person. You may also be charged a fee per transaction, a monthly fee, and an application fee. Some companies may require you to buy or lease equipment, while others may offer an authorization-by-phone set-up with no equipment. Review your needs with the credit card processing company and do your research at various financial institutions or on the Internet.

Do You Need a Grand Opening?

So when exactly do you announce that you're open for business? It's crucial that your grand opening coincides with you being ready for customers. You don't want to open your doors only to provide poor service because you're unprepared. This is especially true for anyone opening a retail business. If your inventory isn't up to adequate levels or the store isn't organized yet, your customers aren't going to be impressed enough to come back.

QUESTION?

Should the business's grand opening coincide with its actual opening?

Not necessarily. Businesses often leave several weeks—sometimes even months—between the two to give themselves a chance to iron out any kinks in their processes before they draw a significant amount of attention (and, therefore, customers) to their location.

If you provide a service, on the other hand, scheduling your time can be a real challenge, especially at first. It's easy to feel that if you don't take every job that's offered, you'll be left twiddling your thumbs in a few weeks with no cash flow. But in the meantime, you're stuck with a punishing schedule of deadlines, and you run the risk of turning out poor quality work. Again, ramping up your business gradually and relying on word of mouth rather than advertising at first can give you the time you need to assess work flow and scheduling.

Once you're ready for a full volume of customers, consider a grand opening. This can be anything from a small announcement in the local newspaper's listing of new businesses to a full marketing push to advertise a grand opening sale. But you don't necessarily need a grand opening, especially if your business is service-oriented rather than retail.

chapter 9

Putting Insurance in Place

When you bring a business into your home, your insurance requirements immediately change, particularly those that deal with liability. While some coverage can seem expensive, consider that insurance is protection against events that are beyond your control. You may never need to make a claim, but in the event of a disaster such as a fire or an accident happening to one of your customers while on your premises, insurance coverage can protect you from extreme financial losses.

Finding Insurance

Home-based businesses have traditionally encountered difficulties finding affordable insurance that suited their needs; however, the growing numbers of small businesses and the self-employed have created a sizeable enough market that insurance companies are responding to with a variety of options. Depending on the size and nature of your home-based business, you might be able to add endorsements (or "riders") to your current policies to cover your business assets and provide some basic liability insurance. This is most likely the case if you have little or no inventory and clients rarely visit you at your home office.

Stand-alone policies for home-based or small businesses are also available that offer a broader coverage than the endorsements provide. These include property and liability coverage, as well as business interruption insurance, limited coverage for loss of valuable papers and records, accounts receivable, and off-site use of equipment.

These choices can be economical because they roll several types of coverage under one umbrella. Depending on your situation, however, you may find that your needs are better met by buying coverage a la carte—picking and choosing specific policies to meet the particular insurance needs of your business.

E ALERT!

Describe the nature and scope of your business accurately when you apply for insurance—otherwise, your insurer can deny you compensation if you have to make a claim. Failing to mention the pottery kiln that's on the premises could cost you everything if it results in the insurer refusing to pay a house fire claim.

The range of coverages and the prices charged for them varies widely from insurer to insurer. It's important to research the kind of coverage you need ahead of time, and then to shop around. If you don't know where to start looking, simply open the phone book or ask other home-based businesspeople who they would recommend.

Because many insurance professionals work on a commission basis, some can be quite sales-oriented, applying a fair amount of pressure to sign right away. Don't do this unless you're certain that it's the coverage you want—the policy will still be there tomorrow, after you've had a chance to think about it and to consult your accountant or other advisor.

Insurance Agents

Insurance agents represent one insurance company: They could be employees of that company, or self-employed. You may find that your current insurance agent is perfectly qualified to help you with the additional coverages that your business needs and that you may even qualify for discounts for holding several policies with the same insurer. If your agent isn't able to help, however, you'll need to investigate other insurance companies. You can call those insurance agencies direct, doing the footwork yourself, or you can talk to an insurance broker.

Insurance Brokers

Insurance brokers are independent of the insurance companies: Think of them as an intermediary between you and the insurers. Their advantage is the ability to offer you a variety of coverages from different insurers, therefore allowing you to pick and chose the plans that are right for you. This can save you time and money: You let the broker know what you're looking for and your budget, and they'll advise you on whether your expectations are reasonable and how best to obtain the coverage.

Associations

Insurance tends to be more expensive when you're just one person or one business. The premiums drop whenever insurers are covering a large number of people or businesses, because the risks (the claims) are spread out over a wider membership. For this reason, many trade, professional, auto, college alumni, and even social organizations offer insurance coverages for their members. If you're having trouble finding affordable policies, you could join one of these associations simply to access the insurance they offer.

Property Insurance

If you own your home, you almost certainly have some kind of property insurance (and if you don't, you need to find it—now). This protects your home, including the building and most of its contents, in the case of fire and smoke damage, burglary and vandalism, and possibly earthquake and flood (although insurers may not offer coverage in certain geographic areas that are vulnerable to specific kinds of natural disasters). Your current policy may provide you with some level of coverage for the loss or damage of property that's used in a home-based business—but that coverage is probably small.

FACT

Avoid making frequent small claims on your property insurance. Each claim can increase your insurance premium, and a pattern of frequent claims can even lose you your coverage. Pay for the small damages or thefts yourself and save your property insurance for when it's really needed.

Consider increasing your policy to cover the full replacement cost of any equipment used in your business, as well as the cost of any home improvements you've made specifically for the business. In addition, even if your insurance policy covers you adequately for your business property, let your insurance representative know (in writing) that you've launched a home-based business. Being completely straightforward with the insurer now can help get your claims paid later.

Home Office Insurance

If your current property insurance coverage either doesn't cover your business or can't be supplemented, you need to look at a policy that deals specifically with home offices, home-based businesses, or small businesses. Remember that you'll need to cover office furniture, equipment, books, computers, inventory, signage, and even a building, if the business is located in an outbuilding on your land.

Renter's Insurance

Just because you don't own your home doesn't mean you can't insure what's in it. Renter's or tenant's insurance will cover your personal possessions. You may also be able to obtain endorsements or riders for the policy to cover business property and limited business liability coverage, although they tend to be smaller than those available to homeowners.

Auto Insurance

Auto insurance includes both property coverage (damage to or theft of your vehicle) and liability coverage (claims against you related to the use of your vehicle). A certain amount of business use may be covered under your current policy, but if your home-based business will be making extensive use of your car, truck, or van, you need to discuss your policy and its limits with your insurer. There may be state- or province-mandated minimums for liability coverage for commercial use, for example.

ESSENTIAL

> Even if you think your policy covers business use, be sure to let your insurer know if your vehicle use is changing—for example, if you're no longer driving it downtown to work every day and instead you're using it to deliver goods to the customers of your home-based business. Insurers appreciate—and in fact demand—full disclosure.

Your needs may change considerably if the vehicle is registered in the business's name or if your employees will be riding in or driving the vehicle. And if you have employees who use their own vehicles for your business (not for commuting, but for delivery, for example), you need to add non-owned auto insurance, which covers you and your employees while they're driving their own vehicles.

Liability Insurance

Most home-based businesses will be sole proprietorships or partnerships. As such, the law sees you and your business as inseparable. If a liability claim is successfully made against you and your insurance isn't adequate, then you face losing your personal assets, including your home. It's one thing to lose money when a business fails—it's quite another to lose your family home because you failed to insure yourself adequately.

Casualty (Liability)

This covers you against claims made by others against you for injuries or damages that happen on the premises or as a result of the work you do or the products you sell. These claims might be for property damage (a customer's car is damaged while on your property), personal injury (a customer slips and falls while on your property), or product-related injury (a customer is punctured by a nail from the birdhouse that you built and sold to her).

Your homeowner's policy likely includes some liability insurance, but it may not include coverage for liability claims made as a result of business you conduct on your property. You'll need a business liability policy or endorsement/rider.

Umbrella Liability

This is added coverage against catastrophic losses or claims. In today's "sue first; ask questions later" world, you could well be facing a liability claim in the millions of dollars (a writer is sued by someone they quoted in a newspaper article, for example). An umbrella policy will upgrade your basic auto, homeowners, or business insurance policies to cover such situations.

FACT

You can reduce the cost of insurance by increasing deductibles (the point at which the insurance kicks in) or reducing your coverage. Especially in the case of liability insurance, it's wiser to increase the deductible, because reducing your overall coverage can leave you vulnerable. The point of insurance is to guard against catastrophic losses.

Industry Specific

Some home-based businesses have special needs. Lawyers, doctors, and even cosmeticians may need professional liability insurance (malpractice insurance), while horse training or boarding facilities or guide services often require specific coverages. Check with the trade association for your profession or business to determine what extra coverage you need and where to find it.

Business Interruption

As part of your business insurance package, consider insuring yourself against the economic losses that might result if something forced the business to close either temporarily or permanently. Your property insurance may cover rebuilding in case of fire, for example, but what about the income you're losing while you rebuild?

If the business policy that you're considering doesn't include this, ask your insurer how much it would cost to add it—it may be a small price to pay for the survival of your business in case of a future catastrophe.

Overhead insurance is related to this. While disability or business interruption insurance may cover income, overhead insurance covers expenses such as rent, salaries, utilities, insurance premiums, and interest payments related to the business in case you become ill or injured.

Personal Insurance

In addition to the insurance for your business activities, you should revisit your personal insurance needs in light of starting a home-based business. How will you handle health insurance, for example, if you're no longer employed elsewhere? What happens if you become disabled? Your previous employer may have offered a life insurance policy as a benefit—should you consider taking out life insurance now that you're on your own?

Health

As health costs continue to climb, health insurance has become an issue for everyone—individuals, small businesses, large corporations, and, of course, home-based businesses. In fact, many people consider the cost of health insurance to be a significant barrier to starting their own business.

While Canadians will likely be able to find reasonably priced private health care plans to supplement their government health coverage (usually offering a buffet of benefits, including varying dental plans, prescription reimbursement and health care practitioner coverage), Americans may find that individual health insurance comes with a hefty sticker shock.

In this case, first investigate whether you qualify for the "COBRA" coverage your employer may be required to offer when you leave. This could provide the current level of coverage from your employer plan, at your current cost, for up to eighteen months. Also check whether it would be practical and cost effective to add yourself to a spouse's policy if he's continuing to work outside the home.

ALERT!

> Don't put off obtaining health insurance to when you think you can better afford it. The later you leave it, the more likely you'll end up with a medical condition such as heart disease or cancer either in yourself or in a family member, which can limit your ability to qualify for health insurance.

Of course, you can also buy health insurance as an individual from a carrier in your area, but it would be wise to also check the rates offered by trade associations that you belong to (or could join) or organizations that cater to home-based businesses or the self-employed, such as the National Association of the Self-Employed.

Also keep in mind that it might be more economical to sign up your business for a group policy. Even if your business has no employees and covers only you as a sole proprietor, you can still qualify for a group plan.

One other avenue is to buy health care coverage that's limited to "catastrophic" situations. Instead of buying insurance that includes coverage for your routine costs, you'd pay for regular checkups and medicines out of your own pocket. Your health insurance would only kick in at a certain expense level or deductible, such as $5,000, or in the case of hospitalization. It may be a more affordable way to ensure that you won't be financially ruined by a significant injury or health condition.

Disability

What would happen to you and your family if you were disabled to the extent that you could no longer earn a living? You not only won't be earning an income, but your care could turn into a financial burden as well. Disability insurance is designed to replace at least part of your income, allowing you and your family to survive financially in case of a disabling accident or illness.

Disability insurance for home-based businesspeople or the self-employed has been one of the toughest coverages to qualify for and to afford, but it is available. Buy as much insurance as you can afford (and that the insurer is willing to give you—they often want to see financial statements from the business to prove how much you're currently making).

FACT

Some insurers limit their long-term disability payouts to five years, on the grounds that many people are disabled temporarily, rather than permanently. But you need to look for longer coverage (usually up to age 65)—after all, if you're permanently disabled, it's not going to help you if your benefits end at year five.

To make disability insurance more affordable, lengthen the amount of time before your benefits kick in (moving the date from thirty to ninety days can provide a significant reduction). But beware of going with an "any occupation" plan: This means that if you're disabled and can no longer do your own job, the insurer can refuse to pay as long as you're able to work at any other occupation. "Own" occupation covers you specifically for your occupation (e.g., writer, golf pro), but is more expensive. "Regular" occupation can be a middle ground between the two, covering you as long as you're unable to work at any occupation that's close to your current occupation and that you'd reasonably be qualified or could retrain for.

Critical Illness/Long-Term Care

Critical illness insurance and long-term care coverage are two increasingly popular coverages to consider. Critical illness insurance pays you a specified amount of money if you're diagnosed with a covered illness such as cancer and often helps you find qualified treatment facilities. Long-term care coverage covers the length of time that you could reasonably expect to be in a long-term care facility or nursing home—often about three years.

Life

If you pass away, are you leaving your family with financial problems as well as grief? Life insurance is meant to provide income to those you leave behind, as well as to pay estate taxes and funeral expenses. If you're single, without financial obligations, you may not need life insurance. But if you have a family or debt, you need to think about it.

For the home-based businessperson, especially those in a partnership, life insurance plays another role. If, for example, you are partners with a nonfamily member, his spouse might inherit the partnership share of the business if he dies. If she doesn't want the business, you'll need to buy her out—but you might not have the money to do that. To avoid this situation, partners may agree to take out life insurance policies, naming each other beneficiaries, with the proceeds to be used specifically for the buyout of the business. You might also want to consider life insurance for any key individual whose death might jeopardize the business.

ESSENTIAL

When it comes to types of insurance, term (which provides a specific amount of money) is the cheapest. Other types, from whole life to universal, generally include an element of savings. The one you choose depends on what you can afford and your family situation.

To calculate how much insurance you should buy, consider how much would be required to buy out your share of the business (in the case of partnership life insurance), or how much your family would need to live on (in the case of personal insurance). Include future costs such as college educations for your children.

Worker's Compensation

If you have an employee, part-time or full-time, you must purchase worker's compensation insurance, which covers employees who are injured in the course of doing their job. This is true regardless of whether you are a sole proprietor, partnership, or corporation. If you have employees, you must have the coverage, unless your industry is specifically excluded from the requirement.

If you are organized as a corporation, then you and any other corporate officers are employees and must be provided with worker's compensation. Even if you are not taking a salary from the corporation (and thus would not receive income if you were hurt on the job), your medical costs for any job-related injuries would be covered.

As a sole proprietor or partner, you are not an employee, so you don't qualify personally for worker's compensation. You only have to carry it if you have employees who work for you. Check with the state or provincial government office that handles worker's compensation coverage to obtain application forms, premium rates, and coverage details.

Preparing for the Worst

As part of your insurance coverage, you should have a disaster recovery plan. If a fire burns down your home-based business, what's your first step? Will you even have the phone number of your insurance agent at hand? Do any clients or vendors need to be notified? And if your roof leaks, exposing valuable inventory to water damage, what are your local storage alternatives?

E ALERT!

You need to take all reasonable precautions to protect yourself, your business, and your customers. In the event of a disaster, you also need to do whatever you can to mitigate—reduce—the damages (such as moving furniture or office records to higher ground if there's a flood threat).

If you can imagine the worst-case scenario ahead of time and consider your options, you'll be much better off if a disaster actually occurs. Take the time to develop a disaster recovery plan: identify key information such as accounting records, client lists, and major written projects, and then copy the information and store it off-site in a safe deposit box or with a friend. Take videos or photos of office equipment and inventory samples and store them off site, too. If you have employees, make them part of the planning so that they know their roles and can be as helpful as possible during the crisis.

chapter 10

Legal Issues

When it comes to the legal system, what you don't know can definitely hurt you. Consequently, there are times during your home-based business venture when you should consult a lawyer before proceeding. Think of legal advice as a tool that will help to minimize the risk inherent in running your own business: After all, the upfront costs of hiring a lawyer on a consulting basis will likely be far less than hiring one to extricate yourself from a legal conflict after the fact.

When You Need a Lawyer

If you're wondering whether a lawyer is worth the cost, ask yourself one question. Are you comfortable risking your entire business on your own knowledge of contracts, liability, real estate, taxes, and/or estate planning? Assess the risk involved in doing things without legal advice. Even if you're comfortable with some tasks and their risks (registering a sole proprietorship on your own, for example), it's wise to seek help when things get more complicated (taking on a partner).

ALERT!

> Books and software programs that guide you through everything from establishing a partnership to incorporating a business might be good for research, but these reading materials are no substitute for legal advice. In fact, this kind of partial or incomplete knowledge could expose you to significant risk: If you make a mistake incorporating your company, for example, you may not have the legal protection from liability that you're counting on.

There are some obvious times when you'll need a lawyer—if you're filing suit against someone in anything other than small claims court, for example. But you should also consider bringing a lawyer on board right from the beginning of your start-up process even if you're a sole proprietor. A lawyer can advise you on the most appropriate structure for your business, and as the business issues grow more complex over time, they'll have a clear understanding of your operation.

If you're starting a corporation, professional legal advice will help you avoid mistakes that you'll pay dearly for later on. If you're starting a partnership, a lawyer is pretty much a must. Most partnerships dissolve at some point—sometimes amicably, but often in conflict. Partners need an agreement that includes an exit strategy, detailing when and how each partner can leave the business or buy out the other partner(s).

Contracts

Many home-based businesses operate on little more than handshake agreements between client and service provider—and that might be fine in a lot of cases. However, your lawyer can help you identify those times when a written contract is preferred and can help you make sure that the contract protects your interests.

Intellectual Property Protection

Intellectual property refers to work that you've created and therefore own the rights to—from inventions to books. If you need to apply for patents or copyrights or if you'll be creating a product (such as software, writing, or graphic arts) and then selling the right to use it (licensing it) to others while you retain ownership, then you'd be wise to have a lawyer with experience in intellectual property review your contracts. This also applies if you're hiring independent contractors to create the intellectual property on a "work for hire" basis (meaning that you own whatever they create for you).

Equipment and Real Estate

Will you be taking on a long-term lease of equipment, such as vehicles, construction equipment, computers, or food preparation equipment, or real estate? You'll want to consult your lawyer to ensure that the lease agreements have enough flexibility and protection for you and your business. A tax lawyer or financial expert can help you work out whether a purchase or lease makes more economic sense for your business.

ESSENTIAL

If you're considering buying a franchise or an independent business or you're selling or franchising your own business, you also need legal advice. Have your lawyer review all of the contracts and paperwork to ensure that the terms and the fees are reasonable and that you're protecting yourself both legally and financially.

Similarly, if you have concerns over real estate, either existing or future, a lawyer can provide strategic advice. They can, for example, investigate local zoning regulations if you don't want to do it yourself and apply for a variance if necessary for your home-based business.

Lawyers can also sort through complications regarding multiple owners of your home. If you're starting a business in a house you own with your two sisters, they can outline your rights and responsibilities and help you avoid potential conflicts.

Tax and Estate Planning

Your law firm may have a tax specialist, lawyer, or accountant who can help you structure your business to minimize your taxes. The more taxes you pay, the more reason to get all the help you can. And, of course, if you run afoul of the IRS or the CRA, your lawyer can help negotiate with them to come to a reasonable settlement.

Tax issues may also be part of estate planning. Will your business survive you, perhaps being taken on by a spouse, son, or daughter after you retire or pass away? If the business has value beyond your own involvement in it, you'll want to consult a lawyer to help organize the transition. You may also want to consider the possibility of marriage breakdown and make plans for the business in case that happens.

Collections and Bankruptcy

Does a major client owe you a lot of money? You might turn it over to a collection agency, which will take a percentage of any money they collect, or you might use the persuasive power of your attorney to help collect what you're owed. (Sometimes, a letter from a lawyer is all that it takes.)

You may also face the situation where one of your customers declares bankruptcy, leaving you in a sea of creditors who are all looking to recoup as much of their money as possible. A lawyer can help you maximize the amount of money you receive when the customer's assets are divided up.

In a worst-case scenario, you may be facing bankruptcy yourself. A lawyer might succeed in keeping you out of bankruptcy court by negotiating with your creditors. If you do file for bankruptcy, a legal specialist can help you keep as many assets as possible.

How to Find a Lawyer

If you're going to spend money on legal advice, make sure that you get the best advice that you can afford. Law, like so many professions, has become highly specialized. It's unlikely that you'll find one lawyer who can handle every possible legal need you might have. But you might find a law firm with a well-rounded group of attorneys who can help you in most instances.

FACT

Lawyers charge either a flat fee for a particular service or an hourly rate. Expenses such as faxes will be extra. You'll likely use a lawyer on an as-needed basis rather than a retainer basis; in some cases such as suing a competitor for improper action, the lawyer might take the case on contingency, earning a percentage of any monetary award.

Try to work with a firm that has experience representing others in your field. If you work with horses, for example, you'll want someone who knows the liability issues. If you fix cars, you'll want someone who has experience with issues such as the regulations for proper disposal of chemicals and waste oil.

The Question of Size

As a home-based business, you aren't likely to be a large client, so you may find it difficult to get the attention you want at a large, prestigious firm. On the other hand, having a large firm on your side can sometimes intimidate the competition should you find yourself in a legal conflict. If your business involves significant risk (selling wooden play equipment for children or installing underground fuel tanks, for instance), you'll want as much legal horsepower as you can afford.

You'll most likely find that a small- or medium-sized firm with reasonable business experience—which is willing to call in help when a specialist is needed—will work well for you. Or perhaps a one-lawyer shop can handle most of your garden-variety needs, but knows when to call in the cavalry for special situations. Above all, you want someone you trust—

someone whose advice you'll listen to, but who will let you make your own decisions.

Finding Lawyers

Ask other small businesspeople, your accountant, or your local chamber of commerce for recommendations. Perhaps you have a personal lawyer who has a partner or knows someone else who specializes in business law. You can also check with local bar associations for legal referral services.

Setting Up an Initial Interview

You need to work with a lawyer that you can feel comfortable with. To find that individual, interview several potential candidates. Many lawyers offer free thirty-minute consultations, but paying a lawyer's fee for half an hour may well be a good investment in time and money.

When you sit down with your prospective lawyer, ask about his or her experience with business issues in general and with your field in particular. How do you think this lawyer would handle issues that he or she had little or no experience with?

It's also a good idea to clarify the fee structure. If you call to ask a simple question, for example, are you billed a minimum of fifteen minutes? Is there a flat fee for an initial consultation on a given legal matter? Ask for a ballpark estimate on a relatively simple matter—reading over a sample contract, perhaps—and compare it to quotes from other lawyers.

How big is the firm? What other specialties does its lawyers have? Do they make an effort to ensure that you feel comfortable in their offices? Keep in mind that it's your money you're spending: There are no stupid questions, and if the lawyer makes you feel that way, find someone else. You want to work with someone who respects your desire to understand how things work.

Working With Your Lawyer

A good lawyer-client relationship works because both parties take responsibility for making it work. You should be able to have your phone calls returned in a timely way, for example. Invoices shouldn't contain any surprises, you should be kept up-to-date on ongoing matters, and the advice and information your lawyer provides should be accurate and practical for your specific situation.

ESSENTIAL

It only makes sense to be completely honest with your lawyer, even if you know you're in a mess because of your own mistake—this is why conversations between lawyers and clients are confidential after all. A lawyer can only provide you with good advice if you share all the facts.

In return, you should be prepared to provide straightforward, complete, and accurate information to your lawyer. You also need to respect your attorney's time and pay your bills on time too.

Reducing Legal Costs

Legal costs can skyrocket quickly if you're not watching them very carefully. Think strategically when it comes to obtaining legal advice. It's better to bring a legal issue to your lawyer's attention as early as possible. For example, asking your lawyer to help you create a good contract will be cheaper and more efficient than asking the lawyer to help you get out of a bad contract that you signed in ignorance.

There are ways to reduce costs, however. These include:

- Being organized. Have your paperwork and records in order and available will save time (and, therefore, money).
- Doing some work yourself. You may be able to create an agreement or contract for your lawyer to review, rather than having her create it from scratch—the more work you do, especially in routine matters, the less you'll owe the lawyers.
- Working with paralegal staff. A paralegal's hourly rate is less than a lawyer's—if the matter is routine, don't insist on sitting down with your lawyers; work with their staff instead.

Keep in mind that good lawyers will work with you to save you money on legal fees: They understand that small home-based businesses generally have tight budgets. But it's important to pay your lawyer what she's worth for the work she does too. After all, she might be saving you from significant risk.

Small Claims Court

There's one legal avenue available to you in certain disputes that's specifically designed to allow you to represent yourself—small claims court. Generally limited to small monetary disputes, small claims court is often used by businesses and individuals to help collect debts that are owing to them or to sort out contractual disputes. Small claims courts are governed by state and provincial law, so monetary limits and legal areas differ depending on where you live. In the United States, small claims procedures are also available at the federal level in Tax Court.

FACT

Small claims court limits vary from $3,000 to $25,000 in the United States, depending on your state, and from $5,000 to $25,000 in Canada, depending on your province. If your claim exceeds the limit, you may still be able to use small claims court, but you'll need to waive your right to any amount that's over the limit.

The main advantage to small claims court is that it simplifies the court procedures so that laypeople can handle the process without requiring the services of a lawyer. Therefore, it reduces potential legal costs significantly. And if you win your case (proving that your client owes you the money, for example), you can ask for the court's help to enforce the judgment against your client.

Before Small Claims Court

First, check that the statute of limitations hasn't run out on the issue that you're trying to resolve. Time periods vary, but generally they give you a reasonable period in which to discover the problem, attempt to solve it, and then apply to the court for assistance.

You've very likely attempted to collect the debt or sort out the contract situation several times already. But if you're considering small claims court, you need to do it one more time, in writing. If you're trying to collect a debt, for example, you'll send the debtor, by certified mail, a request to pay the money and a time limit for payment, letting him know that it's your final request for payment. You also need to say that if you don't receive the money by your deadline, you'll take the debtor to court.

E ALERT!

> Check with local business associations or court systems to see if mediation or arbitration might be available for you to use instead of going to court. These conflict resolution mechanisms are actually required before you go to court in some jurisdictions, and they can be very effective at coming up with creative solutions to issues.

Of course, you need to keep copies of all correspondence regarding the matter—if you speak to the other party on the phone, for example, note the time and date of the call, and what you spoke about. Print out copies of e-mails that you've sent or received. You're looking to support your side of the case as strongly as possible.

Before you make the final decision to file your suit, ensure that you're clear on your aims and on what the court can achieve for you. If, for example, a client owes you a large chunk of money, but they've just declared bankruptcy and have few assets, you're going to have trouble collecting the money even if you win your suit. Think about whether the suit is worth the time and trouble it's going to take.

Filing in Small Claims Court

Once your deadline has passed, you can go ahead and file your small claims lawsuit. You usually need to do this in the small claims court that's closest to where the other party lives or does business.

ESSENTIAL

If the other party lives out of state or province or a significant distance away, then you should rethink small claims court due to the travel costs involved. If the money involved is worth the travel time and expense, go ahead—otherwise, consider writing it off as a bad debt instead.

The local county clerk's office can advise you on which paperwork you need and how to go about filing it. There's usually a small fee involved in filing, so be prepared. Also ask what actions you need to take next: You'll likely have to notify the other party (the defendant) by officially "serving" him.

If you'll need to call witnesses to court, make sure that you understand the time frames and methods needed to give them sufficient notice to appear. Again, your county clerk can give you the right advice.

Your Day in Court

It's essential that you prepare adequately for your time in front of the small claims court judge. Have all of the paperwork that backs up your case organized and available. Copies of letters, contracts, independent assessments of damages in the case of a business vehicle accident, eyewitness statements—bring along whatever will help the judge decide that your story is the more credible one.

FACT

In addition to the money you're owed or the amount that you're claiming in a contractual dispute, you can also request that the court award costs to cover your expenses, such as fees that you've paid to file the court case, travel expenses, or lost work time. Just ensure that you keep the expenses reasonable and under the monetary limit.

It also helps to rehearse what you're going to say, but keep in mind that small claims court judges understand that you're not a lawyer. They'll often help you out if you're having trouble with the procedure. Just try to be as clear and concise as possible: Remember that courts are incredibly busy places, and the judges don't want or need to hear long explanations. Keep it short and simple.

Following Up

If you win your case, you'll then have a judgment that you can enforce. Check with the county clerk to find out what avenues are available to you to help you collect the amount awarded. Often, you can return to court to ask for help, which might take the form of placing a lien against the other party's property or garnishing their wages.

If you lose, check with the clerk to find out what the appeal process is and how soon you need to file the appeal. Then sit back and decide whether it's really worth spending additional time and money on an appeal. Keep in mind that you'll likely need to prove that the judge made a legal mistake—simply disagreeing with the decision isn't going to be enough.

chapter 11

Setting Up Your Home Office

How much of your home will you need to turn over to your business? The space needs of a home-based business will vary widely, depending on whether you're focused on repairing cars or preparing accounts. However, there are some concepts that all businesses have in common—like the desk space and the computer where you'll handle the administrative duties. As for the rest, you need to assess what you need, compare it to what you have, and come up with whatever's left over.

Keeping Home and Home Offices Separate

One of the biggest challenges facing you as a home-based business owner is to achieve a balance between work and the rest of life. One of the best solutions is to have an office with a door that closes.

That door defines the boundary between your personal life and your work life: Not only can you shut the door and walk away at the end of the day, but you can better shut off those after-hours work calls that you'll be tempted to answer. "Out of sight, out of mind" may be a cliché, but it's accurate. If you're still having trouble leaving your work behind, imagine that the door is locked and won't re-open until tomorrow morning. Your spouse and your children will thank you.

The door also helps you manage the rest of your family: When you're in the office and the door is closed, you're at work. That means that the situation needs to be serious before they knock on the door and interrupt you. If it helps, provide age-appropriate examples of "serious" situations to help your children understand what you mean. Whether the child can have a snack before dinner is not serious. Setting the kitchen on fire is serious.

Which outlines another point: Trying to work while also trying to care for your children is an even bigger challenge. This situation will get easier as they grow older and can play more independently, but as any home-based business parent will tell you, the crying will always start just after you call your client. You've been warned.

Assessing Your Needs

The key to determining your needs is to know your chosen business as well as you can before setting up shop. Are you a retail business? Will customers or clients be visiting often? Will more than one customer or client be coming at once? What kind of storage will you need? How frequently will you need access to that storage?

One of the most effective ways to approach this is to imagine yourself spending a typical working day in your home-based business. "Walk" through every task or process, jotting down the office space and all its contents that you'll need to get the tasks done. You'll then have a reasonably comprehensive basis on which to build.

ESSENTIAL

If you're setting up your desk and computer in a corner of the family room, be sure to enlist the opinions and advice of other family members who will be using the space. If they're involved in setting it up, they'll be less likely to complain about your use of the space later.

The Office-Based Business

Many home-based businesses require an entire office—bookkeeping, accounting, freelance writing, editorial services, graphic design, and legal services are examples of businesses that all center on an office space. Ideally, you'll have an extra room in your house—with a door that closes—that you can transform into a space that's dedicated solely to your business. This is particularly important if your clients will be visiting your office: You need a place where they'll feel comfortable discussing their needs with you.

If you don't have a separate room, you'll need to get a little more creative. Look for an area in the house that's as private as possible and could be converted to office space. Basements often hide useable space, if they have a proper concrete floor and wall. You'll need to be mindful of dampness and flooding problems, of course, but you may be able to turn it into an office with some damp-proofing paint on the walls, a little basic carpentry to create a partition, and a couple of hundred dollars in professional electrical work.

ALERT!

If you're looking at any kind of renovations, research and comply with all local fire and building codes, and obtain any needed building permits before you start. Basements, attics, and garages may all present fire exit issues, so be sure to put your safety first.

Similarly, walk-up attics can offer potential office space, but they often face a problem with heat, which can be very hard on computer equipment (and you). Perhaps this can be cured with a whole-house fan or a window air conditioner. Or perhaps there's one end of your garage that, with some simple renovations, could become an office?

Assess your office space honestly—from the perspective of your clients. If it's not appropriate, you might have to plan on meeting clients at their offices instead, at least until you can work out a different solution to office space. You can always set aside funds as you go forward to create a more workable office space, especially if your business will grow with any speed. The most successful business owners decide how much they can make do with for the time being, and plan for changes at certain stages of financial success.

The Non-Office-Based Business

Of course, if your business deals with a retail, manufacturing, or repair operation, you have less flexibility in dealing with space issues. You need a considerable amount of space, and you very likely need to accommodate your customers, too.

FACT

Sometimes, an outbuilding is the only real solution to a space issue—businesses such as auto repair would fall into this category, for example. The administration needs of this kind of business can be met with a desk and computer that are set up in a reception area within the main space.

You may need to look at major changes to the house itself. Can you reasonably turn a rarely used formal living room into a retail shop, for example? It might work if you can effectively close it off from the rest of the house, to preserve your family's privacy. If you have a walk-in basement or a fully enclosed porch or sunroom area that might work, too, as could a garage, especially if you turned the large door into a wall with an entry door and a window.

Client Concerns

If your place of business needs to accommodate client visits, there are other considerations. First, check that local zoning regulations allow customers to visit your home-based business (some don't). Is there adequate parking on the street or in the driveway or will your customers be blocking other family members' vehicles?

For a retail or repair business, it's ideal to have a separate entrance to your home that leads directly into your business space. Make sure that it's clearly marked, inviting, and well lit: Show your customers that you're expecting them and that you care about initial impressions. Flowering shrubs or container gardens can be an inexpensive way to make that impression.

ESSENTIAL

Have a friend conduct a "trial run" before you welcome your first customer to assess anything that's inappropriate or unsafe—from dog toys on the lawn to a loose railing on the steps up to the front door. Is your house number clear, are there adequate places to park, and is there somewhere for customers to hang their coats?

You also want to avoid having your customers walk through or even see the private areas of your home. It's absolutely essential to keep your pets confined, as well. Not only can they be a huge liability issue, but some people are allergic to pets such as dogs and cats. A sneezing client will be an unhappy client.

Solutions for Small Spaces

You may have a finite amount of square footage for your office, no matter how creatively you look for space. In this case, consider separating your records storage from your office area, perhaps putting a filing system in the attic or basement (first solving any heat or dampness problems that could damage the stored items). Off-site storage for records that you don't need to access frequently might also be an option.

In terms of making the best use of the space that you have, try multifunction furniture. You can find computer desks, for example, that resemble armoires when the doors are closed. Open up their doors, and shelves flip down to create work surfaces, filing drawers roll out, and the computer's ready to go, with a bulletin board space on the back wall of the desk.

You can also make use of awkward space in your home for bookshelves and storage areas. Look at the spaces under stairs, for example. Can you fit a small desk and a set of wall shelves into an unused alcove on a stair landing perhaps?

Making it Functional

Before you begin to buy or borrow anything to put into your office, consider the empty space. If the walls need painting, now's the time to do it before a paint job entails moving bookcases or filing cabinets. If your home-based business involves customer or client visits, then you'll need a color that "fits" your business image (perhaps a heritage color for an antique store, for example), but if it's just you in your office, choose whatever will make you happy. Yellow is considered a productive color; blue is soothing; red and orange are energizing; and green is grounding.

What's on the floor right now? Carpeting can make the room warmer, if that's an issue, while laminate flooring is very easy to install and tends to be hard-wearing too. If the hardwood needs refinishing, now's a good time to do it, before you start hauling in furniture. If you're installing new carpet, refinishing hardwood, or painting give the room a few days to air out before you start working in it—even fumes from latex paints can be unhealthy to breathe.

QUESTION?

Can following feng shui principles help my business succeed?
Commonly defined as the Chinese art of placement, feng shui certainly won't hurt. Principles include not sitting with your back to the office entrance, locating your office in your house's "wealth" corner, and using moveable items such as mirrors or candles to redirect energy flow from negative to positive.

You also need to consider wiring and lighting. Does the room have adequate lighting and electrical outlets? Can you place your computer and office equipment on the electrical circuit without overloading it and causing a fuse to blow or a circuit breaker to trip? You'll likely be in the office during daylight and evening hours, so assess the lighting from both respects. Can you meet your needs with floor or desk lamps or do you need an electrician's help to rewire the overhead lights?

Outfitting Your Office

Although you'll need business-specific furniture and shelving for retail and other operations, the basics will be very similar for all businesses, especially those that are office-centered. You'll need furniture, filing space, storage space, shelf space, and sitting space for at least yourself, if not your customers, too.

You may already have some of the furniture you need. If you're outfitting on a budget, however, check out used office furniture stores and classified newspaper ads for great bargains. But whether you're buying new or used, be sure to measure the space you have available inside the office, and the doorways and halls through which large pieces of furniture will have to be moved, before you head out shopping. That beautiful rolltop desk isn't going to do you any good if it won't fit through the office door. In fact, just to be sure, take your tape measure with you.

FACT

Even if you're on a budget, consider splurging on something for your office that you really love, like a piece of art or something that's going to be really useful (like an oversize desk). You'll be spending a lot of time in the office, so you need to make it a place that's both welcoming and functional.

Although it might sound frivolous, consider what will make you happy to spend the entire day in your office. Would a bird feeder outside your office window help? How about a comfy floor cushion for the dog, who might be your main company during the day while the kids are at school? Don't overlook these items, because they can add a great deal of enjoyment—and, therefore, motivation—to an ordinary day at the office.

Desks and Chairs

Whatever you choose for a desk, make sure that it's computer friendly. Desks can be high-end and very stylish, of course. Think about your needs: If you're an architect whose clients will be visiting, you need your office to reflect your style. This could include a matching set of cabinets or bookshelves to go with the desk or even a custom-made set of furniture.

At the other end of the scale, a door slab stretched between two pine bookcases might be enough to get you started or you could opt for a simple pressboard work surface that's available inexpensively at an office store. These come with holes in the backboard for the many connection cords to slip through as well as keyboard holders and monitor shelves.

You'll also need a comfortable office chair that suits your computer table or desk. Office supply stores keep many on hand—sit in them all and slide the chairs up to one of the display desks to ensure that you find it both sturdy and comfy. Be sure the seat fits, both from back to front and from the seat to the floor.

ALERT!

If you're buying a used office chair that's on wheels, ensure that it meets today's safety standards. Older chairs that have only four floor supports are vulnerable to tipping if you lean too far in them; you need at least five floor supports—look for the "star" pattern.

Buy the highest quality that you can afford. Your chair affects your posture and your back, so if you're uncomfortable, you'll not only be less productive, you might even be risking your health. Also assess whether you'll need chairs in your office for clients: Make sure the chairs are close to the same height as yours (to make conversation comfortable) and pleasant to sit in (unless you want to keep the meetings very short).

Bookshelves

You'll likely need at least one, if not several, bookshelves in your office, if for nothing else than the raft of manuals that come with the electronic equipment you'll need. Maybe you have a few professional books that you like to have on hand, and you need a nice spot to stack that monthly trade journal.

Bookshelves range from the most basic pressboard styles to those that look more like pieces of furniture. A fairly expensive solution is to have built-in shelves installed—but keep in mind that once they're in place, they can't be moved, which might limit your flexibility as the office grows.

Filing Cabinets

If you're going to have plenty of work, research, or client files, you'll need to start off with a substantial file cabinet. Consider what kind of documents you'll be storing, and choose either legal or letter size (or one that can accommodate either). A regular desk typically comes with at least one file drawer, which is ideal for those active files that you need within easy reach of your phone or computer, but you'll most likely need at least one filing cabinet for less urgent files.

Other Handy Items and Extra Supplies

After you've spent hours at your desk, a little change of scenery can help remotivate you. An easy chair where you can comfortably read a report or trade journal is ideal if you have the space. You might also want to invest in a small stereo, so that you can listen to music if that helps you work or feel connected to the outside world through news and talk shows. Choose one with a remote control so that you can turn down the volume when the phone rings.

ESSENTIAL

Additional tables can be very useful if you work on projects that require spreading out and if you have room in your office for them. Sure, you could use the kitchen table, but you'll quickly tire of cleaning off your project papers whenever it's family mealtime. You'll also need space for equipment such as computer printers or fax machines.

While you don't want to rival your local office warehouse for extra office supplies, be sure to always have extra printer ink or toner cartridges on hand, as well as a good supply of paper. You also want good stock levels of any other office supply that's essential to the business—such as courier envelopes. But be sure that you can store these extra items where they won't be damaged by moisture or heat.

Office Services

You may find at least at first that you handle most office services such as document shredding and cleaning yourself. However, as you get busier, you need to consider the value of your time. If you're charging $50 an hour, would it be cheaper for you to spend an hour a week cleaning your office or for someone else to come in and do it for you?

Cleaning

It might not be reasonable to hire a cleaner just to come in and deal with your home-based business area, but you might want to add it to the list of cleaning duties if you already use a cleaning service. This is especially important if you have clients coming to the office: A clean and tidy office gives you a professional and credible image even before the meeting starts. Otherwise, be prepared to clean the office yourself: Dusting, vacuuming, and taking out the trash are non-negotiable every week.

Document Shredding

If you deal with confidential matters, any potentially sensitive information that isn't going to be filed needs to be shredded. If you simply throw it out in the trash, it's vulnerable to the local critters tearing it apart and spreading the papers all down the block—and even to corporate espionage, depending on who you're working with. You could buy a document shredder, but if your volume is high, consider using a document shredding service where you can drop documents off or that provides a pick-up service.

Trash Collection

Is the kind of trash that your home-based business generates within your community's service limitations? Do you pay by the bag for trash service, for example, or is there a bag number limit? If so, be sure to budget in the extra costs that your business will generate. You also need to ensure that you're complying with all hazardous or environmentally unfriendly waste rules, such waste oil disposal, and recycling as much material as possible. Ask your waste management service or your municipality or county office for advice.

Ergonomics

Home offices can be hazardous to your health. A poorly positioned chair and keyboard can result in wrist problems like carpal tunnel syndrome that can actually prevent you from being able to type, while a chair with poor lumbar support can leave your back aching at the end of the day. It's worth your while to not only buy the best chair you can afford, but also to set up that chair and your office properly.

- Your chair height should be between eight and ten inches from the underside of your work surface.
- Your feet should fall flat on the floor; avoid crossing your legs.
- Your chair back should be adjustable vertically so that the curved section cradles the lower back.
- Your chair seat's length should reach from your knees to the base of your spine—this aids circulation in your legs.
- Your armrests should support your arms and shoulders, but should not impede the ability to push close to your desk or worktable.
- Your chair and desk should be positioned so that your elbows are at a 90-degree angle when you're using your computer keyboard, and your forearms are parallel to the desktop.

In addition to setting up your office properly, think about using it properly. Take regular breaks from the computer to rest your eyes and to stretch your muscles. Think about your posture: If you have a tendency to slouch, this can impede deep breathing and actually make you feel tired. Make it a habit to correct your posture every time the phone rings—imagine that there's a string attached to the top of your head, pulling you upright from your scalp: Your shoulders will naturally straighten.

chapter 12

Home Office Technology

From accounting to customer list management, technology is streamlining much of the administrative work involved in running a business. But it's doing much more than that—in many cases, it's actually making the business more profitable by saving time . . . and time always means money. Depending on your business, you might simply need a basic computer set-up and a cell phone—or you might need a high-powered computer capable of managing sophisticated graphics and a phone system to match. Whatever your needs, there's technology that can help.

Office Telephones

The most important feature of your office phone system is a second, dedicated telephone line for the business so that you're not sharing the phone with your family. Sure, you could opt for a cheaper "distinctive ring" feature, which is a separate number that shares the main phone line, ringing differently when a call comes in on that number—but imagine how frustrated you'll be if you're sharing that main line with chatty teenagers. Even if you live alone, a second line can be useful to help you establish a boundary between personal and business calls.

Of course, if yours is a business that will need more than one phone line, factor that into your plans right from the start. Talk to your local phone company about small business options—they likely offer a number of service packages that can reduce the cost of the phone lines.

ESSENTIAL

Check that the ringer on your office phone can be shut off completely. That allows you to work undisturbed if you need a stretch of uninterrupted time and also means that you'll be less tempted to answer the phone after hours (assuming that your business doesn't need to deal with after-hours calls).

Phone prices have dropped so low that most phones of reasonable quality now come equipped with features such as speakerphone, hold, and speed-dial functions. These are all very handy, but make sure that you test them out with a friend or family member before using them for the first time—to avoid inadvertently cutting off a potential client. If your phone comes with short cords, you can buy longer versions to make it easier to place the phone where it's handiest for you to reach.

If you're considering a cordless model that will allow you to answer the phone even if you're working in another room of the house (or on your deck!), opt for a good quality digital model. Look for a phone with excellent acoustics, little interference, and security against eavesdropping.

Invest in a headphone system if you'll be spending a lot of time on the phone. Tucking the phone between your ear and your shoulder as you write notes is a surefire way to cramp up your neck muscles. Just make sure that the headphone provides clear reception, for you and your caller—test it out before using it for the first time.

Handy Phone Features

Phone companies offer a number of handy features that you may want to consider. Caller ID is definitely worth the cost, since there will be times when you want to screen your calls (and most business phones have the capacity to display the caller's number if you subscribe to a caller-ID service). Knowing that it's a key client calling means you can choose to pick up the phone, even if you're in the middle of a large project.

Call waiting, however, can be problematic. Although it's handy to know that someone else is calling while you're on the phone, ignoring the beep can be difficult—and if you toggle back and forth to answer one call while you're already on another one, you run the risk of seriously offending the original caller. Having voice mail on the line, so that the second caller can leave a message, may be a better option.

FACT

Once you determine all of the features you need for your phone system—including number of lines, Internet access, calling features, cell phones, calling cards, long distance and toll-free numbers—talk to your phone company about a package deal. The phone company will often reward you with discounts for bringing it all of your business.

Call forwarding reroutes an incoming call to another line if you're on the phone or away from your desk. This is especially useful if you're on the road a lot or if you work out of a different location periodically. You can usually turn the feature on and off as you need it, selecting whichever number you need the phone forwarded to.

Long-Distance Plans

It's impossible to avoid the deluge of special offers from long-distance telephone providers these days. To choose the most suitable one, first figure out where you'll be calling most frequently and when, and then look at which provider gives you the best deal. Ensure, however, that you choose a reputable company that provides good customer service—you don't need the hassle of unreliable phone service.

ESSENTIAL

Even after you make your long-distance choice, monitor what other phone companies are offering. You can always switch providers, but it's also worth contacting your existing provider and asking if they can give you a better deal. They monitor the competition, too, and might match the offer or provide other benefits.

Toll-Free Numbers

For businesses that draw customers from a wide geographic area, toll-free numbers are a relatively inexpensive way to encourage customers to contact you. People are much more likely to call to ask questions if you're footing the bill, and once you have the customer on the phone, you can determine exactly what he needs and how you can provide it.

Your local phone company likely has a number of toll-free packages available. You'll want to monitor the usage, especially at first, to make sure that you've chosen the best package for your needs. When you're speaking with customers, keep in mind that you're paying for the call, so that you walk the line between effective sales and running up your phone bill.

The Digital Option

Using Internet technology to make phone calls, often called Voice over Internet Protocol (VoIP), is becoming increasingly available with its major advantage being saving cost over regular "land" lines. Its major drawback is that it does rely, of course, on your Internet connection—so you may find an occasional problem with "dropped" calls. The same land line features such as local and long-distance calling, voice mail, and call forwarding are also often available, so the technology is definitely worth looking into, especially as voice quality and call reliability have improved significantly over the past several years.

Watch for hidden costs in VoIP phone plans, which are often offered as a "flat fee" service per month. Find out what that monthly fee includes (such as calls within the state or continent), what it doesn't, and what happens if you make calls that are outside the plan's fee. Also check out activation costs, taxes and other government fees, and cancellation fees.

Staying in Touch

In today's fast-paced world of communications, customers expect instant access to you, or close to it. They expect to have e-mails and phone messages answered within hours, if not instantly. In some cases, a recorded message on the phone will mean that they'll move on to the next company on their list that provides similar services—they won't even leave a message.

You need to assess how critical it is that you're in constant contact with your clients, and plan your technology purchases to suit that. If you're a plumber offering twenty-four-hour emergency response, for example, a pager may be crucial. For accountants, however, there's very little that can't be resolved the following business day (except, perhaps, during tax season), so they can afford to rely on phones and voice mail.

FACT

> In many areas, you may be able to have your cell phone share your office number. This can be useful if you expect to be out of the office (on sales calls, for example) a lot. This solves the problem of giving your clients more than one number to contact you or call-forwarding your office phone.

Cell Phones

Cell phones have become virtually essential in today's business world. Many people still resist them, not wanting to become "tied" to their phones and accessible at all hours and places to their clients. If that's an issue, you may choose to turn the phone off during the times you prefer not to be disturbed, allow calls to go to your voice mail (put the ringer on *silent*) so you can review the messages and answer them at your leisure or simply don't give out the number to clients.

You'll still have the phone for emergencies (if you're stranded by a vehicle breakdown, lost, or stuck in traffic and running late), but you won't constantly be interrupted by its ringing. If you do need to stay in touch, you can use the cell phone to check your messages back at the office, or you can forward your office phone number to your cell phone number (check that your network will let you do that).

Cell phones can also help you make the most efficient use of your time—you can return phone calls while you're waiting to pick the kids up from soccer practice, for example, or make sales calls when you're out of the office but between meetings.

ALERT!

> Numerous studies have proven that cell phones, even ones that use headphones, can contribute to vehicle accidents. Even if your area allows the use of cell phones in vehicles, make sure that you stay safe: Don't talk and drive at the same time—find a safe place to pull over, and then make or answer the call.

Cell phone features and payment plans change so frequently that the best advice is to shop around for the deal that offers the best price for the features you need—which may include compatibility with your office phone (for forwarding), e-mail/Internet access, clear reception, and reliable coverage for the areas in which you travel.

Handheld PDAs

Of course, regular cell phones are just a starter toy when compared with the computing power of a personal digital assistant (PDA). These mini-computers range from basic models that store your diary, your contact list, and your task list to much more sophisticated models that connect wirelessly to e-mail and the Internet, take photos, and even incorporate a cell phone.

The more you're away from your desk, relying on mobile technology, the more sophisticated your choice of PDA will likely be. Figure out what you'll need it for, and then choose a model that fits those needs. You'll need to determine which operating system (or software) you want to use, including how important it is to have mini-versions of the software that's on your main computer.

Also review how much external memory storage it comes with (and whether there are one or two slots for storage), how much internal memory it has (especially if you'll need to work on large files such as spreadsheets), and how easy the screen is to read (color helps). Some PDAs come with thumb keyboards; others with pens—you can learn to use either quite effectively.

FACT

It's easy to get caught up in buying electronic gadgets because they're handy and cool, or buying more advanced (and more expensive) gadgets than you really need. Instead, focus on the tools that you need to communicate professionally and equip yourself with the tools that fit those needs.

Answering Machines and Services

Many business-type phones come with an answering machine built into them, but these desk-based answering machines are increasingly being replaced by voice mail systems. The voice mail services—usually offered through your local telephone company—have the advantage of taking messages while you're on the phone as well as when you're away from your desk. A client won't end up with a busy signal—they'll always be able to leave you a message.

If you do decide to use a desk-based answering machine, ensure that it has clear reception and recording so that both your outgoing message and your clients' incoming messages are clearly audible. Opt for a machine that provides plenty of time for clients to leave messages.

ESSENTIAL

Test your answering machine or voice mail by calling your office number from a different phone. Check that your outgoing message is clear and professional and leave a test message on the system so that you can check that incoming messages are clearly recorded and that the system is operating properly.

If it's important to you that callers speak to a real person instead of a recording when you're unavailable, you can opt for a live answering service. Many professionals, such as doctors or contractors, choose this alternative. It can mask the fact that you're a home-based business by making it sound like you have reception staff. Speaking to a real person can also be more reassuring for clients—it provides a personal touch that a machine cannot.

Computer Systems

If you only need a business computer to handle basic tasks such as word processing, accounting, and e-mail/Internet access, you can pretty much walk into your local electronics outlet and pick any model. You'll need to be more careful about your choice, however, if you need to handle large graphic, spreadsheet, or database files.

Your best approach is to first assess your needs, both current and future. If you're not handling graphic design now, for example, but you've identified it as a potential business line a year or so down the road, you'll want to buy a computer that can handle memory-hungry graphic software and files or that can be upgraded to handle them. The extra cost to build in the capacity will be much smaller than buying a brand new system next year because the existing computer can't handle it (or can't be upgraded effectively).

Research the kinds of computer systems that will meet your needs. Become familiar with the terminology and the minimum and optimum requirements that you'll need. The Internet and electronics store flyers often provide good background information and pricing examples. Then you'll be ready for the stores or Internet outlets themselves. If you choose one that has noncommissioned salespeople, you're less likely to find a hard-sell approach.

FACT

> The *PC World* family of magazines and Internet site (*www.pcworld.com*) provides well-researched and trustworthy background information on electronics purchases of all kinds, but especially computer systems. Their ratings for popular models can be particularly helpful, since they're often categorized for home- or small-office users.

Desktops and Laptops

Today's laptops have the capability of most desktops (albeit at a slightly higher price), but provide portability as well—and can serve as desktops if they're attached to a desktop "docking" station. If you expect to be out of the office on sales calls most days or if you're going to be traveling frequently, pick a laptop. If portability isn't an issue, go with the cheaper desktop (you can always buy a more basic and less expensive laptop as a backup in case of desktop failure or for the occasional road trip).

Your system requirements will be determined by what you'll be using the computer to do—effectively, the kind of software programs that you'll be using on it. For a good guide, check the software boxes or their manufacturer's Web sites to determine the system requirements for each program.

The computer's processor (CPU) determines how quickly the computer runs—the faster the processor, the more expensive it is, but you don't want to skimp here. Look for Pentium 4s and up, or their equivalent. Installed memory is a good indicator of how well your computer will perform and how many things you'll be able to do at once on it—look for at least 512MB, but buy more memory if you can. The hard drive stores your data, so size is again important—for the flexibility to work with digital photo files, for example, you should be looking at 40GB and up.

When it comes to graphics, most mid-priced computers will come with a perfectly adequate graphics card for average users; if you have specific graphics needs, however, ensure that your card, memory, and processor can all handle your needs.

Removable file storage devices include recordable CD and DVD drives (having both gives you the greatest flexibility). The popularity of "keychain" type USB file storage devices means that the best computer designs have USB ports on the front of the unit for easy plug-in.

Monitors

Gone are the days of bulky monitors taking up acres of desk space. Prices are now so low for the digital flat-panel LCD monitors that the minimum you should be shopping for is a seventeen-inch model, especially if you'll be working at the computer a lot. For those working on screen with large spreadsheet, graphics, or database files, a nineteen- or twenty-one-inch screen will be invaluable.

ALERT!

To reduce glare and reflection on your computer screen, place your monitor so that it's not facing or directly opposite the windows in your office. You can also buy inexpensive glare shields that fit over the monitor to help reduce the strain on your eyes.

Printers

You basically have a choice between inkjet and laser printers in either less expensive monochrome (black), and more expensive color models. They all have their pros and cons, centered on three major features: speed, resolution, and cost.

Inkjet printers are the least expensive models, often thrown in for free with a computer because the manufacturers really make their money on the ink cartridges that you'll be buying over the life of the printer. Overall, their print quality isn't as high as laser printers, but if you buy a better inkjet printer, it will handle photos and graphics well, although probably slower than a laser (some inkjets that are dedicated photo printers rate particularly high on quality).

Laser printers are faster and generally produce better quality printing than inkjets, and monochromes in particular have dropped in price to the point where they're giving inkjets a run for their money—especially since toner cartridges for laser printers can be less expensive than the print cartridges for inkjets over the life of the printer. Color laser printers are the top of the print quality and price scales, but they will be worth the investment if your business relies on producing high-quality color documents.

Other Computer Hardware

There's plenty of other equipment that links into a computer system, including scanners, digital cameras, and digital camcorders. If you'll be using two or more computers in your home-based business, you should also look into networking capabilities so that you have one main "server" that lets all of the other computers share the system including its files and peripherals such as printers. Again, start with your needs, and then look at model features.

FACT

Wireless technology that connects computer system components without cabling is becoming increasingly available. Be aware, however, that wireless Internet connections may not be secure. Research your system as well to find out if it's compatible with the wireless component.

Software

Most computers come equipped with an operating system (usually Microsoft Windows) and other software. An office suite that comes with word processing, visual presentation, spreadsheet, database, and time management applications will likely cover most home-based business needs.

You should also invest in an accounting software package—you simply set up the accounts and enter in your income and expenses, and it creates reports and financial statements for you. Most will even link to income tax preparation software released by the same manufacturer, making tax time less onerous. In fact, many accountants actively encourage you to submit electronic bookkeeping files to them along with your paper receipts—and this will certainly reduce your tax preparation costs.

Your other software needs will depend on your business. If you're not sure what you need, check with local entrepreneur centers or your professional or trade association to see what's popular with other business owners. A contact management system (which lets you store information about clients, vendors, and other key people) will be very useful.

Faxes and Photocopiers

Many home-based businesses will find that their fax and photocopying needs can be met effectively with a multifunction computer printer that handles printing, scanning, photocopying and faxing all in one. Opt for a model with a flatbed scanner, which can handle photocopying items that won't fit through a document feed.

While multi-function machines are handy, you may want to choose a stand-alone fax with a separate fax phone line if your business will be relying on faxes a great deal. Whichever you choose, check the model's memory capacity—the more memory, the better. This is handy if the paper runs out or jams while the machine is receiving a fax; the fax machine simply stores the fax in its memory until you can sort out the problem.

Similarly, if you'll be doing a lot of photocopying, a dedicated photocopier will be sturdier and more flexible than a multifunction machine. It will likely offer a number of sort and sizing features that aren't available in smaller models. Photocopiers tend to be expensive, however, and can require regular servicing: It's worth considering leasing a machine (which gives you quick access to technical help or a replacement if the machine goes down) rather than purchasing one.

The Internet

Internet access isn't an option for a home-based business; it's a necessity. Although dial-up services that use your phone line are cheap, they're also slow. You should be aiming at a minimum service speed of 56K to make viewing Web sites and downloading information as painless as possible. In many areas, high-speed Internet access is available through both phone lines (an option that doesn't tie up your line with a busy signal) or through your cable television system.

QUESTION?

I live in a rural area without high-speed Internet access—is there a solution?

Yes—you may be able to obtain high-speed access through satellite television providers—it's more expensive, of course, and can be affected by atmospheric conditions, but if your business relies on connecting with customers through the Internet, it might be worth the cost.

Once you know how you're going to connect with the Internet, you'll need an Internet service provider (ISP). This could be your local phone or cable television company or an independent company. Look for one that's reliable and has plenty of technical help available. Services that don't provide twenty-four-hour technical help (with a real person on the line) may be okay if you're technically savvy, but if you're not, you'll appreciate having a friendly voice on the other end of the phone.

Most ISPs provide the proprietary hardware and software needed to connect you with the Internet (you'll pay at least for the hardware) and will either give you detailed instructions on installing it or will send someone out to install it for you. Then it's just a matter of connecting!

Technical Help: DIY or Speed Dial?

There comes a time with all technology when it fails. A computer hard drive crashes, giving you nothing but a blank screen with a cursor blinking unhappily at you, or the fax machine jams irretrievably. At that point, you have a decision to make: You can do the repair yourself, or you can call in an expert.

Of course, if the machine is on warranty, then you call the experts. If you're lucky, they'll come to you; otherwise, you'll be trucking the machine into the nearest repair location. Try to get an estimate on how long it will take for the repair—renting a loaner might be worthwhile if it means that your business is up and running while the machine is being fixed. Also check the terms of the warranty and ask for a cost estimate if it's not fully covered—if it's going to cost hundreds of dollars to fix a machine that can be purchased for only a little more than the repair bill, opting for a new machine might make sense.

If it's not on warranty, and you're familiar with the technology and happy to tinker, then go for it. But if you're not familiar with the technology, consider picking up the phone and speed dialing the experts. Sure, you may be facing a repair bill of $50 an hour or more, but consider how long it's going to take you to (a) learn what you need to know to fix the problem, and (b) actually fix it. And that assumes that you don't compound the problem while you're trying to fix it. In the long run, it can be a lot cheaper to have someone else handle the repair.

chapter 13

Daily Operations

Once the flurry of start-up activity fades for your home-based business, you need to settle into the daily operations of actually producing the goods and services that you're offering and dealing with your customers and clients. Your launch should have given you a strong foundation for the business; now, you need to build on that foundation to work toward your business goals. Time management, professionalism, and organization are key elements that set the stage for you to do your best work.

Professionalism

Whether you're turning your hobby into a business, operating part-time, or planning a major business venture, the way you run your home-based business will greatly affect how your customers perceive you—and your products. From your advertising to your telephone manner, everything about your business operation sends a message about your goods or services and how you treat your customers. You need to make sure that it's the right one.

FACT

> Being serious about your business doesn't mean you have to be humorless or hopelessly conventional. How far you let yourself go depends on your personality and the nature of your business. As long as you present yourself as organized, reliable, knowledgeable, and skilled, you may be also be able to indulge your sense of humor with fun slogans and logos or casual clothes.

Plenty of home-based businesses achieve profit status without being professional, of course—but the business world is more competitive than ever, and you want to do everything possible to enhance your chances of success.

Communication

The success of any business depends on how effectively it communicates with its customers and potential customers. Communication takes many forms—from signs on your lawn to phone conversations. In every case, put yourself in your customer's place: Ask yourself what kind of information you need to receive, how best to receive it, and what will either encourage or discourage you from buying the goods and services.

For example, if you're a small tour operator, you should have a Web site that prospective clients can visit before they call you. You can describe each of the tours you offer and provide price listings and booking information—all of which can cut down on the time you need to spend on the phone with each client.

If you're a plumber, on the other hand, your communication issues might be that your customers need to reach you quickly in an emergency. Consider a pager or answering service so that your customer doesn't hear your sleep-blurred voice when you answer a late-night call, but they still get a call back from you right away.

ALERT!

Make sure that you follow through on price, quantity, or credit terms that you offer customers, whether in conversation, formal correspondence, or e-mail—your customer might rely on that information and consider it a contract. Similarly, follow up in writing to protect your interests if a customer or supplier gives you details about orders or deliveries.

Which communication method you use will depend partially on how important the information is. Important communications with legal implications should go by mail in all cases (particularly because you can request that the recipient sign for the mail, thus proving that they've received it). Daily back-and-forth communication that isn't sensitive or confidential can go by e-mail, while matters that need an immediate answer or that involve some delicate personal discussion, might be better done by phone.

The Written Word

Whether you're producing flyers, brochures, letters, or a Web site for your business, you need to make sure that they are well written. Remember—they may be the first impression that someone receives about you. If your written communications are misspelled, poorly worded, or confusing, your customers will get the impression that your work could also be substandard, even if you're a carpenter and your work has nothing to do with the written word.

If writing isn't your strength, you have two options: Learn tips and techniques to improve it or hire a professional to either write the material to your specifications or edit the material that you've written. Community colleges and other continuing education programs offer plenty of business writing courses that will give you a head start, and computer word processing software can also help (through templates and spelling/grammar checks). To find writers, check with local writers' associations or with other business people for recommendations.

FACT

In our technology-dominated business world, the value of a handwritten note is more important than ever. Thank-you notes, quick apologies for minor mistakes, and congratulations for business or personal success can carry much more meaning when you take the time to write them out by hand. Even "thank you" written on an invoice can help build customer relations.

E-Mail

E-mail may well be the most frequently used method of correspondence for your business, and although it's seen as informal, you shouldn't treat it that way. Instead, give it the same weight and importance that you would a formal letter. Use a greeting and a signature line (so that people know who is contacting them) and ensure that you include your contact information below the name in your signature line. Also ensure that you spell-check the e-mail before you send it.

Although you can find plenty of fancy graphics to use in e-mails, resist the temptation: these may not display effectively on all computers, so it's best to stick with a clean, easy-to-read, text-based message. And never send pictures or other attachments with your e-mail unless the recipient is expecting them: Many attachments these days include viruses, so people may delete the e-mails unread if they arrive with attachments.

Speaking of virus protection, ensure that yours is always on and up-to-date. If you end up with a virus on your computer because you've opened the wrong e-mail attachment, it may take you days to have the system fixed. Even worse, you could inadvertently send it to everyone on your address list—not the best way to impress your clients.

If you're using e-mail regularly for business, you should be checking it regularly: at least two to three times daily. People tend to expect virtually instantaneous responses to e-mail. While this might be unreasonable, you should be responding as quickly as possible—at least within twenty-four hours—particularly to inquiries about your products or services.

ALERT!

> Make sure that you follow through on price, quantity, or credit terms that you offer customers, whether in conversation, formal correspondence, or e-mail—your customer might rely on that information and consider it a contract. Similarly, follow up in writing to protect your interests if a customer or supplier gives you details about orders or deliveries.

Phone

One of the quickest ways to be taken seriously as a business is to develop a phone manner in keeping with the nature of your business. Try to answer the phone in a way that will immediately let the caller know that they've reached the correct number. It's fine to shorten the name of your business if it's a long one, but potential customers should never have to ask if they've called the right place. Adding a simple "May I help you?" in a friendly, confident tone invites the customer to tell you what they need.

To help cultivate a telephone voice that will foster good customer relations, ask a friend to give you feedback about your phone voice. Have the friend make a typical customer call—perhaps at an unexpected time—and ask you typical questions. Ask the friend to tell you about your phone voice. Is it friendly? Do you sound pleased to hear from the caller? Do you sound as if you're welcoming their business? Do you speak clearly?

These may seem like obvious elements of a good phone manner, but experience with businesses of all sizes shows that all too often, these elements are lacking. In fact, if you're having rough day, or you're in the middle of a project, it might be better to let the phone go to voice mail (and, of course, reply to it as soon as possible) rather than picking it up brusquely—as you might if you were committing one of the following phone faux pas.

The Surly Busy Bee

Overstressed and busy with something else, the owner answers the phone with a one-word "Yeah?"—as if to say to the caller, "This had better be worth my time, pal, 'cause I've got bigger fish to fry." When the caller hangs up in disgust, this owner may have just lost a huge contract.

The Mumbler

Not completely comfortable talking to others, the proprietor answers with an unintelligible "Heluh, this mmph . . . henrimph, can im oss grmpp?" forcing the caller to ask, "Is this Henry's Upholstery?" If you're going to have a phone, don't make the customer work hard to use it. Speak clearly. This goes for any of your employees too.

The Shouter

After an initial greeting, the owner says, "Hold on, would you?" and then shouts to coworkers or kids or barking dogs, "Hey, keep it down there! I'm on the phone, for crying out loud!" The customer, eardrum now ringing, is embarrassed for the owner and loses confidence in him as a businessperson.

ESSENTIAL

Your voice communicates a lot more information than simply the words that you use, even over the phone—it also says a lot about your mood. Try saying the same sentence twice, once while frowning and once while smiling. Hear the difference? So will your customers.

The Challenge

Often practiced by auto parts counter help and other "technical" business owners. Every phone call or approaching customer is viewed as an opportunity to show off how much more they know about the product. If you're in the know, the service is fine. But woe to the customer who doesn't yet understand the intricacies of the product. Humiliation is the only way out. Don't make your customer pay homage to your superior knowledge just to get courteous service.

The Cynic

"We can't fix that, nobody can fix that. Within two weeks, are you kidding? Can't be done. You're wasting my time." Yes, sometimes customers ask for what seems to be the impossible, but remember that you're trying to develop a relationship with people who need your product or service. Look at this as an opportunity to talk the customer into something more realistic. "Well, my schedule is busy within that time frame—what if I were able to get it to you by Friday the nineteenth?" Be helpful, and your customer will respond positively.

The Invisible Man

A frequent technique of various contractors. They're out on the job all day, don't get back until it's too late to return phone calls and somehow forget to call back. During boom times, they have enough business to get away with this, but it's bad policy for the long term. Even if you're too busy to take more business, make a point of calling back prospective customers and letting each of them know you appreciate his call and would love his business at another time. Help him out with the name of a colleague if you can. This simple courtesy will keep you going even when economic times are tough.

The Chatty Cathy

You wonder how they ever make any profit, since they spend all day talking. There's nothing wrong with taking an interest in a customer and making polite small talk—you'll even make some great friends from your customers this way—but bring it back to business in a timely fashion and wrap up the conversation so that you can get back to work . . . which is ultimately what the customer wants, too.

In Person

Even if you're not a retail operation, you'll need to meet with customers, vendors, and other people occasionally. Remember that as the business owner, you are the image of your business. Presenting yourself in a professional manner—matching your clothes to the business, and ensuring that you're well groomed—helps you to build other people's trust in you and the business. This applies even to businesses such as landscape design or contractors. Sure, you're going to get dirty during the course of the day, but at least start out with a clean T-shirt that has your business name and logo on it, and you'll send a much better message than if you show up in a ripped T-shirt that needs washing. When you meet with customers, try to project confidence and self-assurance. If customers sense that you know what you're doing, they'll have more confidence in you and will feel better about spending their money with you. Look the customer in the eye and smile. Use a firm handshake and be personable.

Meeting Customer Needs

As you consider the best way to run your business day-to-day, start by considering the needs of your customers. What time of day will they expect to interact with you? Will keeping your business open only on weekends work for them? The answer, of course, depends on your business. If you're a contractor, plumber, or electrician, you may be able to establish regular daily work hours, but—depending on the project's deadline—you may have to work some evenings and weekends as well. Your customers may also expect you to be available on a twenty-four-hour basis in case of emergencies.

FACT

It's tempting to keep a home-based business open long hours, but you'll be fresher, more creative, and happier if you limit those hours. Track when most of your business takes place, and set your times accordingly: If 9 to 11 A.M. brings only a few sales, for example, open at 11, and use the other two hours for business administration.

On the other hand, if you do business across the country, you might need to make yourself available at different hours to suit your customers' time zones. Or, if you're a genealogist, helping people to track down their ancestors, your customers may find it most convenient to speak with you in the evenings or on the weekends.

Setting Regular Hours

Based on your business, your customers, and even your suppliers (if you're a florist, for example, and need to take delivery of perishable items), there's likely a natural timetable for your business to be open or for you to be at your desk. You may be working on your own, but your work schedule will still be influenced by those other factors. The key is to be predictable.

Even if you're operating part-time, your customers should always know when they can find you. If they have to chase you down or leave several messages before you get back to them, you'll lose their business. Setting regular hours has an added benefit: It lets your customers know when you're not available too. This makes it much easier to establish those much-needed boundaries between your home business and your home life.

If regular hours aren't practical, at least make it easy for people to reach you, perhaps by providing cell phone or pager numbers. Just be sure that when a customer calls, you call her back as soon as possible: You can even leave a message saying that you'll return her call within, say, two hours—whatever's practical.

Listening

It's amazing what you can learn when you listen to your customers—that means really listening to what he's saying and valuing it. Not only will he tell you what his needs are, but your approach will send the message that you respect his opinions and appreciate his time.

Try to employ the principles of "active" listening even if you're on the phone: Focus your attention on your customer, lean forward slightly to indicate that you're interested, and take notes if it's appropriate to do so. Perhaps summarize the key ideas to indicate that you've not only heard, but also absorbed what's been said and ask questions to help the customer expand on what she's saying.

Anticipating Needs

Listening to your customers can help you anticipate needs that they're either unaware of or not expecting you to fill. Say, for example, that you operate an auto repair shop. Your customers bring their vehicles to you with the expectation that you'll repair them. Perhaps you're chatting with a customer one morning, and she mentions that one of her concerns is breaking down after hours.

Perhaps this is an opportunity for you to anticipate this customer's needs. If her vehicle breaks down after hours, and she doesn't have some kind of auto club membership, she'll need to phone a tow truck. Maybe, you have a windshield sticker or a travel coffee mug printed with your "24-hour phone response line," and you've set up an agreement with a local towing company to give your customers a break on the price of a tow. If a customer breaks down, she calls you, and you call out the tow truck, which then tows the vehicle to your shop for repair.

ESSENTIAL

In many cases, when you anticipate a customer need, you're actually finding new and creative ways to help retain your customers—either through the provision of new goods and services that are related to your existing ones or through adding value to those existing products.

Making Promises

It should go without saying that if you make a promise to a customer, you need to keep it. However, businesses break this rule all the time. Perhaps a contractor promises to phone a customer back with an estimate within twenty-four hours, but instead he never calls. Perhaps a retail shop owner promises to call a customer when new stock comes in, but in the rush of activity, the promised phone call is forgotten.

When you make a promise, first ensure that it's one that you can keep. Then make a note of it, so that you don't forget. And if you get busy, the stock doesn't come in, or you're not able to keep the promise for whatever reason, at least call the customer to explain. She'll likely understand and will appreciate that you took the time to let her know.

Following Up

Following up on promises and commitments is an important element of running a professional and reputable business, no matter what goods or services you offer. And it's not just customers who need to see that: It's also important to suppliers and other vendors, your financial institution, your professional advisors such as accountants and your employees.

This includes meeting deadlines—perhaps ensuring that your accountant receives all of your completed bookkeeping records on time, so that your tax return can be filed. Or it might mean renewing your association memberships and issuing your invoices in a timely manner. It definitely includes paying your employees on time.

Remember that not following up or missing deadlines makes you look disorganized and ineffective—and therefore less trustworthy.

Organizing Yourself

Staying organized doesn't come naturally for everyone, but it's critical to running a home-based business. You need to be maintaining accurate, up-to-date records and file correspondence so that you can find it when you need it. The best reason to do so is that you'll save time and make things easier for yourself in the long run, especially when tax season arrives.

However, you need to stay organized for your customers, too. They don't want to waste time while you search for a product catalog or an invoice. They want to feel confident that you're in control of your business and can help them with their needs. So help your customers to feel that way: Keep confidential files in a safe place; back up your computer data regularly; and keep your business records current.

Finding Your Style

Office supply stores have all kinds of storage containers from magazine files to four-drawer wall cabinets. You not only need to figure out which suit your business best; you also need to know which suit you best. If you're happy putting things away in filing drawers, and you know where to find them later, that's great. But if you're more comfortable with piles of paper all over your office, a filing cabinet's not going to work for you: You need to find a system that keeps those piles corralled and tidy-looking but still lets you work with them.

If you're having trouble getting or staying organized, consider calling in a professional organizer who deals with small businesses. You can opt for a one- or two-hour consultation to keep costs down or for the full deal, where they help you set up the system and even help you to work with it. There's also software available to help you manage the contents of your filing cabinet.

Finding Time

If dealing with customers or large projects often keeps you hopping, consider setting aside a time each week that's dedicated to keeping up with filing, cleaning, and organizing. Whatever your schedule, just pick a time when you know you'll have an hour or so to deal with the tasks and keep up with it regularly. The once-every-six-months pile removal method isn't recommended.

Effective Time Management

Presenting an organized and professional image to the world requires a certain amount of time and energy, but it's worth it, since it saves time and boosts sales in the long run. It's also much easier to do if you're already managing your time efficiently.

ALERT!

If you're paralyzed because you're facing numerous tasks and finding it difficult to focus, turn the tasks into a list. Label the list in terms of priorities: A for top priority, B for mid-range, and C for lower priorities. Within each category, number the tasks 1, 2, 3, and so on. Start with the A-1 task and work down.

Unfortunately, even if you consider yourself an organized person, time won't always cooperate with you. That's when you reach the end of the day, having worked so hard that you can barely keep your eyes open, and yet there's barely a dent in the "to-do" list. However, if you start with a routine that works for you, your family, and your customers, and you do whatever you can to make your days more efficient, you'll be able to limit those kinds of days.

Establishing a Routine

Part of your routine may well be established by your customer's needs—retail and repair shops need regular opening hours, for example, so that your customers can rely on you. And you'll also need to factor in your family's need to have you around. However, outside those hours, you should pay attention to when you're naturally at your best.

If you're a morning person, set the alarm and get your day started early—and don't expect to be able to work late into the night at peak efficiency. If you're a night owl, then work an opposite schedule. If you know that you have a mid-afternoon slump, don't schedule mind-bendingly difficult tasks then—plan on doing something that requires less brainpower at those times.

Saving Time

There are a number of tips and techniques that you can use to save yourself time in a work week. The good news is that many of the following will also help you reduce your stress level:

- Keep enough key office supplies, such as printer toner or ink, on hand so that you won't be in danger of running out in the middle of a key project.
- The above caveat includes postage supplies—rates for various letter and parcel weights are available at the post office sites on the Internet or through brochures, so it's just a case of obtaining a scale (or even a postage meter) and putting on the correct stamps.
- Establish an account with a local and/or long-distance courier—you'll be able to use your account number to book pick-ups and manage your account online.
- Save up your errands so that you do them all at once, perhaps weekly, instead of popping out of the office every day.
- Use the Internet to replace out-of-office trips whenever possible and practical—for online banking, library research, and office supply shopping, for example.

Giving Yourself "Thinking" Time

It's essential that you build time into your schedule simply for "thinking" or recharging your batteries. You can't work, or focus on work, all day and every day. You need time off, but you also need "work" time that isn't scheduled for actual work. This recharging time lets you step away from the "busyness" of your usual day, so that you can see the big picture again, which is often lost among the details.

There's a reason that employees have coffee and lunch breaks, and vacation days. Try giving yourself coffee breaks in your living room or on your deck every morning, or take yourself out for coffee or a meal once a week, or even book a weekend retreat away from home periodically. However you achieve it, this change in scenery gives you the chance to put the small stuff back in perspective and to consider the larger questions, such as the business's direction, or your next big marketing push.

chapter 14

Managing Employees and Contractors

Even if you enjoy the sometimes solitary nature of owning a home-based business, there may come a time in your business when you need help. This is more likely to be an issue early in the life of the business if you're in a retail environment—but even if you offer services and don't want the business to grow any larger than you can handle on your own, you may still benefit from expert assistance in a number of areas.

Assessing When You Need Help

Business owners often struggle with knowing when to bring in help and how to do it—to the point where it's often a crisis that prompts the hiring process. It's better to handle the issue proactively, so that you have people in place before you hit that crisis point. But how can you tell when you need help?

FACT

How much is your time worth? It might be worth paying a professional such as a bookkeeper, payroll specialist, or accountant if they can do the task in less time than it would take you—especially if they might be more efficient at the task than you would be.

First, think about contingency planning. What would happen to the business if you were ill or called away on a family matter for several days? Could you close down for those days—and would you want to? If staying open is your priority, do you have someone you can call on to pinch-hit for you?

Now think about the natural volume of your business. Do you have peaks and valleys—and can you handle those peaks on your own? How about the business's growth rate—is it starting to outstrip your ability to handle it all yourself? You should also consider your skills and experience and any potential gaps in them. Hiring an expert could save you the learning curve involved and allow you to focus your energies on your own areas of expertise.

Employing Spouses and Children

There are certain advantages to keeping the business "all in the family." After all, if you have to pay someone to help in the business, why shouldn't that someone be your spouse or your children? It keeps your business profits close to home and involves your family in the business, perhaps allowing your family members to better understand and respect your work. Children in particular can learn a great deal about the entrepreneurial world by helping you out—and it's possible that they'll gain a new perspective at the same time. There are, however, some pitfalls to be aware of.

First, you need to treat an employed spouse or child exactly as you'd treat any other employee for tax and benefit purposes. Taxes and other employment-related deductions, such as pension and unemployment insurance, need to be withheld; worker's compensation premiums need to be paid if they apply; and wages need to be reported to your employees and to the tax office annually. Your spouse or children will also need to file a tax return of their own. Just as important, however, are the personal considerations. Ask yourself honestly whether you and your spouse communicate well enough to work together? Will you have difficulties accepting business ideas or criticism from him or her? Will you be able to maintain the boundaries between your work and your family life? Do you view employing your children as a way to help teach them responsibility or do you expect that they'll already be responsible?

If you decide to go ahead with hiring a family member, make sure that his duties and responsibilities are clear, both to you and to him. Discuss your expectations and his so that opportunities for confusion and conflict are limited. And don't forget to thank him for his contributions, just as you'd thank any employee.

Contractor Versus Employee?

In many cases, a business doesn't need an employee; in fact, employees require more responsibility of the business owner and might even be a financial burden during slow periods. No matter how the business is doing, an employee still needs to be paid (both wages and benefits, although part-timers may have fewer benefits), and you still need to handle all the administration that goes along with payroll and other employee issues.

A contractor, on the other hand, can be brought in whenever the volume of work warrants another person's assistance. They can be paid by the hour or by the task (e.g., a flat fee for weekly bookkeeping), and there's little administration involved: You simply write a check for their services. There are no benefits involved, so you're not paying for those (although their hourly rate is likely higher than an employee's to account for the fact that they're paying their own benefits). They also don't come under labor rules for issues such as lay-offs or firing, which can streamline those processes.

It may appear that contractors are the way to go, but you need to assess that carefully. First, can you find someone who's willing to do the job on a contract basis? And, second, even if you can, will the government consider this person to be a contractor? If the answer to either of those questions is "no," you need to go the employment route.

ALERT!

> Both the IRS and CRA have strict rules about when contractors become employees. If your contractors are doing so much work for you that they could be considered employees, the tax office can make that designation for you, making you liable for significant tax arrears payments. Check with your local tax office for the rules.

Generally, a person will be considered an employee if you have more control than they do over the duties or tasks that he's performing for you. For example, if the person works at your office, using your equipment, to do tasks that you assign to him, in the way that you specify, he'll likely be considered an employee. Other factors include the significance of the hours or contributions that the person makes: If he's working for you forty hours a week, in this case again, he'll likely be considered an employee.

The Question of Pay

How much you'll pay your employees or contractors depends on a number of factors. How much you can afford to pay is an obvious issue, but so is the "going" rate for their services. In general, the greater the responsibility or skill level that's required, the higher the pay will be.

If you can't afford the going rate, one solution might be to go with a part-time employee who may provide fewer hours than you really want but who will be more productive in those hours than someone who would accept a lower rate of pay for full-time work. You might also be able to find sales professionals who will work on a part- or full-commission basis so that their pay is pegged to the amount of business that they bring in. You can also consider bringing someone in as a limited partner or offering her some kind of equity in the business in return for a lower-than-industry wage. This situation often offers a greater incentive for her to work hard because she plays a role in the success of the business. This requires careful thought, however, as you may not wish to dilute your share of the business—and this step definitely requires legal advice.

QUESTION?

If I can't afford to pay much, how can I attract staff?
Think about other benefits that you can offer potential employees or contractors. Perhaps employees would be interested in flexible schedules to work around school hours, telecommuting from their home, or professional development opportunities. Perhaps you can barter with contractors to trade your services for theirs.

Writing a Job Description

The first step in hiring either an employee or a contractor is to establish the ground rules: What will he be doing, how will he do it, and what qualifications or experience does he need in order to do it? Writing a clear job description will answer all of these questions and having a job description has other advantages too.

First, it lets your staff know exactly what's expected of them, which can avoid a lot of problems later on. If you have more than one person on staff, it can help you to avoid areas of overlapping responsibility that can cause conflict between staff members. And it also provides a starting point when you're evaluating your staff.

When you write the job description, you should separate it clearly into sections that cover the duties, responsibilities, competencies, and qualifications that you expect of the person who will be doing the job. You should also consider whether you need the person to sign a nondisclosure or non-compete agreement. As long as the agreement is enforceable by law, the person's signature on the agreement means that she's agreeing to keep your business matters confidential or that she can't start a directly competing business or go to work for a competitor in a certain geographic area or time period, as applicable. (You'll need legal advice on such agreements, since the courts will not usually allow you to prevent someone from practicing her trade or profession in a reasonable manner.)

E FACT

Don't be fooled into thinking your business is too small to worry about formal job descriptions. Your compliance with government regulations (such as labor laws that govern overtime and nondiscrimination) will often be judged by your job description. Consult with small business development offices or a lawyer if you have any concerns.

Position Summary

This short paragraph should briefly describe the scope of the job and its duties. It should also explain how the job fits into the business as a whole (who the person will be reporting to, and managing, if that's applicable). The position summary can also include a brief description of the business itself to put the job into context.

Key Duties and Responsibilities

This is a list of the specific duties that the job entails and might also include the responsibilities involved in those duties. For example, if you're looking for help in your retail store, one of the key duties would likely be staffing the cash register. The responsibility associated with that duty is to balance the cash in the register with the register tapes at the end of the shift. It can also be helpful to break down the duties into the time involved (e.g., staffing cash register: 30 percent; restocking shelves: 20 percent; assisting customers: 50 percent). If the position involves any occupational hazards or irregular hours, they should be noted here.

Core Competencies or Abilities

Here, you'll list the key competencies and abilities that the person will need to do the job. For example, your retail assistant may need to be able to stand for long periods of time, lift boxes of stock (within reason, say, 30 pounds), and enjoy finding solutions to customer questions.

Qualifications

This section deals with the education, training, and experience that you expect the person to have. You can ask for minimum education levels (such as high school graduation or college diplomas), specialized training (such as in handling workplace hazardous materials, if you're in manufacturing), and the amount and degree of experience (such as time in an equivalent position). This is also the place to list the skills required, such as good mathematical skills and an ability to work well as part of a team.

Application Process

Finally, the job description should list how to apply for the job, whether it's by resume or application form, for example, and whether you want applications submitted by mail, in person, or via e-mail, and when the deadline is. Also note whether you will accept phone call inquiries about the job, and whether you'll be contacting only those accepted for an interview.

The Hiring Process

Whether you're hiring employees or independent contractors, you want to focus on finding the best person for the job. No business can afford to hire the wrong people, but for a home-based business—where there are likely fewer financial resources available—it's especially important to bring in people who are assets rather than liabilities. Once you have the job description in place, you can start the hiring process.

ESSENTIAL

Decide whether it's important to discuss the issue of wages in the job description. While you may not want to let your competition know what you're paying, it can weed out many job applicants for whom the pay wouldn't be appropriate. If you don't want to be specific, try stating a pay range.

The hiring process doesn't need to be complicated, but it helps if you have a clear idea of any testing or interview questions that you'll be using. Then it's just a case of finding qualified people, reviewing the applications, and putting the test and/or interview process into play.

Where to Find Qualified People

Depending on the position that you're trying to fill, a classified ad in the local newspaper might be fine. But there are plenty of other avenues to consider. First, let people know that you're looking for someone—it might be that a colleague or friend knows of someone who comes highly recommended.

FACT

If you need to save time looking for qualified people, employment agencies can be an effective solution. An employment agency will charge you a higher rate for the individual's hours or a fee for the job placement, but their access to a pool of personnel can mean the position is filled much more quickly—which can help you out in a crisis situation.

For intern or student help, you can contact local schools, colleges, or universities or a local hire-a-student office. Professional associations often offer a job listing service, and, of course, there are plenty of options on the Internet. If you use an Internet service to post the job description, be sure that you're specific about its geographic area to reduce the number of applications you'll have to deal with. Also, don't overlook sources such as senior citizen's groups, particularly if you're looking for experienced part-time help.

Assessing the Applications

First, sort through the applications quickly, separating them into three piles: no, for those who don't meeting the qualifications; maybe, for those you're not sure about; and yes, for those who are clearly well qualified. Then go through your "yes" pile to come up with a short list of people (anywhere from three to ten, depending on the job and your requirements). If you have time or you need to, also check your "maybe" pile.

Testing

If skills such as carpentry, math, or writing are essential for the position, you might wish to set up a test for your short-list candidates. This test should be something that's relatively quick to administer and to take and directly applicable to the job at hand.

ESSENTIAL

Qualified professionals such as accountants are likely to be unimpressed with the idea of taking a test so be sure that testing is appropriate. Similarly, avoid asking skilled applicants to take a test that will basically provide you with free samples (such as carpentry or magazine articles). This isn't ethical.

The Interview Process

Once you have the short-list down to between three and five candidates, bring each of them in for an interview. You know by now what their qualifications are: The interview is an opportunity to see how each presents himself or herself personally and to elicit further details about his or her experience. You might also find out how each of them would solve difficult work situations that he or she might find himself or herself in. Be sure that the questions are fair, that you ask them of all the candidates, and that they never cross personal boundaries.

Checking References

The point at which you check references is flexible: You can use it to help short-list candidates or as a final step before hiring your number-one pick. Just be sure that you do check them. While it's unlikely that a prospective hire will give you a reference that will paint a poor or lukewarm picture of him, you may be surprised at what you'll learn. You could also check qualifications. For example, a quick call to your local college could confirm whether someone did actually graduate from a diploma program.

Working with Employees and Contractors

Clear communication is the key to a good working relationship with employees and contractors. That starts from the first day that they're working with you. The job description gave you a clear place to begin in terms of expectations: This can be reinforced with an informal discussion when they arrive at the workplace. Don't forget to ask each of them what their expectations are to make sure that you're both working with the same assumptions.

Be clear and specific with your expectations not just for the job as a whole, but also when assigning specific tasks. If you need something done in a particular way or time frame, let the employee or contractor know. Also do whatever you can to foster a collegial and positive workplace. A quick thank-you card to a contractor who came through for you in a crisis will always be appreciated. Buying everyone pizza for lunch during an inventory count will make a tedious job a little more pleasant.

Pay both your employees and your independent contractors on time. They're relying on that income for their own livelihood; it's your responsibility to ensure that it's there for them. Consistently paying your contractors' invoices sixty or ninety days late is a good way to lose their services or at least to have your work take a much lower priority for them. Contractors have every right to institute terms on their invoices such as interest or penalties for payments received after a certain date (usually thirty days after the invoice date).

Handling Problem People

A careful hiring process can help to reduce your need to handle difficult employees or contractors. But you might still find yourself with someone who either isn't as competent as you'd hoped he'd be or is causing you other problems (such as not showing up on time, not putting in a good effort, or alienating customers). If it's a one-time issue and doesn't recur, then perhaps he was just having a bad day. But if it does occur again, you need to deal with the situation—immediately.

It can be tempting to avoid the issue, because it's difficult to deal with someone who's not performing well. However, remember that this is your business and your livelihood. You have certain expectations, and—as long as they're reasonable—your employees need to meet these expectations. Besides, not dealing with performance problems sets a precedent that allows the individual (and others who work with you) to believe that poor performance or behavior is acceptable.

ALERT!

Be sure to check any government regulations that apply to your business in terms of an employee discipline or termination process. If you don't abide by these regulations, you could find yourself facing—and losing—an expensive wrongful dismissal claim. Obtaining legal advice is a good idea.

Talk to the Individual

Whether the person is an employee or a contractor, have a private conversation with her—preferably at a time when neither of you is stressed—about whatever issue you're having with her. Be specific about where the problem is and ask for her assistance in solving it. You need to be clear, but tactful, because putting her on the defensive will be counterproductive.

During the interview, ask open-ended questions (that can't be answered with a simple "yes" or "no"), make sure that you obtain all the facts involved in the situation and focus on the actions or attitudes that are the problem. You're trying to let the individual know that you're not criticizing her personally; you're aiming to correct a specific problem or behavior.

FACT

It's much easier to handle a difficult conversation with someone when you're not angry or upset yourself. If necessary, give yourself time to cool down before addressing the issue—this will help you maintain control over the conversation and will avoid making the problem worse.

Document that you've had the conversation with the individual and let him know that you'll be following up. If he needs additional training time, make sure that you provide it. If he's identified any problems within the relationship or the business that are affecting his performance, decide how you're going to solve these problems.

Give Him or Her a Chance

Depending on the situation, you need to give the individual an opportunity to improve. Of course, if the issue is one of theft or other major dishonesty or if you're dealing with a contractor, and there's no hope for the working relationship, you can move more quickly. Usually, however, it's better to try to solve the performance issue. After all, going through the hiring and training process all over again will be costly in terms of time and money.

You may wish to use an "escalating" discipline process where you start with an informal or verbal discussion, then go to a verbal warning, and then to a letter that clearly states the problem and the expected solution in writing. If you have to eventually fire the individual, this sort of process will help you establish a solid basis for the termination. Whatever process you choose, however, it must be consistent for all your employees.

Letting an Employee Go

As unpleasant as it might be, you might not have any choice but to terminate an individual's employment or work with your business. If that's the case, ensure that all of your documentation is clear and that you've followed all applicable government regulations. Then, make sure that you're fully prepared. First, decide when to tell the individual. It needs to done in person (not over the phone or via mail), in a place that's private and, if possible, neutral. Time the talk for the end of a work week or a work day. If you think the person might cause a problem when you terminate him or her, have someone else present. Talk to your lawyer about whether this is appropriate.

Have the person's last paycheck (including benefits such as vacation pay, if applicable) and all other necessary paperwork with you at the interview. Follow up with any further paperwork promptly. If a contractor needs to bill you, let her know that she should send you her bill up to and including that day and that you'll send her the check for the agreed-upon work immediately. You don't want to be hurtful during the interview, but you do need to be firm and clear about the reasons for the termination.

chapter 15

Selling Your Product

It's not enough to produce a great widget or keep a clean set of accounts books. You also need to get your products and services in front of potential customers and that means selling. Being a salesperson might have been the last thing on your mind when you started your home-based business, but it's a crucial factor in your success. If sales doesn't come naturally to you, read motivational books about selling, arm yourself with a sales plan, and practice: You'll be well on your way!

Making a Sales Plan

Your customer research (Chapter 4) and your marketing plan (Chapter 5) will give you an excellent place to start developing a sales plan. Jumping haphazardly from one sales effort to the next is not the best way to go about selling your product or service. Instead, a sales plan helps you to further identify your target market, prioritize your leads, and track your success.

FACT

Your target market analysis includes who your customers are, where they are located, and demographic information (such as age, income, family size, and education), or your market analysis could cover defining characteristics for business or government clients (business or office size, location, customers, and services provided).

Your sales plan is simply a document that establishes goals for the number of leads or potential customers whom you want to reach and the number of actual customers that you want to attract. Those leads can be divided into strategies that will achieve them.

Sales Leads

Your sales plan should list the various sources of customer leads (these should come from your marketing plan strategies, such as word-of-mouth recommendations, drive-by inquiries, and phone directory inquiries), how many leads you expect to generate from each source, the percentage of those leads that you think will turn into actual customers, and how many customers that translates into.

For example, if you're in the pet grooming business, and you've set a goal of $30,000 in revenue for the year with the average revenue from a grooming session at $40, you need 750 grooming sessions a year. If your average customer has their pet groomed three to four times a year, you'll need approximately 200 different clients.

While all of this can be difficult to estimate when you're starting out, the advertising representatives from various media and your network contacts, such as other members of trade organizations, should be able to help you with some of the information you need. If you keep track of your leads and customers—including asking customers where they heard about you—in the first year, you'll be able to greatly improve the accuracy of your estimates.

Timing

Your sales plan also needs to schedule your sales efforts. The time you spend on selling will be affected by how busy you already are, any seasonal variations in your business, and the strategies that you plan to employ (trade shows may only happen a few times a year, for example, while telephone directories generally have an annual deadline for the print edition). Research these factors, to establish an annual calendar that shows which sales efforts you'll be making and when.

ALERT!

> Ensure that you're ready to handle the workload that could be generated by your sales efforts. If you're just starting out, your major push could wait for a month or so after you open your doors to give you time to work out any bugs in your daily routine.

Keep in mind that your sales plan timing needs to be reflected in your business plan's revenue projections too. If you're planning a major promotional sales push in April and May, then your business should show a corresponding jump in revenue as a result of that push. If you're a retailer, the increase should be immediate. If you're a contractor, however, you may not see the revenue jump for several months after you make the sales.

Tracking Sales Effectiveness

The goal with any sales plan is to maximize the return on your efforts. To refine future efforts and keep costs in line, track the results of every promotion you try. How many calls did the ad in the local weekly generate? How does that compare with your radio campaign or your direct-mail special offer? Which seems to work best at bringing leads in and which offers the highest conversion rate of leads to actual paying customers?

In this way, you'll be able to compare the costs and the effectiveness of various sales efforts. As you plan your future sales, these past results can help you to put your time and resources to work where they'll create the best effect.

Managing Customers

One of the best ways to generate sales leads is through your current satisfied customers. Ask them diplomatically to recommend you to their friends, coworkers, and relatives. One of the most effective ways to do this is to offer them some sort of incentive to do so to ensure that it's a win-win effort for everyone. You could, for example, offer your customers discounts or free services when they bring in a new customer for the first time. Or you could give your customers discount coupons to give out to potential customers.

You should also be looking at other noncompetitive businesses to find opportunities for joint marketing efforts where your customers overlap. Using the pet grooming example, you could contact veterinarians, kennels, and pet supply stores that don't have a groomer on staff and advertise your services on their bulletin boards or in their customer newsletters. You can also take this further, by suggesting that you buy advertising cooperatively in local venues such as newspapers—that means that you pool your money to buy joint advertising space that perhaps neither of you could afford on your own.

Customer Information

The easiest way to keep track of your customers, both actual and potential, is to enter their contact information into some kind of database or contact management software. This allows you to quickly pull up either your entire customer list or only those customers who fall into certain categories, such as those living in specific areas.

The contact information, whether it's e-mail or regular addresses or phone numbers, allows you to let people know about special sales, for example, or the arrival of new merchandise. Or you can send them newsletters with useful tips that are related to your business.

It's key, however, that you store, use, and protect personal information with great care. When you collect the information, let the customer know how it will be used—and, preferably, that it won't be shared or sold in any way. If you send the customer e-mails or regular mail, always let him know how to contact you if he wants to be taken off the mailing lists and respect his request immediately.

FACT

In the United States, personal privacy and consumer protection matters (such as the Children's Online Personal Privacy Protection Act) fall under the Federal Trade Commission. In Canada, all businesses, no matter how large or small, must comply with the terms of the Personal Information Protection and Electronic Documents Act (PIPEDA).

Customer Retention Techniques

While you're focusing on increasing your customer numbers, don't forget that you already have a group of people who are familiar with and feel positive toward your business—your existing customers. They've already purchased from you: Assuming that it was a good experience, these customer don't need to be sold on your product or service.

Think about ways that you can reinforce that positive feeling. Send these customers useful discount coupons, for example, as a thank-you for their previous purchases. Offer discounts when two or more specific products or services are purchased at the same time. Give your customers a special day when they can "sneak a peek" at new merchandise before it's offered to everyone else. Make your customers feel special in some way, and they'll keep coming back.

Learning to Sell

For some people, selling comes naturally—they've never met a stranger and feel comfortable talking to almost anyone about almost anything. For others, especially those who like the idea of being on their own in a home-based business, the idea of becoming a proactive, outgoing salesperson can be intimidating. You do, of course, always need to be yourself, but you can also learn the techniques of effective selling. These techniques could include gaining a customer's interest when he walks in the door and going from interest to closing the deal.

Start with creating your sales plan and following it. Continue by listening to your customers. When you're speaking with them, point out the benefits of your product or service, and how it meets their needs. If it helps, imagine that you're speaking with friends or family and that you therefore have a friendly, receptive audience.

ESSENTIAL

> Whether selling in person or over the phone, practice your pitch. Write it down and then rehearse it until you no longer need the script—although keeping a few key statistics or phrases handy can help. Ask a friend to pose as a customer to let you practice in a low-pressure situation and improve your skills.

Many great salespeople (who often make excellent motivational speakers) have published books on effective selling techniques. Reading these can help boost your own effectiveness, as can taking workshops or courses at local colleges or continuing education programs. Also develop a keen eye and ear for salespeople: When you find someone who's either very good or very bad at what they do, take note of what's working for them, and what isn't—and apply it to your own techniques.

Relationship Marketing

If your business relies on selling an item only once to each customer, you might not be concerned about the concept of relationship marketing. If you're hoping, however, that each customer becomes a repeat customer, you should be. Relationship marketing recognizes that the customer is more than a number or a commodity for your business; she's in fact a person with needs and wants.

Relationship marketing, then, is just what it sounds like: establishing an ongoing relationship between you and your customers so that customers see you as more than just a business. Customers should see you as someone they trust and value, even if they're just stopping by once a month to pick up pet supplies. You can achieve this by adding value to their purchase of your goods or services. This might mean staying in contact with them perhaps by a monthly newsletter containing pet care tips. Or it could mean ensuring that you're always available to them by phone or in the store to answer their pet care questions. However you approach this, you're offering them more than just pet supplies: You're becoming someone on whom they rely.

FACT

Part of relationship selling includes establishing trust and credibility. If you're selling on the Internet, consider applying for certification or membership in a program such as the one offered by the Internet Business Standards Association (*www.internetstandards.org*). Their certification indicates to customers that you've made a commitment to certain standards of conduct.

However you let your customers know about your products or services, make sure that your communications and your sales pitches foster your image as a person or business that they'll feel comfortable dealing with. If there's ever a problem with an order or a job, a good relationship will make it easier to solve.

Needs-Based Selling

Once customers respond to your marketing strategies, you need to move them from "interested" to "sold." To do this, focus not just on the features of your product or service, but on the benefits that those features offer. Talking about benefits changes the focus from what you're selling to what your customers need. Obviously, whatever it is that you're selling is designed to meet your customers' needs, but by focusing on needs first and features second, you connect much more effectively.

For example, you offer a high-quality dog grooming service. But what's the benefit to your customers? Maybe it's a cleaner house and less time spent vacuuming up pet hair. Maybe it's a healthier, happier pet, because a well-groomed coat helps prevent skin irritations.

Figuring out the benefits often begins with identifying customer needs. Are your customers looking for convenience and saving time (need)? Your service offers a convenient location and flexible hours (features), allowing them to drop Fido off on the way to work and pick him up later (benefits). Do your customers want only the best for their dogs? Invite them for a facility tour, where they can see that you keep things spotless and use only the best shampoos.

Selling Face-to-Face

You've no doubt experienced both good and bad salespeople. The latter demonstrate zero understanding of or interest in your concerns or situation, they don't listen, and they often rattle off a prepared speech or feature list. Bad salespeople have a set selling style that works with a certain percentage of customers—but they miss a lot of sales because they annoy too many qualified customers.

Bad salespeople often have irritating habits. They don't look you in the eye, they interrupt, they fidget, or they look over your shoulder to see if a better prospect is coming along. They dress poorly. They ignore you to answer the phone or deal with a colleague on a minor matter. They are pushy rather than helpful. They make you, the customer, feel unimportant.

Good salespeople, on the other hand, are good listeners. They want to hear about your needs, and they look for opportunities to point out how their product or service meets those needs. They are well groomed, present themselves professionally, meet your gaze, and tell you what you want to know. They make themselves available, at your service, but they also give you room to consider and decide on your own if you prefer. They do well in business because they make customers feel as if they're making the right decision in buying their products or services.

When you're selling face-to-face, let your pride in your work show. If asked to compare your product or service to a competitor's, take the high road: Stress the positive aspects of your product without bad-mouthing your competition. Talk to your customers and establish a relationship. Smile and be happy to see them. Listen to their problems or needs. Ask leading questions to get them to tell you more; avoid questions that can be answered by a simple "yes" or "no"—you want to learn more than that. Give good advice based on your knowledge and show them how your product or service will fill their needs and benefit them.

Selling by Phone

Phone sales are more difficult than face-to-face selling because it's harder to gauge a customer's reaction. But the phone is a valuable tool, and the better you get at projecting confidence and developing a pleasant phone manner, the more you'll sell based on incoming or outgoing calls.

Phone Manners

Try not to sound rushed. If a customer took the time to look up your number and call you for information, then they are likely a good lead and thus valuable. Remind yourself that every call could be your next big customer—and treat the caller with the respect you would give someone who represented a large chunk of your business. Keep your voice bright and friendly—you should sound as if you're happy to hear from them.

E ALERT!

After a while, you'll find it easy to recognize someone who's just fishing for information, isn't really committed, or just wants to chat. Bring the conversation to a timely end, but remember your dependence on good word-of-mouth referrals. Be courteous, tell the person that you'll "let her get back to her day," and give her a cheery goodbye.

Your job on the phone is to find out what a customer needs and quickly let him know how your product or service can help. If it's a complex need, invite him to stop by or ask for his address (e-mail or postal) so that you can send him printed information (and then follow up on that promise). Be helpful.

Telemarketing

Telemarketing is one way to use the phone to contact potential customers, but you need to make a lot of calls to turn a lead into a customer, so it's time-intensive. Also, you risk irritating a lot of potential customers along the way (how happy are you when a telemarketer calls you at home?). Instead, it might be more worthwhile to call highly qualified potential customers or past customers on a regular basis. Do you have a list of customers who haven't made use of your services in a while? You could call to remind them of what you offer and to find out if there's any particular reason for their absence—you'll gather some valuable feedback and no doubt generate some sales, too.

You could also use telemarketing as a follow-up to a direct mail or trade show campaign. If you create a response card that's sent to a geographic area or filled out at the show, you'll be able to call those who returned the card. That way, you're spending your phone time with good leads, rather than getting hung up on by people who have no interest in your service.

Selling by the Word

When you're corresponding with potential customers by e-mail, through your Web site or through direct mail and other printed correspondence, your sales techniques need to be tweaked so that they work even though the customer can't see the enthusiasm in your face or hear it in your voice. You need to transmit it through the words that you choose and the design on the page.

It's always critical to put the most important or most attention-getting information first in order to "hook" your customer into reading further, but this counts even more when it comes to electronic documents that can be deleted or left behind at the click of a mouse. You also need to make sure that your documents of any kind are well laid out or designed. You don't want your customers to be confused or even intimidated when they look at your page, whether it's on a computer screen or sheet of paper.

Ensure that you have a good balance between text and white space so that the document looks easy to read. Use bullet points to help achieve that balance and to highlight key items. Use exclamation marks and techniques such as bolding certain words to emphasize your main points—but don't overuse them. They tend to lose their impact when used too frequently and could lead to fatigue or distraction for the reader.

ESSENTIAL

Writers use many techniques to make their words more powerful. Using the word "you," for example, can connect your readers to the text more personally. And using active verbs (run, walk, sell) instead of passive verbs (instead of to be use is, are) could add power and energy to your writing.

Above all, make sure that the document reads well—that your spelling, grammar, and punctuation reflect well on you and your business. If this isn't your strongest point, have someone such as an editor read it over. Remember that this is your first impression: Make it a good one.

chapter 16

Network Your Way to Profit

Every one of the most effective marketing techniques for your business involves the concept of networking: building contacts with people in a mutual effort to increase success. Imagine this looking like an intricate spider's web in which each filament leads to several others, all of them connecting to and depending on each other. That's the key to successful networking, whether you're hoping that your contacts can provide you with information, referrals, or sales: networking starts with sharing; the process is as much about giving as it is about gaining.

Evaluating Your Current Network

You might be surprised to learn just how connected you are, even if you haven't yet launched your business. Start by looking at the people who are already in your circles. Who are your friends, neighbors, and acquaintances? If you belong to a moms-and-tot's playgroup, for example, and your business focuses on children's toys, think about ways in which you can help out the other moms.

You don't want to turn the networking into a sales pitch because that runs the risk of alienating the other moms. However, there would be nothing wrong with having the business sponsor coffee, juice, and treats each week, perhaps with a stack of discount coupons available on the same table. The other moms can take the discount coupons if they're interested, but they're unlikely to feel that you're putting them in a position where they'll feel obligated to.

ALERT!

> You cannot, of course, take customer lists or any other proprietary information with you when you leave your employer nor can you expect preferential treatment in the contracting process. You should also be wary of breaking the terms of a legal nondisclosure or noncompete agreement that was part of your employment contract.

You may also find that contacts gained from your previous employment can be useful. Making an effort to stay in touch with key people—perhaps going out for lunch together occasionally—will help you stay on top of what's happening in the industry, and might even bring you opportunities for sales or referrals.

Perhaps your old office is looking to outsource certain services, for example, and one of them is exactly what your business focuses on. You'll likely know who to approach within the company to ensure that at least you're notified when the outsourcing contract comes up for tender.

Don't forget that your contacts include suppliers and others on the periphery of your business such as accountants or bookkeepers. They likely have wide networks themselves and so could offer interesting insights into the industry and perhaps even referrals to other businesses or individuals with whom you might want to work.

Building Your Network

You should keep two things in mind about networking: It could help improve your business sales, but—perhaps just as important—networking could also provide key information about the industry or demographic in which you're operating. Networking could, for example, help you track trends and new developments. You might also pick up great tips from fellow business owners on issues from bill collection to reliable suppliers to tax strategies.

Whenever people get together to talk—regardless of the subject—energy builds. Just because that energy isn't directly related to your business doesn't mean that it's not useful or important. With that in mind, consider these strategies for building your network.

Set Goals

It's easier to find networking opportunities that will work for you if you set goals. What are you hoping to accomplish with your networking, and who do you want to meet? If you'd like to improve your contacts with suppliers, for example, it makes sense to go to events where they're likely to be present.

ESSENTIAL

When you're at networking events, wear your nametag on your right-hand side, where it's more visible when you're shaking hands. Speak clearly when you introduce yourself. Use a firm but comfortable handshake and hold drinks, etc., in your left hand so that your right hand is free (and not wet with condensation) when you shake hands.

Join In

Joining organizations is one of the best ways to expand your network quickly. And there's certainly no shortage of membership-based organizations that are looking to expand: You just need to pick the one that's right for you. It might be a professional organization (for human resources or communications specialists, for example), a trade association (for contractors), or a business-related group (such as your local chamber of commerce or business improvement area).

FACT

Whichever organization you join, make sure that you're committed to its goals or vision: If there's a discrepancy there, chances are good that you won't be networking with the people who would best be able to help you. In addition, you may be viewed as less credible within the organization, which counteracts your intention.

Structured Networking

A follow-on from joining a membership-based organization is to sign up with a local networking organization. These often offer networking events from small and informal get-togethers to larger and more structured affairs. They may also offer helpful workshops or tips for networking.

Look for Opportunities

While you never want to hassle anyone, you should look for chances to network even when you're not at an event that's billed as a networking opportunity. This could be in venues as varied as airplanes, the beauty salon, the grocery store line-up, and social events. Remember that you're not trying to "sell" anything. You're sincerely interested in the other person and their interests, and you're looking for common ground.

Effective Networking Tips

The best networking is *not* the same as selling. Networking is far more subtle. It sets you up as credible and helpful and lets people extrapolate that to the products or services you offer. If you're not naturally outgoing, you might think of networking as more of a chore than an opportunity—facing a room full of people and choosing who to introduce yourself to can be a serious challenge. If that's the case, try starting small perhaps with smaller networking breakfasts run by the local chamber of commerce where you're seated at tables. It also helps to rehearse some good opening lines—everything from a thirty-second summary of your business to questions about the other person's business. Offering to staff the registration table is an excellent low-pressure way to meet people.

ESSENTIAL

Networking is a long-term effort, so it's important not to expect instant results from a single event or contact. In fact, you might find contacts paying off months or even years later. It's best to think of networking as an ongoing process that builds on itself over time.

Before you head out to do any networking, ensure that you have your business cards with you. Put them in a suit pocket where they won't be crushed or in an exterior pocket of a purse or briefcase so that the cards will be easily available when you need them. When you hand one to the other person, try to ensure that the card is oriented so that the recipient can read what's on them. When you receive a business card in return, always take the time to read it and perhaps comment positively on it before you put it away.

Listen and Practice Small Talk

Especially if you're not comfortable at networking events, you might worry so much about introducing your own business that you monopolize the conversation. You'll learn much more about opportunities if you listen to what other people are saying. If you're concerned that you're talking too much, start asking questions instead and make them open-ended so that they can't easily be answered with a simple "yes" or "no." The bonus is that if the other person is nervous, he'll appreciate the fact that you're making it easy for him to contribute to the conversation.

Many people put way too much pressure on themselves when networking, thinking that they have to be scintillating and interesting. Well, that helps—but there's nothing wrong with starting a conversation with small talk. The weather may be a cliché, but it works. So does a positive comment about the food being served, the wine, the venue, or even the number of people in attendance. You just need to get the conversation started.

If you find there's an awkward pause, you might want to use it to excuse yourself and circulate. (Convenient excuses include refreshing your drink, finding the facilities, or heading for the food table.) Or, you could ask the group of people you're standing with a question in order to generate discussion: Try asking what their favorite restaurant is or where their best vacation ever took place.

Connect Other People

A key factor in networking success is building the positive relationships with people that lead to your reputation as helpful and knowledgeable—as someone that people want to do business with. You might not need the services of the interior designer that you met at a lunch presentation, but perhaps you know someone who does. Passing along the designer's contact information might be useful for both parties, who might well appreciate your gesture.

FACT

You can also work on introducing people to each other along the lines of: "Bill, I'd like to introduce you to Nadia, an interior designer who specializes in commercial offices. Nadia, Bill is an attorney with Roberts & Associates." They'll likely appreciate the connection, but they'll also notice that you took the time to remember their names and their background.

Link Up

If you're really uncertain about showing up at an event and "working the room," try going with a friend or trusted colleague who's more comfortable with networking. Agree beforehand that you can stick with her for a little while before striking off on your own—watch how she integrates herself into groups of people, for example, or how she introduces herself and you to others.

If you're at an event and you notice someone you know, it's entirely acceptable to move toward the group of people he's with and stand just off to the side but within his line of vision. His reaction should be to notice you and to invite you into the group and introduce you. If he doesn't, you shouldn't take it personally. He might be speaking about confidential matters with colleagues—simply smile, nod pleasantly, and move along.

Protect Your Image

You've spent a lot of time and thought on presenting the right image for you and your home-based business. Keep in mind that you need to protect that image. Since networking can take place anywhere—even over the backyard fence or at the local gym—be aware of how you're presenting yourself. Of course, no one expects you to wear a tie or full make-up to an exercise class, but you still need to project that professional, credible image. You never know who'll be on the stair machine beside you.

Follow Up

It's no good making contacts with plenty of people if you never follow up with them. If someone has expressed an interest in your business, even if you think that she's perhaps just trying to sell you something, don't dismiss her out of hand. Follow up to see where the contact might lead. You can send her a short e-mail, letting her know that it was a pleasure to meet her, for example. If you talked about something specific, even if it wasn't business-related, and you have some information (a Web site link, for example) that might be interesting to her, send it along.

ESSENTIAL

There's no reason why you can't ask someone if he would mind if you followed up with him. Perhaps he seemed interested, but it's not the right time to go into details with him. Ask if you can give him a call at another time and be sure to make the call.

Show Appreciation

This goes back to the golden rule: Treat people as you would wish to be treated. If someone refers a client to you or gives you a great tip, be sure to thank her—a quick handwritten note might do the trick nicely. If the referral or tip turns into paying work, it wouldn't hurt to make a bigger gesture such as a bouquet of flowers or gift basket. Your public image will shine if you let people know that you appreciate their efforts.

How Not to Network

You never want to inadvertently rebuff or turn off the very people that you're trying to connect with when networking. The following items are surefire ways to annoy your potential contacts:

- Focusing only on yourself or your business
- Over-selling yourself or the business
- Looking around the room to find a better contact than the one you're already talking to
- Expecting instant contacts
- Monopolizing one or two people for long periods of time
- Handing out your business cards impersonally as if you're dealing playing cards

You need to approach the networking process with an attitude of respect toward your fellow networkers and a genuine sense of interest in their business or interests. Think about what would make you feel most comfortable in a networking situation, and make an effort to be that person for other networkers.

The Volunteer Effect

When people are looking for jobs, they're often advised to volunteer as a way to meet potential employers or build their skills. It's no different for a home-based business owner: Volunteering can boost your network significantly. You may also gain skills or experience in areas that you've identified as weak or perhaps add to your resume in areas of strength. And as you're volunteering, you'll be building considerable goodwill in your community.

ALERT!

> Before you volunteer, assess how much time per week or month you have to devote to this particular cause or organization and be upfront about the commitment that you can make. If you find volunteering is interfering with time that you really need to devote to the business, find a way to gracefully scale back.

Even if you're too busy or you travel too frequently to volunteer in an ongoing capacity, consider volunteering for specific events or projects that have a clear (and short) lifespan. You'll still be contributing, but you won't be trying to juggle an ongoing commitment with your other responsibilities.

Volunteer from the Heart

There is no substitute for the energy, commitment, and enthusiasm that you generate when you're volunteering for a cause that you sincerely believe in. You need to be there first for the cause or the organization and second for your personal or business goals. Anything else will quickly become transparent to those who are volunteering with you, and you run the risk of losing their respect—which is partially why you're there in the first place.

Match Volunteer Efforts with Your Goals

Assess which of your personal or business goals you want to work toward with your volunteer efforts. Then, find an organization that you believe in and that would help you achieve those goals. Finally, look at the volunteer opportunities within the organization to find one or more that would work for you.

If you're looking to expand your contacts within your industry, for example, you could look at joining a trade-based association, or—if your industry is well represented within its membership—the local chamber of commerce. Then narrow down your volunteer participation to a committee within the organization where you'll likely find members of your industry. If, on the other hand, you've identified that you need practical experience in leadership and people management, consider an organization in which you can take such a role.

FACT

Be prepared to put in your time as a worker before you take on a leadership role. You might, for example, volunteer within the organization to begin with, next move on to a committee of the board of directors, and then perhaps to running for a position on the board itself.

Committees also work well if you're looking for ways to increase specific knowledge areas. Say that you want to improve your public relations skills in relation to the business. Volunteering to work on (but not lead) the public relations committee of an organization will give you insight into how public relations works and the various tasks that go into managing a PR campaign. As long as you ask for direction when you need it, you can learn a significant amount simply by observing and by being part of the team that's doing the work.

The Advisory Board

Many entrepreneurs understand that along with their strengths as businesspeople, they also have the occasional weakness. To offset those weaknesses and to provide insight, alternative points of view, and much needed moral support, think about taking networking one step further to setting up an advisory board. Studies have shown that entrepreneurs who regularly turn to advisors generate significantly more revenue growth than those who don't.

An advisory board can be several people (anywhere from about three to seven) whom you believe can help guide the business and provide you with advice—including legal professionals, financial planners, and business experts. These might be retired businesspeople, business school teachers, or entrepreneurs in other industries (that is, people who wouldn't consider you in competition with themselves). Although some advisors would be willing to volunteer their time, you should consider paying them a certain sum—perhaps $500—per meeting or paying them in stock if cash is an issue.

ESSENTIAL

When you're looking for advisors, you should look outside your immediate circle of friends and family. You need frank, unbiased advice rather than that given through the filter of an existing relationship where someone might be more concerned about maintaining that relationship.

An advisory board works best when you set up a regular meeting time—say, quarterly. You might consider meeting for lunch or for dinner (you pick up the tab). Create an agenda for those meetings, focusing on strategic issues. You might start off with a report on how your business is faring, include income and expense figures, and revised projections. For example, your goals and any changes to them or a particular problem that you're encountering could be on the agenda.

Explain your view of the problem and any solutions that you've come up with, and seek their counsel and input. Ask as many questions as you need to in order to understand their advice. And keep in mind that the answer you're looking for is probably there, but you need to be willing to hear it: Listen actively.

chapter 17

Advertising

It can be challenging when you run a home-based business to let customers and clients know about the products or services that you can offer them: Zoning regulations may restrict your use of signage, and you're not exactly located in a high-traffic shopping mall. That's where advertising comes in—as part of your marketing plan, it can help you reach out to your target market, letting potential customers know what you can do for them and how to contact you.

How Advertising Works

When you advertise, you're essentially paying to promote your business, whether you're printing and distributing flyers or appearing in a television commercial. This is not the same thing as publicity (discussed in Chapter 18), which you don't pay for. If you purchase a quarter-page ad in your local newspaper, for example, that's advertising. If the local paper interviews you about the opening of your business and then runs a story about you (for which you don't pay), that's publicity. There's room for both in your marketing plan.

FACT

There are two main types of paid advertising: ads, which you design yourself; and advertorials, which often resemble regular news stories, but which you've paid for. Ads tend to be more attention-getting, but advertorials can look more credible or authoritative than ads. Consider which matches your image best.

Cost, of course, is the disadvantage to advertising. In major metropolitan areas, the leading newspapers, radio stations, and televisions stations are often out of reach for home-based businesses. The danger is that unless you've carefully considered your market and your message, you can spend a significant amount of operating funds on advertising that doesn't generate the response you want. The advantage of advertising, however, is that you have control over the content, timing, and often the placement of your ads. This is particularly important if you're planning a grand opening sale or some other time-sensitive event.

Ads

Ads are the traditional version of advertising: Whether they're running in print, radio, or television media, ads look or sound distinctly different from the news stories, features, or programs that they interrupt. Ads are often graphic or pictorial in nature and use logos, drawings, and fancy text effects to draw attention to their content.

Advertorials

Advertorials, on the other hand, are designed to resemble the other stories or programs in whatever media they're appearing in. In fact, their name comes from the combination of "advertising" and "editorial" (editorial refers to the nonadvertising content in the publication or program). In a newspaper, for example, advertorials will look much like another news story with columns of text and possibly a photo, although they're often labeled with phrases such as "special advertising feature." The difference is that you've paid for them just like you would for regular ads.

Creating Your Image

Before you consider any kind of advertising, think about how you want your customers to perceive your business: Your business image needs to reflect your vision and your goals for it. Of course, that vision also needs to appeal to your target market.

If you make teddy bears, then a "cute" image would represent your product accurately and would probably appeal to your potential customers. If you haul away junk cars, "cute" is unlikely to work unless you can use it a humorous way. And if you're an accountant, humor might be a tricky concept to pull off, because you need an image that reflects your professionalism and credibility.

Creating an image is a balancing act. You want to stand out from the crowd so that customers will remember you, but you don't want to stand out for the wrong reasons and inadvertently turn your customers away. If you're unsure of the image you want to portray, you can use some easy ways to figure it out.

Start with the product or service that you're offering and list all of its attributes—any words at all that you could associate with it. (For those teddy bears, the list could include: cute, cuddly, handmade, baby-friendly, custom-made, high quality, huggable . . . you get the idea.) Then think about the benefits that people would associate with your service and list them. (The vehicle removal service's list might include: convenience, helping the environment, improving the neighborhood, deterring crime, etc.)

Now look at your lists. Which of the words best describes what your business is all about? That's an excellent place to begin brainstorming ideas for your image. While you could certainly do this on your own, it could be useful to enlist the help of a friend or family member here: The energy that's produced in brainstorming from more than one perspective often results in excellent ideas.

ESSENTIAL

Many businesses use advertising agencies or public relations specialists to help them create an image or a marketing campaign. Agencies and specialists aren't cheap, but if they produce creative ideas that fit the business, the investment pays off. Assess, though, whether you really need them—and ensure they're a good fit for you and your business before hiring them.

Business Name

As discussed in Chapter 8, your business name is often the first impression a customer gets of your business. As you develop an overall image for your business, the name should fit the picture and support your promotion efforts. If it takes you five minutes to explain what your business name means, it's probably not helping you. Pick a name that communicates clearly to potential customers the product or service you provide or an important element about the business that you want them to remember.

Slogan

A short, snappy slogan can reinforce your image while providing more information about the business than a name can convey alone. You can add it to business cards, flyers, stationery, and pretty much any piece of advertising that you produce—repetition reinforces the slogan and makes it easier for your target audience to remember it. To be safe, you should check that no one else is using the slogan that you've come up with, and you should protect yourself by trademarking it, to ensure that no one else can use it without your permission.

Logo

Like a slogan, you don't necessarily need a logo, but it can help to reinforce your image, and gain the attention of your customers. Logo development ranges from computer software clipart (free for use) to custom abstract designs created by a graphic artist. As you might imagine, the former is far cheaper than the latter. If you're graphically inclined, give it a try but don't be afraid to spend the money on a professional if the logo is important to you. It needs to look good and work for the business.

ALERT!

> If you're developing the logo yourself, ensure that you're using your own original art or design or what's known as "clipart"—banks of images that are free and available for public use. Otherwise, you open yourself up to a lawsuit from the art's rightful owner.

It's important that your logo is versatile. You'll want to use it on letterhead, envelopes, business cards, invoices, and possibly on bags, packaging, signage, advertising, etc. Make sure that your logo works well in one color—four-color logos look great in four colors, but when they run in a black and white newspaper ad, they sometimes lose definition. And, if you're having stationery printed, one- or two-color printing will be significantly cheaper.

Stationery

Ideally, any printed piece of paper coming out of your business should work to reinforce the image you want to promote. While all of the basic printed pieces that you'll likely need—such as letterhead, envelopes, business cards, and notes—are available in blank form for you to print from your own computer, seriously consider having these items professionally printed.

Office supply stores offer a wide range of templates and designs to choose from, and they can often print your stationery, particularly business cards, quite cheaply.. Think about your computer printer: If you have an expensive laser printer that will produce a top-notch professional result, then by all means go for it at home. But if your printing capability is not high quality, you run the risk of having business correspondence that looks cheap and unprofessional (business card stock with perforated edges is a particular giveaway). This is unlikely to be the image you're going for.

You'll need to choose paper for these printed pieces. The number of different colors, weights, brightness, and textures available are astounding—pick something that appeals to you and that reinforces your business image (bright colors might work well for an event planning business, less well for a lawyer).

Targeting Your Audience

Thanks to your business plan, particularly your marketing plan, you should have a clear idea of whom your customers are and what their key characteristics are including their ages, family type, buying habits, etc. You should also know where they're located whether around the corner or across the country. All of these factors need to be part of your advertising decisions.

Most media organizations, from newspapers and magazines to radio, television, and many online businesses, have what's known as a "media kit." It's available free of charge to potential advertisers (that's you) and outlines the demographics of their audience. It lets you know how many people make up their audience, where they are, and should also list the various advertising costs, the deadlines for each edition, and the subject material of upcoming special editions or sections.

Compare all of this information with your target customer, your business, and your budget, so that you can select the best matches. To evaluate how effective they are, you could choose one outlet at a time, which will give you a clear idea of how successfully each is reaching your customers. Or you can choose several—when your customers contact you, ask where they found you, to gain a sense of which outlet has been most effective.

Setting Your Budget

It's often said that the true cost of a business location is the cost of rent plus the cost of advertising to get your customers to come to that location. Whether you sell your products and services from a physical shop in your home or a virtual site on the Internet, it can cost you both time and money to let potential customers know where you are. In many cases, you'll be able to keep the expense down by being creative—if you don't have much cash, you can work at gaining free publicity or at generating word of mouth advertising, for example.

Although small business consultants may suggest a figure such as 2 to 4 percent of your gross annual sales for your advertising budget, it's difficult to make sweeping generalizations: Too much depends on the type of business you operate, its location, and how quickly you need to get customers in the door. And, of course, you might be limited by the amount of working capital you could come up with. For a more accurate guideline, contact a trade association that deals with your type of business and ask for some average percentages for a business your size.

FACT

Publishers and broadcasters base advertising rates on their costs, but they're also guided by what the market will bear. It's worth trying to negotiate a better rate than what's being offered. Your advertising rep wants to keep your business and will often find a way to help, either with a discount or another benefit such as better placement.

You can also track the competition. Note where your competitors are advertising and how frequently, jotting down ad size, positioning, timing, and color use. Check the phone directories and other media—even bus advertising. You can ballpark costs by asking the advertising reps from each of the media outlets about their rates. Multiply the rates by the ad frequency, and you'll have a reasonable idea how much your competitors are spending.

Although it's fine to try new media and new publications in search of additional customers, beware of buying an ad just because it's cheap. Even an inexpensive ad is wasted money if it doesn't reach your target customers.

Your Own Web Site

There are few businesses today that wouldn't benefit from having their own Web site. This is particularly important if your business relies on customers who aren't in your geographical area, but even if that doesn't describe your situation, customers are increasingly using Web sites to make purchases online or at least check out the business.

If you have a retail or repair business, for example, customers can review the scope of your products or services ahead of time (can they bring in their lawnmower to your small engine repair shop, for example, or do you only handle motorcycle engines?). They can also find out key information, such as your hours of operation and your location, if those are applicable.

Image

From an image standpoint, you'll want to make sure that your Web presence echoes the rest of your business. Most important, make sure that it's easy to access and understandable. If your home page (the one that opens up first) is difficult to read or the site itself is confusing to navigate, most customers won't stick around to figure it out; they'll move on to another site, and you'll have lost them.

Hosting Services

Many Internet service providers (ISPs) make a limited Web page available as part of the monthly fee for Internet access, while trade associations and other membership-based organizations will offer reasonably simple Web site services as a membership benefit.

You should consider a dedicated hosting service, however, especially if your Web site needs high-volume capacity, secure sales options, or other special requirements.

Domain Name

Many hosting services and Web site development companies will help you to register and purchase a domain name (this is your site's address and is usually preceded by "www"), or you can obtain the name yourself by contacting a registration company directly. It's best to choose one that incorporates your business name if possible or your primary products or services to make sure that customers can find you quickly and easily. Generally, keeping a domain name short and simple works well.

Web Site Development

With the software currently on the market, you can develop your own site without too much trouble, although taking courses at your local community college will definitely help. However, think about how much time it's going to take you and how much you may—or may not—enjoy the process. When you factor in the money you could be earning instead of learning about Web site development, it might be cheaper to hire someone who specializes in it.

Also check with your hosting service, because they often offer easy-to-use templates that you simply enter your text or graphics into, and—like magic—they appear on the Web page. The templates work best if you can find one that suits the business image you want to portray and that is organized in a way that suits your needs for a Web site.

ESSENTIAL

> Especially if the site is your primary advertising or purchase point for customers, you need it to be very reliable, and ensure that it's resistant to being hacked or hijacked by other users. And if your customers are providing sensitive personal details such as credit card information, your privacy and security measures need to be top-notch.

Of course, if you're looking at developing a site that will let customers purchase items and pay for them online, you'll need a more sophisticated site than most templates will provide. You'll want to talk to a Web site developer or designer in that case. Look for one that specializes in small businesses: Web site designers often understand that your budget is limited and might be able to use templates in some areas to keep your costs down.

Design Tips

One frequent complaint from Internet users is that Web sites aren't updated frequently. Don't set yourself up for an impossible task by promising regular updates and new information if you can't keep up with it. If you know you don't have the time or the budget for updates, create a site that focuses on information that doesn't change such as your contact information and basic products or services.

ALERT!

> Designers might want to add fancy features such as pop-up boxes, or pictures or phrases that move on the page as you move the cursor. For the most part, these items just annoy your customers so avoid using these features.

In addition, make sure that your site loads quickly and doesn't contain massive graphics that will slow down a customer's computer. Clean, clear designs work best for most sites. Cut out the clutter and ensure that the site is easy to navigate—make it easy for customers to find key information, especially your contact information, which should be on each of the pages that make up your site.

Key Words

Talk to your Web site designer about the search words that people are likely to enter into Internet search engines when they're looking for the goods or services that you offer. You, of course, want your Web site to appear as high as possible in the search results. Designers use formulas to calculate how often and where the key words should appear on the site in order for the search engines to recognize them. Even after the Web site has been launched, keep an eye on how it's doing in the search ratings. If its placement suddenly seems to fall off, talk to your designer about why it's happening and what you can do to solve it.

Other Internet Advertising

Even if you're not ready to host your own Web site, you can still advertise on the Internet. It might be particularly helpful to you if you need to attract customers with a narrow interest focus from a wide geographic area—if you're running a specialty quilt supply business by mail order, for example.

Consider placing ads on sites for publications related to your business: trade, special interest, and business-to-business publications. Or consider running a contest in a Web ad to drum up new business. Of course, Internet advertising likely works best when a potential customer can click on the ad and go straight to your Web site—so consider launching one, even if it's just a simple one-page site.

FACT

Community and networking work especially well on the Internet. If you have a Web site, you can ask other Web sites to include links to yours in return for putting a link to their Web site on yours. Just make sure that these "reciprocal" links go to places that complement your business and fit your image.

Print Advertising

Print advertising of some kind, whether it's a newspaper insert or an ad in your community association's newsletter, is the most commonly used form of advertising for many small businesses. This is because it's relatively inexpensive compared to other forms, such as radio and television, and it has the potential to reach plenty of customers.

Brochures and Flyers

One of the simplest forms of advertising is a sheet of 8.5" × 11" paper, folded three times (trifold) to create a brochure or flyer. Home-made used to look exactly that: home-made and on the cheap; however, today's computer printers are improving the look and feel considerably. You can produce it yourself or take the design (usually in an electronic file) to your local office supply store or print shop. You could also hire a writer or writer/graphic designer team to prepare the brochure and deal with the printer.

Then, of course, you need to deliver it. Maybe you just need it to send out on request or to have on hand at trade shows. But you can also hand deliver it to specific neighborhoods—either under your own power or through a flyer delivery service.

Newspapers

Newspapers usually sell ads based on a price per column inch. The rate will depend on the market, the circulation (the number of customers it reaches), the competition, and the newspaper itself. Paid-circulation major dailies will likely charge more than free weeklies, for example.

You can buy "run of paper" ads that might be placed anywhere within certain sections of the newspaper or you can request specific positioning such as up-front, or sports—although you'll pay for a premium ad or location to guarantee your spot. Of course, you can always try classified ads, if you think they'll reach your target customer. As always, gauge the response rate to find out if something's working; if it's not, change it.

Magazines

Magazines tend to be much more expensive than newspapers because they have higher costs (all that glossy paper) and because they have better longevity—a newspaper tends to get read a few times and then recycled; magazines may stick around for weeks or months.

Check out the differences between local, regional, and national magazines, and don't forget to consider trade association publications. The latter can be very effective if you're focusing on a business-to-business product.

Telephone Directories

Telephone directories have the advantage of being in virtually every household—plus, when people open them up they're generally looking to buy. The disadvantage is that you're committing yourself to a year of advertising—there's no opportunity to change the text or reduce the size of your ad to improve its response rate or decrease its cost.

For home-based businesses that cater to customers in the immediate area, directories can be a reasonable component of an advertising program. But be wary of taking out large display ads, especially if there isn't much competition for your business.

Direct Mail

Direct mail, when carefully targeted, can be a very effective technique. The mailing lists that you can rent or purchase should narrow down your customers' characteristics as much as possible by: age or income, interest, or zip or postal code, for example. It can be reasonably expensive to obtain the list and then to produce the mailing and send it, but if the list is closely aligned to the customers you want to reach, it could make economic sense. (Note that if you've rented the list, the list broker will likely send out the mailing, so that you can't "steal" the names on it.)

ESSENTIAL

> When using direct mail, create a promotion that encourages quick response such as a sale with specific dates or a coupon that expires. You're trying to get potential customers to make a special effort to spend money in your business—make it worth their while to do so quickly.

Once you begin to build a customer base, you can build your own direct mail list. Find out whether people prefer to be contacted via regular mail or e-mail, for example (e-mail is cheaper for you). Be sure to note in your communication with the people that you won't release their names or information to anyone else. (In Canada, privacy legislation is now in place that all businesses, no matter how small, have to follow.)

Coupon Mailers

One way to use direct mail less expensively is to consider a coupon mailer, in which your coupon is included in a packet along with a number of other coupons. If you've recently received one of these promotions yourself, look at the different companies that are advertising. Are they targeting your customers? Would your business seem out of place in this mailing?

Call a noncompeting business that participated and ask about their response rates. How much business did they get from the coupon? Would they do it again? If so, would they change what they printed on the coupon?

Radio Advertising

Radio stations charge by the length of the ad spot, the frequency, and the time of day. You'll pay more for your ad to air during "drive-time" (morning and evening rush hour) than you will at 2:00 A.M., for example.

Radio stations are often segmented demographically by virtue of their format—from talk to rock and roll. If your business happens to appeal to listeners of one format instead of another, buying radio time could be a smart option.

The disadvantage is that radio is ephemeral: Your target customer has to be listening—actively—at the exact moment the ad airs in order for the message to be delivered. In addition, it's difficult to get details to sink in, such as phone numbers, or the specifics of a sale. Remember, though, that your advertising budget is there to help you build an image and establish credibility among current and future customers. The right kind of radio campaign can help reinforce your name recognition and credibility.

Television Advertising

The growth of cable television has provided many opportunities to advertise far more economically than in the past. Costs are based on the length of the ad spot, the frequency, and the time of day it runs. Often, however, the big hurdle is the production cost for a fifteen- or thirty-second ad. Do you really want your ad—and, therefore, your business—to look cheap?

For many home-based businesses, the best value on cable may be the crawler ads shown on the local access channel or programming guide. They usually consist of text only, so they can be inexpensive and effective.

Trade and Consumer Shows

Annual trade shows, consumer shows, or other events can be excellent showcases for your business. You can generate leads for new customers face-to-face there, try out new sales pitches, trial new products, ask a lot of questions to get a sense of customer needs, and check out your competition in the next aisle.

Any form of promotion, however, only works if you're pitching to the right audience. Try to attend the event as a spectator first, before signing up to be an exhibitor. If that's not possible, ask to see the previous year's program and call a few of the noncompeting exhibitors to see if they thought it was worthwhile. Did they generate lots of business and are they going back this year? And finally, do what you can to get contact information for potential customers—and then follow up with them.

ALERT!

> Be aware of all of the costs to participate, including booth or space rental costs, display development costs, fixtures and furnishings rental, parking, travel, meals, and even the cost to have someone cover your regular location while you're at the show.

Community Advertising

Once the people in your area see that you advertise, you could be inundated with requests to advertise in any number of community outlets: school play programs, local sporting event programs, community group newsletters, and so on. In most cases, those asking you to advertise will be appealing more to your sense of community support than to your business goals.

However, if your research and instincts tell you that you can generate an adequate reader response, then consider it. You can always track your results and reconsider next year. For some home-based businesses, community ads will be opportunities to reach your target audience for a reasonable cost. For others, it will simply be a way for you to support your community. Either way, it's fine. Just be sure that you're clear on your expectations for those ads.

chapter 18

Gaining Positive Publicity

The saying goes that there's no such thing as bad publicity, but it really is better to do what you can to generate positive publicity about your business. And if you think you might have to deal with negative attention from the media, it helps to have a communications strategy in place before they start to call. The good news is that publicity of either kind doesn't come with the same price tag that advertising does—although it can require time and other resources.

Publicity Versus Advertising

As noted in Chapter 17, publicity is not the same thing as advertising. If you advertise in a publication or on a television channel, you generally provide the advertisement, pay for it, and in large part determine when and where and how it's going to appear. You have control over the ad (a plus), but you also pay for it (a minus).

Publicity works differently. First, you don't pay for it. For whatever reason, the media decides that you're newsworthy enough to include in one of their stories. Perhaps you've sent a news release to them about a quirky and fun charity challenge that your business is running, and they've agreed with you that it's something the public should know about it. Or maybe a reporter is researching a story about widgets, found your Web site, and now wants to interview you about them.

So—publicity is free, and it's positive exposure to the audience. What's not to like? Publicity's main disadvantage is that you have no control over it. You can't dictate when the story will run, what part of the newspaper it will appear in, or even whether it will run at all: If the paper runs out of space on the pages, stories get bumped. You also have no control over how you appear in the news story: You simply give your best quotes and hope that they're reported accurately and in context.

Publicity is much less predictable than advertising, and although it's free, the effort to catch the news media's attention can be time consuming. However, it comes with a powerful benefit: If you're quoted positively in a news story, it carries much more weight with the reader than any advertisement you'd place in the same media. The reporter, after all, is unbiased (or should be) and therefore trustworthy in the eyes of the readers, giving you more credibility.

How Publicity Works

You might think of publicity as a huge dance hall. On one side of the room are the editors and reporters representing various media: newspapers, magazines, radio, television, and the Internet. On the other side of the room are all of the individuals, businesses, and charities, etc., that are trying to attract the attention of the media. Since there are far fewer media representatives than publicity hopefuls, filling your dance card is a challenge. You need to stand out from the crowd—in a good way.

You may be lucky enough to have the media stumble on you and your business, and decide that you're newsworthy. But usually, you'll need to approach them with written material that outlines why they should notice you—what your story is and why it's important to their readers.

ESSENTIAL

Just as you focus on your customers' needs to help develop your goods and services, you need to focus on the media's needs when it comes to seeking publicity. Don't just think about what you want to say; think about what the readers/listeners/viewers need or would be interested in, and direct your efforts to those areas.

If the media likes your story, they may take your written material and simply tweak it a little and print it. They might or might not contact you beforehand, so you need to monitor where you've sent your material in case they use the information without letting you know (clipping services will do this for you, for a fee). If they do contact you, however, they'll likely request an interview perhaps by phone, in person, or even via e-mail. At the same time, they may be interviewing other people or gathering information such as statistics. Once the research and interviews are done, the story is produced in whatever form necessary for the media they're working with, and there you are—in the spotlight!

What's Your Story?

The key part of this process is to determine what your story is. Ask yourself why anyone should care about you and your business. What do you offer that's different, unique, or important? (Think about your unique selling proposition, or USP.) Is your business part of a growing trend locally or nationally? Does it require unique training or knowledge that would be of interest to readers?

Are you considered an expert in your field? Do you have a fascinating or famous customer who is willing to be interviewed? Could you offer a reporter an opportunity to personally experience some aspect of your business (such as having him participate in a tour that you operate)?

Remember that the story isn't simply that you exist. There has to be a fresh, compelling reason why your existence is noteworthy. Find that reason, and you've found your story.

Developing a Publicity Plan

If you've decided that generating publicity about yourself, your products, or your business in general will help to drive sales or achieve other key objectives (perhaps drawing attention to a charitable effort, for example), then you need to develop a publicity plan.

Essentially, you'll look at your goals for the publicity, who you want to reach with it, how you're going to reach them, and when the best time to do it is. It's also a good idea to include a budget and to decide how to evaluate the success of your publicity.

FACT

You don't have to manage the publicity process yourself: You can hire a public relations firm or a publicist to plan it and run it. This will cost money, but PR professionals often have excellent contacts within the media and can advise you on the best ways to get your story the right attention.

Your publicity plan can be as simple or complex as you need it to be, depending on whether you want to alert local media to an upcoming event or mount a nationwide publicity campaign for your latest product. For more information about publicity, check out local continuing education and business development organizations for workshops or head to the Internet, bookstores, or libraries. Also read, listen to, or watch the media analytically. Assess where each story might have originated and which kind of stories seem to appeal to the media you're interested in.

Goals

As always, start with your goals. What do you hope to achieve with your publicity? You may want to increase sales, let customers know about a new product, draw attention to a book that you've published, or raise awareness about an issue or a problem. Be as specific as possible with your goals, because they'll guide the rest of the process.

For example, if you're a landscaping company operating in a dry climate, perhaps your goals include increasing your customer list by 10 percent and encouraging people to conserve water in their gardens.

Key Messages

Your "key messages" are the pieces of information that you want to get across to your audiences about your business. These won't necessarily be the direct subject of your publicity, but they should always be present in whatever publicity you release.

Using the landscaping example, your key messages could be that lawns need only one inch of water per week to be healthy, that lawns are watered most efficiently in the early morning hours, and that your business cares about the environment.

Audiences

Next, establish who you're trying to reach; in other words, your audiences. In broad strokes, these might be consumers, local government officials, other businesses in your area, readers of certain types of books, etc. Knowing who your audience is allows you to research their characteristics or to divide people into specific demographics—which then allows you to determine how best to reach them.

Your landscaping company, for example, could be reaching out to an audience of potential customers who are homeowners who care about their lawns and the environment.

Actions

Now it's time to list all of the ways you could reach your audiences (if you have more than one audience, each one might require a different method).

This includes deciding on specific media to target (print, radio, television, Internet, etc.) and how to target each of them (with press releases, personal phone calls, letters to the editor, pre-written articles such as opinion pieces, product placement, etc.).

In the example, you may decide that your local newspaper's weekly gardening section is the best place to reach your audience and that a press release is the best way to get the editor's attention.

Resources: Budget and Timeline

There may be plenty of ways to reach your audience, but only a limited amount of money and time available to you. Establish how much money you have to spend and how much each of your options could cost. This will help you set priorities. Do the same with the time that you have available.

ALERT!

When considering how much time you have, don't forget to assess how much time you can devote to answering the media inquiries and customer calls that your publicity might generate. Have a contingency plan in place—perhaps someone who can help out in the retail store for a few days—in case you get overwhelmed.

Evaluation

Don't forget to assess how the publicity worked. If you sent a press release out to a dozen media outlets, how many calls did you receive from people who read them? How many calls turned into stories? And how much interest did those stories generate for the business and the goals that you wanted to achieve?

Creating a Press Kit

If you're serious about publicity, creating a set of materials known as a press kit will be invaluable. Generally, this includes the press release that's the focus of your publicity, backgrounders or fact sheets to further explain the issue that the press release is focusing on, your biography or business history if that's important, and perhaps photocopies or transcripts of other stories that have appeared in the media about your business.

Depending on the subject, the target media, and the audience, you could also include company brochures, complimentary passes or discount coupons, CD-ROMs with photographs, and other pieces of information. It's easiest to package all of this in some kind of folder, with the contents securely tucked inside.

FACT

Many businesses (particularly those in the travel sector) are now putting their entire press kit on CD or DVD and sending this kit out with a single-sheet press release. The electronic versions reduce paper and postage costs and make it easy to update the information—but you need to know that the recipient welcomes electronic documents.

Businesses often spend significant sums to develop elaborate press kit folders and stationery. This isn't necessary, however: A clean, crisp and easy-to-use folder from your local office supply store will work if your budget doesn't run to expensive designs.

Press Releases

The most common form of publicity for the home-based business is the press release. This is a one- to two-page summary of a newsworthy item and generally includes the following components:

- The release date and the words "For Immediate Release"—which lets the recipients know that the information is not confidential and can be used immediately.
- A title and subtitle that accurately describe the key information contained in the release in a way that's catchy and that encourages the reader to keep reading.
- An introductory paragraph that clearly explains the key piece of information and "hooks" the reader so that he wants to keep reading.

- Several paragraphs that add details, including quotes from key people to create a press release that's ideally one page long (two pages maximum).
- Contact information so that reporters can quickly get in touch if they need more information or an interview.

Backgrounders

These additional sheets of paper in the press kit expand on information contained in the press release, providing further details in case the editor or reporter is interested. These might include the history of the issue, statistics to further support statements in the press release, or fact sheets that list significant details. Each backgrounder needs to contain the contact information that's also listed on the press release.

Writing Your Own Stories

You may feel that a press release isn't the best way to reach your audience—that an article you've written would be more effective. The opinion and editorial pages of newspapers often run these types of articles (commonly referred to as "op-ed" pieces). Analyze the types of articles that the publication is running and use them as a guide for writing your own.

On the Internet

Your Web site is an excellent place to put your publicity material. Many businesses will have section called a "Media Room" or "Press Room" that takes visitors right to the publicity material including press releases, biographies of key people in the business, and links to stories that have already appeared about them. You can also investigate blogging, which allows you to write frequent short articles, somewhat like a diary, that will appear on the Web.

Writing Effective Press Materials

When you're writing your press materials, remember that they're going to journalists. They don't need to be award-winning material, but they do need to be written well. Journalists will often notice errors in spelling and grammar, etc., but—more important—they'll immediately be skeptical about excessive claims or any kind of exaggerated praise that they see.

Reporters are also busy, which is why it's important to keep press materials short (hence the one-page press release) and to put the most important information in the titles and the first paragraph. If you haven't captured their attention by then, the entire press release will likely be consigned to the recycling pile.

ESSENTIAL

For examples of press releases, check out a press release distribution service such as *www.prweb.com*. This kind of service generally lists hundreds of releases that you can look at to see what works and what doesn't. And, of course, you can also use the distribution service to send out your own press release, especially if you're looking for nationwide attention.

In terms of specifics, press releases and backgrounders should be written in the third person (use he/she/it; not you/my/we/our), although direct quotes from key individuals, of course, can be in the first person. Write clearly and concisely and avoid jargon and complicated wording. Use active verbs and avoid passive voice.

Developing Your Media List

You'll want to put together a media list that contains all of the journalists, editors, reporters, or outlets that you want to send your publicity to. If you're focusing on local media, you can assemble the list yourself, simply by researching the media outlets you've identified as important to you.

Every media outlet offers contact information for their editorial staff, even if it's just a central switchboard number—but many list individual editors (such as a newspaper's Business or Features editor) and staff (such as columnists and reporters), along with phone numbers and/or e-mail addresses. Many also list how they want to receive press releases or other publicity information—check the "about us" section on their Web site for staff listings and directions on how to submit story ideas. If you're an advertiser, ask your ad rep to let you know what the policies and procedures are for sending press releases.

QUESTION?

Should I follow up my press materials with a phone call?
Journalists often say they don't like the practice, but a phone call can help you "sell" your story to one of them. If you call, always identify yourself, ask if it's a good time to talk, don't be offended if the person doesn't know who you are, and keep the call short and to the point.

If you're looking for wider distribution, it will likely be too time-consuming to put together your own list, unless you restrict it to ten or twenty media outlets that you particularly want to focus on. Otherwise, you can use a press release distribution service; most of these services operate by faxing or—more commonly—e-mailing the release to media outlets that you can select by audience size, geography, or subject areas.

If you're developing an area of expertise, you can also list yourself in directories of experts or speakers (either print or online). Reporters often use these to find sources for interviews when they're working on stories.

Working with the Media

It's not always easy to work with the media. Reporters are often on deadlines and overworked, and they're inundated with hundreds of press releases, phone calls, faxes, and e-mails every week, all of these letting them know about a great story that they really should run with. You need to stand out in all of that "noise"—for all the right reasons.

It's best to think of the process as relationship building. Especially when you're working with local media, if you're persistent without crossing the line into hassling them, and you provide them with timely, useful information, the reporters will come to see you as a valuable resource.

Be Reliable

Provide useful, accurate information in your publicity material. Check your facts before you send them, especially statistics, claims that might be open to questions, and your contact information.

ALERT!

> If you're quoted out of context or otherwise unhappy with a story that has appeared in the media about you, you can try talking to the reporter or the reporter's editor about it. You can ask for a clarification or correction in a subsequent edition. You could also write a letter to the editor, clarifying your position.

Be Available

If a reporter calls, talk to her right away or at least call her back immediately even if it's just to book a more convenient time to talk. A delay may well see the reporter move on to the next story or the next source. Ensure that your contact information is easily found on all of your press materials including your Web site address.

Be Helpful

If you find something that might make a good story, even if you're not involved in it, send in the idea to an editor or reporter that you're trying to build a relationship with. For your own stories, be prepared to provide photos, if applicable, or to connect the reporter with other resources such as customers or suppliers.

Be Interesting

Depending on your business and your resources, you may be able to do something fun to draw the media's attention. Want to promote your U-Pick Blueberry Farm, for example? Send the paper's newsroom some fresh-baked blueberry pies with your press material. And if you're providing photos, be sure that they're more interesting than the usual "grip and grin" shots.

chapter 19

Bookkeeping

The idea of bookkeeping for a home-based business may seem daunting, especially if accounting isn't in your background. But there's good news—between relatively easy software programs and traditional bookkeepers, you can find ways to keep your books current without turning yourself into a chartered accountant. And if you have a hard time forcing yourself to roll around in the numbers, think of it this way: It's like counting your money—except that it's on paper instead of in your hands.

Why Bookkeeping Matters

Most people don't consider bookkeeping one of their favorite activities; however, maintaining good, clear, organized records will pay dividends. Even if you do nothing more than hand over the bills and checks to someone else, you need to understand how basic bookkeeping and financial statements work.

At a minimum, you need to be able to read your monthly statements and know how much you're worth, how much you owe, what your cash flow situation is, and what you have or need for inventory. You should also be monitoring income and expenses on a monthly, quarterly, and annual basis, to help you make the best decisions about the future of your business. Bookkeeping is how you get to your goals.

Good bookkeeping records are also essential when you're preparing your tax returns, because they ensure that you're deducting everything from your income that you can. They'll also be essential if you're ever audited by the government. You may not have to send your receipts in with your tax return, but the government always reserves the right to ask for the receipts later, to prove that you were entitled to make the expense deductions that you claimed.

Should you ever need to seek financing for the business, solid record keeping will be a strong point in your favor when your financial institution is making a decision. How you track your business finances reflects how well you run your business. No matter how outstanding your product is, poor bookkeeping can make you look like a bad risk.

Do-It-Yourself Options

If you're comfortable with a computer, small business accounting packages make it astoundingly easy to do your own bookkeeping. Most will walk you through the process of setting up the accounts structure and tailoring the books to your specific kind of business. Most also link to tax preparation software, making the entire process even easier.

It helps if you have a basic knowledge of bookkeeping or accounting, but if you don't, there are plenty of ways to learn. Online courses or workshops at local business colleges can give you a great background and help you make the best use of the accounting software program.

FACT

Maintaining your accounts by hand, rather than using a computer, is entirely legal and acceptable. Realistically, however, it works only for the most painstaking of people or the simplest of businesses. Investing a little time in learning the computer software will give you the power to analyze your financial situation—and make decisions based on it—quickly and accurately.

If you enjoy doing your own bookkeeping and if you find it a good way to keep a close watch on your business finances—not just monthly, but weekly and daily—then by all means do it yourself. But make sure that you actually *do* it. Good accounting means regular accounting: Saving your receipts in a big pile that you deal with just before your taxes are due isn't doing your business decision-making any good, and it's a guaranteed source of major stress.

When to Hire a Bookkeeper

It's true that hiring a bookkeeper, or even an accountant, is an expense—and you may be trying to keep your expenses down. However, don't decide to do your own bookkeeping and tax preparation just to save yourself some money. The time you spend on it and the mistakes that you could potentially make if you don't understand what you're doing, could result in missed tax savings that will cost you just as much as an expert would have charged you.

As your business grows in complexity, so too will your need for expert help. It may simply be a factor of time: If you're running out of it, you need to delegate some of your tasks to other people. Think, too, about how much your time is worth. If you're earning $40 an hour for your services, and a bookkeeper would charge you only $25 an hour, it makes more sense for you to pay the bookkeeper's fee and spend that time earning money instead.

If you need to keep your costs down, there are some ways to do it: You can always enter your income and expenses into an accounting software program and send an electronic file to your accountant when it's tax time. Or you can hire a bookkeeper to enter in your receipts while you handle financial statement preparation.

QUESTION?

How do I find a good bookkeeper?
Ask for recommendations from other home-based business owners or from local business resources such as chambers of commerce or small business development centers. Interview prospective bookkeepers, asking about experience, services offered, expertise with your industry, and rates—and check the references they give you.

If you've set your business up as a corporation or if you have employees, however, the added complications may make having an accountant, payroll specialist, or bookkeeper essential.

Preliminary Decisions

Before you set up your bookkeeping system, you'll need to make some decisions including your accounting method and accounting period of your fiscal year. If you plan to hire a bookkeeper or accountant, it's a good idea to sit down with him at this point to discuss what's best for your situation.

American businesses will find IRS Publication 538, *Accounting Periods and Methods*, useful. In Canada, the CRA's *Business and Professional Income* (T4002) can help.

Determining Your Accounting Method

Accounting methods refer to the set of rules that you use to determine when to report income and expenses. There are two generally accepted accounting methods: cash and accrual.

Cash Method

This is the simplest method in which you record income when money is received and expenses when money is paid out. In the United States, it's often used by sole proprietors who have service-based businesses that don't maintain inventory. If your business has inventory, you generally have to use the accrual method. In Canada, however, the cash method is only available to farmers, fishermen, or self-employed commissioned sales agents.

Accrual Method

This method requires you to report income when it is earned (when you invoice your client, for example), regardless of when the money actually arrives. Similarly, you report expenses when they're incurred, even if you don't pay the bill until later. As a result, you'll have receivables (money owed to you but not yet received) and payables (money owed by you but not yet paid) on your balance statements. In the United States, inventory-based business generally must use this method, and it can also be used by any other business that chooses it. In Canada, most businesses have to use the accrual method.

ESSENTIAL

In the United States, you can sometimes combine the two methods, using the accrual method to calculate business expenses, for example, and the cash method to calculate personal items—and there are a number of special rules. IRS Publication 334, *Tax Guide for Small Business* can help.

Establishing Your Fiscal Year

The government requires that you file an income tax return for your business each year. In the United States, you have the choice of using the calendar year (January 1 to December 31) or a twelve-month period of your choice. Once you've made that choice, however, you need to stick with it or apply to the IRS to change it. If you're a sole proprietor or partner, using the calendar year keeps your business on the same schedule as your personal taxes, which makes reporting your earnings straightforward.

In Canada, if you're self-employed as a sole proprietor or partner, you generally need to use the calendar year as your fiscal year. If your business is a corporation, however, you can choose your fiscal year.

Business Versus Personal Expenses

Do everything that you can to separate your business finances from your personal finances. Set up a separate checking account and use separate credit cards for personal and business expenses. If you don't believe that it makes sense for you to do this, at least keep scrupulously detailed records about which expenses are personal and which are business.

FACT

When you need to use personal money for business purposes, deposit that money into the business account to show a clear paper trail. If you do buy something for the business out of your own pocket, reimburse yourself out of the business account so that you have a record of it—or establish a business petty cash account.

Basic Record Keeping

Keep copies of original documents such as invoices, deposit slips, bills, and receipts, all of which should show the date, dollar amount, and description of the transaction, including the vendor. If possible, include the name and address of the vendor and also your business name and address. Write any missing details down on, for example, the cash register tape. If the transaction doesn't come with a receipt (such as a parking meter charge), note down the details in a logbook or on a sheet of paper that can be included in your accounting records.

You also need to keep bank statements, cancelled checks, and computerized records—essentially, if it applies to your finances in any way, keep it. And then organize it: Filing expenses by account and by month, for example, makes it easy to find a receipt if you ever need to refer to it again.

Turning Paperwork into Records

All of the paperwork that involves receiving or spending money needs to be translated into records. You'll do this by entering the transactions into a revenue and expense journal, which can be either paper- or electronic-based (although the latter is much more efficient). This should be done at least weekly. Each income and expense transaction is assigned to a specific account (such as Gross Sales or Office Supplies).

Creating Accounts

The tax forms that you use to report your business activities to the government are a good place to start when you're figuring out what your own income and expense categories should be. They include expenses such as advertising, bad debts, commissions, insurance, office supplies such as computer paper, and travel.

ESSENTIAL

There's a definite advantage to using the government's categories for your expenses: If you use the tax software that's produced by the company that produces your accounting software, your accounting records can be imported directly into the tax software—it automatically translates it into the correct lines and accounts, saving you time.

Tracking Inventory

Retail businesses will also need to keep track of their inventory. This includes merchandise that's ready for sale, raw materials, work in progress, and any supplies (such as packaging) that physically become part of the item for sale. You must be able to identify and value your inventory items, and you need to know the value of the inventory at the beginning and end of each tax year. Keep in mind that if you maintain inventories, you'll need to use the accrual accounting method.

Daily Sales

Retailers with daily receipts should clear the cash register on a daily basis, tracking taxable sales in order to pay sales tax based on your state and city's regulations. Deposits should be made daily or weekly, as appropriate—don't let your revenue sit around the house to get lost or stolen.

ALERT!

> If you need to deposit cash sales, be security conscious. Make the trip to your financial institution during daylight hours, preferably during its opening hours (to avoid using outdoor deposit chutes), and avoid making the trip at the same day of the week or same time. Don't make it obvious that you're carrying cash—avoid making yourself an easy target for robbery.

Capital Assets

Keep particularly good records of assets that will be depreciated over a certain number of years, including vehicles, computers and office furniture. These "capital" assets aren't expensed completely when they're purchased because their life extends over a period of several years. Depreciation (sometimes called "capital cost allowance") allows a certain percentage of the value of these items to be expensed each year instead. In the United States, you may have a choice of deducting these items as an expense when purchased or spreading the expense over a number of years through depreciation. In Canada, you have no choice—it's depreciation.

Business Versus Personal Use Logbooks

For assets that are used for both personal and business purposes (such as vehicles), you'll need to maintain a logbook of activity, noting when and what the use was and its purpose (e.g., odometer readings showing ten miles driven between your home office and a client's office for the purpose of signing a new contract). At the end of the year, you'll calculate the percentage that you used the asset for business purposes. Once you've totaled up the expenses for the year, you multiply the total by your business percentage and that's how much you can claim for tax purposes. If you're audited, your logbook will become essential evidence that your expense claim is reasonable.

Other Records

If your home phone doubles as your business line, it will be useful to log your business calls, including noting long-distance calls. A petty cash log to track small cash purchases that are business-related can also be useful. For travel expenses, separate meals and entertainment costs, and record the name of the client and the purpose of the trip.

Record Retention

In the United States, you need to keep all records relating to your tax return for a minimum of three years, which is when the period of limitations expires for the IRS to review your return (unless you've filed a fraudulent return or not filed at all—but that would never apply to you, right?). If you're claiming a bad debt, however, you need to keep the records for seven years. Employee tax records must be kept for at least four years after the date that the tax becomes due or is paid.

In Canada, tax-related records must be kept for six years after the latest of (a) the end of the tax year they relate to; (b) the date that you filed your income tax return late; or (c) the date an objection or appeal process is completed and the time for filing further appeals expires.

Turning Records into Financial Statements

Each month, the individual transactions that you've entered into your records will form the basis of a number of financial statements. Before you create the statements, you'll need to balance your bank accounts with your accounting records to make sure that all of your income and expenses have been recorded properly. An accounting software package will help you accomplish both the account balancing and the financial statement preparation with just a few clicks of the mouse.

Then, you (or the accounting software) will add up your revenue and expenses to create a profit and loss statement. This statement details your income and your expenses by account for a given accounting period. The statement lets you see how you stand not only at the end of that month, but year-to-date as well. You can also compare the current year's figures (monthly, quarterly, and annually) to those of the previous year.

A cash flow statement compares money coming in to money going out. You can look back to get a picture of previous cash flow trends, but—more important—look forward to check your projected cash flow. This helps you to answer the big question: Will I have enough cash to pay my bills when they're due?

A balance sheet, which uses your accounts to compare your business assets to your business liabilities and investment may also be useful. Essentially, the balance statement lets you know how much your business is worth.

Tracking Your Progress

One of the most important reasons to maintain good records and to use generally accepted accounting procedures is that you can use your monthly statements to analyze the health and progress of your business. Your balance sheet, for example, can help you determine if too much of your cash is tied up either in inventory or in accounts receivable.

The profit and loss statement will be one of your most useful reports, allowing you to compare your income and expenses to your projected budget. When you began the year, how much profit did you expect to have each month? Are you below or above your target? Is there a revenue problem (you're not selling enough) or an expense problem (you're spending too much)? Your statements will let you know exactly where the problem is. It might be, for example, that your cost of goods sold is too high. To solve the problem, you can look at your pricing to see if the market will bear a price increase, or you can try to source your materials at a lower cost.

Look not just at the monthly figures, but year-to-date figures as well. Search for trends. Are your overhead costs rising? Do you need to pass those costs on to your customers in the price of your goods or services?

Or perhaps you need to look again at ways to reduce your expenses. The key to dealing with any business challenge is to catch a problem before it becomes insurmountable and to identify a negative trend so that you can act quickly to reverse it.

ALERT!

> If you extend credit to your customers, check your accounts receivable aging. Are all accounts current? How much of your receivables are over thirty days? Sixty days? Ninety days? By checking this regularly, you can stay on top of clients who tend to be slow payers—and withhold further services to them as necessary. See Chapter 23 for tips on collecting receivables.

Paying Yourself

Many home-based businesses operate on a very tight cash flow model with the owners plowing the profits right back into the business to help it grow. That doesn't mean, however, that you shouldn't pay yourself, too. Psychologically, it's important to feel that the business is providing you with an income.

If you're a sole proprietor or partner, you don't write yourself a paycheck to take money out of the business. Instead, the check or withdrawal is known as an owner's draw (sometimes referred to as a payout of retained equity). The owner's draw is not a business expense that appears on your profit and loss statement; instead, it's reflected on your balance sheet.

In a case where the business is also your livelihood, you should make regular draws, perhaps twice a month, to ensure that you can pay your personal bills on time. However, even if you don't need the income to pay your personal living expenses, it can be a good idea to make a small, regular owner's draw, perhaps monthly. You might decide to put the money back into the business at a later date, but in the meantime, you'll feel the satisfaction that comes with getting paid on a regular basis.

chapter 20

Taxes

Operating a home-based business may help you escape an aggravating commute and frustrating office politics, but you can't escape taxes. In fact, as a business owner, you have more responsibility than ever for record keeping, accounting, tax return filing and—yes—the all-important tax paying. This chapter provides an overview of tax issues in the United States and Canada: although the tax systems differ, many of the concepts are similar between the two countries.

Intention to Make a Profit

If your business is a sole proprietorship, a partnership comprised of individuals, or (in the United States) an S Corporation, the government expects that you're in business to make a profit—if you're not, the expenses that you can claim will be limited (usually to the amount of income that you've made). Corporations operate under slightly different rules, so they can be more flexible when it comes to claiming losses.

However, even if you're not a corporation, the tax systems do understand that some years are better than others and that start-up operations in particular often show a net operating loss. As a result, they may allow you to claim expenses that exceed your income, as well—in effect, allowing you to claim a loss against other income that you have such as that from paid employment. If this is your situation, you'll need to show that you're in business to make a profit rather than just earning income from a hobby. Factors that will be considered in making this distinction include:

- The time and effort you put into the business, including marketing efforts
- Profits and losses experienced in the past
- The qualifications, experience, and knowledge that you bring to the business
- Whether the loss and the expenses you're claiming are reasonable given the nature and stage (e.g., start-up) of the business or due to circumstances beyond your control
- The extent to which you rely on the business for your living expenses
- Your ability to qualify for financing that could assist the business
- Your intended course of action, including changing operational methods to improve profitability
- Whether there is a reasonable expectation that you'll make a profit in the future

Even if you can't claim all of your deductions in any given year, ensure that you document them and retain all of the paperwork, because you may be able to carry them forward or back to claim them against years in which you do make a profit. As a general rule, three years of losses occurring close together will have the government reviewing your status.

Working with the Government

The easiest way to stay out of tax trouble is to follow the rules and guidelines set down by the IRS or the CRA. Both government departments offer a range of resources to help you do just that. Two IRS publications provide an excellent place to start. Publication 583, *Starting a Business and Keeping Records*, and Publication 334, *Tax Guide for Small Business* (for sole proprietors who file Schedule C or Schedule C-EZ with their Form 1040) summarize all of the essential concepts with plenty of examples to help explain them.

FACT

> The best place to look for federal tax information is online at *www.irs.gov* for the IRS and *www.cra.gc.ca* for the CRA. Toll-free phone assistance is available for the IRS at 1-800-829-1040 (individuals) and 1-800-829-4933 (businesses). For CRA assistance in Canada, call 1-800-959-8281 (individuals), 1-800-959-5525 (businesses), and 1-800-959-2221 (to order publications).

The IRS also partners with federal tax specialists to offer a series of Small Business Tax Workshops throughout the United States; and most of these are free. Self-study versions of the workshops are online, the same as small business products such as tax calendars and resource guides, which can also be ordered on CD/DVD. In addition, Publication 1066, the *Small Business Tax Workshop Workbook*, which is used in the workshops, takes you through various helpful examples and case studies, and it is available online and in hard copy.

In Canada, start with the CRA's *Guide for Canadian Small Businesses* (RC4070) and *Business and Professional Income* (T4002). The CRA also provides small business information seminars free of charge and will even offer a staff person visit to your location if you're too busy to attend a seminar.

Contact your local tax services office to register (local offices are listed on the Web site).

Estimated Tax

Because you're self-employed, there's no employer withholding money from your paycheck in anticipation of income taxes that will become due and payable each April. Consequently, you may have to make estimated tax payments on your own, which are usually due quarterly. This can be challenging to calculate, especially in the first few years, when you're not sure what your profits will be. However, it's important to do this as accurately as possible, not only because the government may impose penalties and interest on you if you don't—but because facing the bill for an entire year's income tax can be a nasty shock in April if you haven't been paying quarterly.

In the United States, you need to make quarterly estimated tax payments (April 15, June 15, September 15 and January 15) if you expect to owe at least $1,000 in federal taxes (including income tax and self-employment tax). See Publication 505, *Estimated Tax Payments*, for specifics.

In Canada, you may be paying by installments if you expect to owe more than $2,000 in federal taxes. Payments are due March 15, June 15, September 15, and December 15, and need to include Canada Pension Plan contributions, if they'll be payable, as well. For details, check the CRA's *Paying Your Income Tax by Installments* (P110).

Preparing Your Tax Returns

If you're comfortable completing your individual tax returns and your business structure is a straightforward sole proprietorship or partnership, you likely won't have any trouble completing the tax forms for your business/self-employment. However, if you run into challenges, don't hesitate to hire a tax preparer or accountant. They know the rules and may even find deductions you weren't aware of (including their own fees).

If you're preparing your own tax returns, invest in a tax software program annually. It can't replace expert advice, but this specialized software does make the process much easier—all the forms are included, along with plenty of tips. If you know the tax forms, you can complete them as needed; if you don't, the software walks you through the process systematically.

Business Income

In general, all the money you receive from your business is considered income. For product-based businesses, you'll need to calculate two important income figures. The first one is your gross income, i.e., all the money that you receive from sales of the product. The second is your gross profit, i.e., your sales figure minus the cost of the goods sold.

FACT

"Cost of goods sold" is the total of the costs directly involved in making or buying the product for resale. Assume, for instance, that it costs you $100 to buy the materials used to put together gift baskets that you sell for $250. Your gross income is $250, your cost of goods sold is $100, and your gross profit is $150.

Service-based businesses don't usually have a cost-of-goods-sold figure. They often declare their sales as both their gross income and their gross profit.

Business Expenses

All of your expenses that weren't part of cost of goods sold are then listed, and the total of these is subtracted from your gross profit to come up with your net operating profit or loss. For home-based businesses, some of these expenses are frequently questioned by tax offices, because the place of business and various assets used in the business are often used for personal as well as business purposes. When you use your home for the business, you're also using the home's heat, electricity, and perhaps telephone expenses for the business too. The same goes for your vehicle.

Whenever you're determining your business expenses, the key is to be reasonable. Stopping for a gallon of milk on your way home from a business appointment might not be an issue—the bulk of your mileage was still used for business purposes. But if you try to write off the family's trip to Walt Disney World on the premise that you stopped in to see a client while you were there, you're on extremely shaky ground. Similarly, while the cost of subscribing to a trade publication might well be a reasonable deduction; your subscription to a television listings magazine probably isn't (unless, of course, you can prove that it's a necessary part of your employment as a television reviewer!).

Business-Use-of-Home Deductions

Most home-based businesses will qualify to take the deductions for business use of the home if they meet the key requirements:

- The space is used exclusively and regularly for the business.
- The home is the principal place of business.
- The home is where you meet or deal with customers or clients in the normal course of business.

You can use two different formulas to determine the percentage of your home that's used for the business. One is the area method: Divide the area of your home used for business by the total area of your home. If, for example, your office is 100 square feet of a 1,000-square-foot home, your office is 10 percent of your home.

The other method uses the number of rooms, and applies in particular if your rooms are all about the same size. If the house has ten rooms, and you use one of them as your office, again, you're using 10 percent of your home for the business.

You then multiply your home expenses, such as utilities, insurance, maintenance, property tax, and mortgage interest or rent by your business-use-of home percentage to figure out what you can claim. Note that your ability to deduct business-use-of-home expenses is limited in some cases: In general you can't create or increase a net loss by deducting business-use-of-home expenses. You may, however, be able to carry forward the expense into a year when you do produce a net profit.

In the United States, you'll use "Expenses for Business Use of Your Home" (Form 8829) to figure out the deduction. Publication 587, *Business Use of Your Home,* contains more information. In Canada, check the *Business and Professional Income* (T4002) guide.

Vehicle Expenses

In the United States, you have a choice between claiming actual vehicle expenses or the standard mileage deduction (44.5 cents per mile for 2006 and generally updated annually in the fall for the year ahead). In Canada, you claim actual vehicle expenses.

Actual vehicle expenses include gas and oil, insurance, lease payments, interest payments on loans, licenses, repairs, depreciation, and registration. Once you've calculated your total actual expenses, you multiply that figure by the percentage you used the vehicle for business to come up with the amount that you can actually deduct.

Gifts, Meals, and Entertainment

In the United States, you can claim a maximum of $25 for each gift that you give to clients or potential clients, even if the gift exceeded that cost. Meals and entertainment are generally claimed at a maximum of 50 percent of the allowed expense. For details, check IRS Publication 463, *Travel, Entertainment, Gift, and Car Expenses.*

In Canada, check with either the CRA or your accountant to see if gifts qualify as expenses for your situation. Meals and entertainment also come with a 50-percent limit and are explained in CRA Interpretation Bulletin IT-518, *Food, Beverages, and Entertainment Expenses.*

Depreciation

Some business assets lose value over time. Computers and vehicles are common examples, but any machinery or other property that generally lasts more than a year will depreciate rather than be directly expensed. Inventory for resale is not depreciable, but copyrights and patents are. In general, you deduct depreciation over the life of the asset; however, there are some assets, such as computers, that can be depreciated more quickly, and sometimes even expensed in the year of purchase (which can be an advantage if you had a good revenue year). See IRS Publication 946, *How to Depreciate Property* and the CRA's *Business and Professional Income* (T4200) guide for more details.

Start-up Expenses

You may be able to claim your start-up expenses for the business—that is, the expenses you incurred prior to actually opening your doors to clients or customers. However, this can be a tricky area, so it's best to check your regulations to make sure that you declare the most appropriate date for your business's start. IRS Publication 535, *Business Expenses*, can help. In Canada, check CRA Interpretation Bulletin IT-364, *Commencement of Business Operations*.

Sole Proprietors and Partnerships

As a sole proprietor, you pay income tax on your net profits. Partnerships are similar to sole proprietorships when it comes to taxes—the business itself doesn't pay: instead, the partners each pay taxes on their share of the net profits from the business.

Taxes and Sole Proprietors

In simple terms, as a sole proprietor you add up your revenue, subtract all your expenses, and pay federal and state/provincial income tax on what's left over. When it comes to your tax return, you'll still be filing your individual tax return as usual—but you'll also file additional paperwork that summarizes the income and expenses you're claiming for the business.

In the United States, you file your individual tax return via Form 1040. With it, you'll file Schedule C or Schedule C-EZ: Profit or Loss from Business. You may also need to file Schedule SE for self-employment tax and 1040-ES for estimated taxes.

In Canada, you'll file the usual T1 individual tax return for your province. It needs to be accompanied by the forms contained in the *Business and Professional Income Guide* (T4002) for that tax year: either the T2124 for business activities or the T2032 for self-employed professionals. You may also need to file Schedule 8 of the T1 for self-employed Canada Pension Plan contributions.

Taxes and Partnerships

In general, a partnership agreement determines how distributions (whether they're profits or losses) are to be divided among the partners. If there's no agreement in place, then the distribution is made according to how much of an interest each partner holds in the business. Just as in a sole proprietorship, each partner may have to pay estimated taxes, and (except in the case of a limited partner), self-employment tax.

In the United States, check IRS Publication 541, *Partnerships*, for the details. You'll need to fill out Form 1065, which reports the partnership profit or loss, and Schedule K-1, which reports each partner's share. In Canada, the partnership profit or losses noted on the forms that accompany the *Business and Professional Income* (T4002) guide.

Self-Employment Tax

As a self-employed person who's either a sole proprietor or in a partnership, you're not an employee—so no one's taking income taxes out of your checks, nor are they withholding deductions such as Social Security and Medicare (FICA). There's also no employer paying FICA on your behalf. It can be a shock to discover that you have to pony up not only for your share of FICA, but also for the share that the employer would normally pay.

E ALERT!

In Canada, the self-employment tax equivalent is the payment of Canada Pension Plan contributions. Usually, you and your employer would each pay half of your contributions to CPP. When you're self-employed, you pay the whole amount—calculated on Schedule 8 of your T1 tax return.

Generally, if you make more than $400, you have to pay the tax, which you'll figure out using Schedule SE. This comes in a short and a long form, but most people can use the short form. If you have more than one business (and thus more than one Schedule C or C-EZ, you add up all of your self-employment profits and fill out one Schedule SE.

Taxes and Corporations

Corporations are taxed differently from sole proprietorships or partnerships, because they exist as taxable entities in and of themselves. The corporation pays corporate income taxes on net profits, and the corporation will also pay the employer's share of Social Security and Medicare (or Canada Pension Plan, etc.) charges. If the corporation has paid you wages or salary as an employee, you'll file a tax return just as any employee would.

There are some differences between American corporation types, however. An S Corporation functions similarly to a partnership, with the corporation's profits divided between the shareholders, who then fill out their individual tax returns. Limited Liability Companies differ from state to state, but in general work like partnerships as well with the profits divided between each owner.

Taxes and Employees

If you've hired employees, it's a sign that your business is growing, which is excellent. But with employees comes plenty of paperwork including tax obligations. The following tax and other deductions list the major issues, first in the United States, and then in Canada.

Withholding FIT and FICA

First, you're responsible for withholding an appropriate portion of the employee's wages for income taxes. You need to have new employees fill out a Form W-4 that claims the number of withholding allowances. You determine the amount of tax to withhold based on the tables in IRS Publication 15, Circular E, or a percentage basis as described in Circular E.

You also need to withhold Social Security and Medicare taxes from your employee's paycheck. You report employee compensation and taxes withheld, as well as your employer's share of FICA, on Form 941: Employer's Quarterly Federal Tax Return.

FUTA Tax

As an employer, you pay the federal unemployment tax based on a portion of your employee's earnings. Your state will also have unemployment tax, so the federal system gives you credit for the payment you need to make to the state. The FUTA tax return is filed once a year on Form 940 or 940-EX, and is due January 31 after the end of the reporting year.

Tax Deposits

If your withholding taxes are less than $50,000 for the year—and they likely will be—you need to deposit withheld taxes monthly, no later than the fifteenth of the following month.

In Canada

The system works in a similar way in Canada: you have to withhold income tax, Canada Pension Plan/Quebec Pension Plan, Employment Insurance, and possibly Worker's Compensation amounts from your employees' paychecks and remit those amounts (along with any employer's contributions) to the appropriate government entity. Each year, you'll provide your employees with a T4 slip that lists the deductions so that they can fill out their individual tax returns. For information, obtain from CRA the Payroll Deductions (Basic Information) guide and the Payroll Deductions Tables for your province or territory. If you're having trouble figuring it out, call your local tax services office: They'll even send someone by to give you a hand to get started.

Taxes and Independent Contractors

Independent contractors are not employees; they work for themselves, performing services for you while not under your direct control and are responsible for paying their own income taxes. In the United States, ask for a Social Security number or EIN before the contractor starts work and have the contractor sign a Form W-9 too. In Canada, you need the contractor's Social Insurance Number or Business Number.

In the United States, if you pay one independent contractor $600 or more during a tax year, you need to file Form 1099-MISC with the IRS (with a copy to the contractor), identifying the type of payment, amount, who made the payment, who received it, and the recipient's taxpayer identification number (EIN or SSN).

In Canada, you may have to report amounts of $500 or more paid to a self-employed contractor. Check with the CRA to determine if this situation applies to you.

Collecting and Reporting Sales Tax

Home-based businesses that are selling merchandise in a state or province that charges a sales tax will likely have to charge their customers the applicable sales tax, and remit it in turn to the state/provincial government. Your first step is to apply for a sales tax number in your state or province and then to set it up in your accounting records so that you keep track of the tax. Check how often you'll need to remit the sales tax. It will be at least annually and more often quarterly.

If you travel out of your state or province to consumer shows, you may be required to collect and pay sales tax on those sales to the host state or province. Check with the state department of revenue or provincial ministry of finance to find out if this applies to you.

ESSENTIAL

In Canada, businesses with income of $30,000 in a tax year, or any quarter of a tax year, must register for the Goods and Services Sales Tax (GST) or Harmonized Sales Tax (HST). You'll charge the tax on your goods and services, subtract any tax you've been charged on business expenses, and remit the balance to the CRA. Call 1-800-959-5525 for registration/information.

Dealing with an Audit

The government uses audits as a way to ensure that the tax returns submitted are, in fact, accurate. They generally select files for several reasons: your return may have raised some questions; your partner may be being audited;

information may have been received from a source that indicates there's a problem with your return; your type of business is being examined more closely, in general; or, in fact, it may be a completely random, luck-of-the-draw selection.

In some cases, you'll simply be asked to send in the receipts or documents that apply to a specific part of your return. Ensure that you make copies of those documents before sending them by registered mail before the deadline set out in the request.

In other cases, an auditor may visit your home-based business to conduct a thorough review of your records. This can be intimidating, and it will certainly be time-consuming. You'll likely need to familiarize the auditor with your business and possibly even with the industry that you're in. Before the auditor's arrival, go through your records to make sure that they're as organized and complete as possible. You should also talk to your bookkeeper or accountant—they may be able to provide advice, and (although it may involve additional costs) even be present when the auditor visits if you feel you don't have the knowledge to deal with the auditor's questions on your own.

ALERT!

Whatever happens during the audit, remain calm, collected, and polite. Becoming argumentative or defensive isn't going to help, and it may well hinder your cause. Do your best to explain the issue to the auditor, but if you're not getting your message across, save your argument for the written appeals/objection stage of the process.

You'll later receive a letter detailing any changes to your tax return(s) that the auditor is recommending and the process that you can follow if you object to those changes. If you do want to object, it's definitely time to bring in some expert help. In the worst case scenario, where you're facing an additional tax bill that you don't have the money to pay, you should be able to work out a payment arrangement with the IRS or CRA. You'll be charged interest on the outstanding amount, but that's better than being hit with penalties for nonpayment on top of everything else.

chapter 21

The Personal Side

In Chapter 1, you established that, yes, you do have the ambition, initiative, and resourcefulness that's best suited for home-based business ownership. But once you get past the excitement of opening the business, you might find a variety of personal challenges waiting for you. You need to set goals for yourself and stay motivated on the path to achieving them, and you might find yourself dealing with the issues that come with the isolation of a home-based business. There are solutions, however—and being proactive with them helps.

Setting Goals

Whatever the nature of your challenge on any given day, it will be easier to deal with if you've set yourself clear goals. Without goals, you have nothing clear to work toward, which means that your day-to-day focus can lose its edge. Goals can be flexible, however—there's no reason why you can't change them as you go or add new ones.

If you miss your goal, it's not the end of the world; it simply means that you need to reassess what you're aiming for or perhaps how to achieve it. In the meantime, you'll find it useful to remember the popular S.M.A.R.T. acronym for goal-setting. Making your goals Specific, Measurable, Attainable, Realistic, and Timed helps you on your way, as does writing your goals down.

Specific Goals

The best goals are those that are specific enough in nature to offer a clear path. It's not enough to say that you want to improve your professional development. Instead, you need to be specific: For example, you could set a goal of taking two online courses in the next year on sales techniques and on bookkeeping. In fact, if you noted the source of the classes, that's even more specific . . . and even better.

Measurable Goals

The concept of measurable goals is directly connected to specific goals. If the goal isn't measurable, how will you know when you've achieved it? How will you know when you're making progress? "Increase sales" is something that most business owners would like to do, but it's not measurable in a meaningful way; even an increase of one or two sales could technically mean that the goal was achieved. In this case, it would be more effective to set a goal of increasing sales of gift baskets by 15 percent compared to the previous year.

Attainable Goals

An attainable goal is one that you have control over. If you're writing a book that you want to have published, for example, you might think that your goal is to have a publisher publish your book. But you really have no control over what the publisher does or doesn't do, so it's not fair to set yourself this goal. Instead, set a goal that you can attain, i.e., to send the book proposal or manuscript to ten agents and ten publishers, for example.

Realistic Goals

It's easy to set goals that sound great, but that are, in fact, unrealistic. Think about the time and resources that you have available to you and the effort that it will take to achieve the goal. The goal should feel as though it's stretching you, but not that it's unachievable. For example, if you want to increase publication of a newsletter, it might not be realistic to go from six to twelve issues a year in the space of a year—but going to eight issues might be achievable and beneficial to your business.

Timed Goals

The best goals have a time frame attached to them. For example, in the gift basket example, increasing sales by 15 percent in the next twelve months is specific, measurable and timed—and powerful. Keep time frames in mind when you're setting goals, so that you're setting short-, mid- and long-term goals. In fact, some of the shorter term goals might be ones that help you achieve longer term goals.

FACT

Some motivational experts believe that it also helps to phrase your goals in the present tense, as if they're happening now: e.g., "I am increasing sales by 15 percent over the next twelve months." The theory is that this sends the message to your brain that this is your reality.

Staying Motivated

The first step to staying motivated is to understand what actually motivates you in the first place. Consider why you started your home-based business. Was it for a sense of control, for greater money, more creativity, or the opportunity for innovation, for example? Whatever it was, you need to find ways to use that motivating factor to maintain your enthusiasm for the business—to keep you making those phone calls and greeting those customers.

ESSENTIAL

Maintaining a support network can help if you're struggling with motivation—friends who understand your business can cheer you on or deliver well-aimed stronger encouragement when it's appropriate. Or consider hiring a personal business coach. They often host weekly conference phone calls or online sessions specifically for maintaining motivation.

How you tap into your motivating factor is just as personal as the factor itself. If inspirational quotes help you, put them on your computer screensaver. Perhaps make your goals visual by putting pictures of them (e.g., a shiny new car) in your office or by mounting charts (e.g., number of new clients per month) on your bulletin board. Whatever inspires you, do it.

Control

If you started your business because you wanted more control over your work life—especially if you were looking for more personal time—be sure that you've structured your business to achieve it. Maybe in the summer you can start your work hours at 7 A.M. and shut down at noon to take the kids to the beach or the pool. Save your bookkeeping for two hours in the evening when your favorite classical music radio program is on. Quit your week at 3 P.M. on Fridays. You're now in full control—so do something with it!

Money

If the chance to work for your own profit rather than someone else's is a prime motivator, it can be tough to keep going at first when revenues might still be modest. Perhaps it would help if you found a money-making angle for everything you do, even if it doesn't at first seem that the task is directly related to the bottom line. You could sign up for a class that's specifically geared toward increasing sales, bringing in new clients, or even cutting costs, for example.

Creativity

When your motivation is creativity, you might not have any difficulty when it comes to dreaming up new products or new ways to sell them—but the more routine tasks of administration or bookkeeping might be a major problem. Try positive reinforcement by promising yourself a reward (perhaps the new exhibit at the art gallery?) for getting them done. Look for ways to make the tasks more interesting—perhaps by putting on some energetic music. If it's still a problem, consider hiring someone else to do the admin, while you focus on the creative side of things.

Innovation

Innovation is exciting, but it's tough to sustain. You may be totally psyched while you're developing a new product, for example, but lose enthusiasm when you're dealing with day-to-day product sales. To keep your motivation up, focus on your goal-setting (perhaps sales of 10,000 improved mousetraps will give you the financial resources to develop the next product, for instance). It can help to attend conferences or maintain online links with other inventors or innovators, since just talking about innovation can reignite your enthusiasm.

Professional Development

One of the best ways to sustain your creativity and your enthusiasm is to ensure that you're looking after your own professional development. If you're an employee, your company will often pay for you to take all kinds of training courses, workshops, and even college certificates or degrees. Your company knows that the knowledge and experience you're gaining will be valuable. Think of your own business in the same way.

To spend your money and your time where they'll provide the best return on your investment, consider your goals. There might, for example, be "holes" in your business operations knowledge. Perhaps you need to take some workshops in bookkeeping or tax management? Or a seminar to help make your sales presentations more powerful?

You can also look at what would make you (and the business) more valuable to your customers. If you're a public relations specialist, for example, it might be useful to go through the certification process offered by one of the industry associations to back up your experience with an industry-recognized educational standard.

FACT

You won't have a problem finding courses to take: In fact, there's a huge selection out there, offered by private training companies, colleges and universities, business development offices, and local school boards. If you'll have trouble scheduling a multiweek course, look for one-day workshops or seminars.

Boosting Productivity

One of the most effective ways to boost productivity is to schedule your toughest tasks, or those that require the most intense focus, for the time of day when you're naturally at your best. This could be first thing in the morning for an early bird, or it could be early evening for a night owl—but it pays to go with your body's natural rhythms.

If there's too much to do, your focus can be scattered in too many directions, making it impossible for you to settle down to any one of the tasks. Instead, assess where your priorities are and focus only on those. Once you start moving through the list, the momentum naturally builds.

Don't forget to make time for yourself. It's easy, as a home-based businessperson, to spend all of your personal time on your business. Taking some time off keeps your mind clear and your outlook fresh, allowing you to make the best decisions possible in your business.

Beating Procrastination

It's the bane of many home-based businesspeople…the temptation to put off tasks and projects that you either don't want to do or that are so large they seem impossible to accomplish. Perhaps it's the intimidation factor of the blank page that's putting you off or simply that you dislike bookkeeping so much that you'd rather clean your office than sit down with the growing pile of receipts—but the result is the same. You end up facing an urgent deadline because you delayed starting the project in the first place.

ALERT!

> You will need to balance your to-do lists with what's actually achievable by one person in one day. If there aren't enough productive hours in the day to complete all the tasks that you've listed, it's very easy to become "paralyzed"—also known as the "deer-in-the-headlights" look.

You need to figure out what's really going on. Are you having a hard time starting, for example? Are your thoughts distracted by all of the chores that are waiting for you? Are you so fatigued by a long stretch of extreme work hours that your brain is looking for a break? Establishing what the problem is will help you figure out what the solution is.

If it's all the household chores (or the fridge or the television), set yourself some ground rules, e.g., no chores or even on turning the television news until a certain time of the day or until a certain number of tasks are completed. Take a thermal carafe of coffee or tea into the office so that you have no excuse to wander the house. If you can't be trusted to limit your time on computer games, remove them completely from your home office computer.

Conversely, try establishing a reward system if you'll respond better to positive reinforcement. One or two hours spent focusing on work gives you half an hour to take a walk or make yourself a (healthy) snack.

In a similar vein, make sure that your office is somewhere that you actually want to be. If it's down in a dingy basement or it's a cramped, awkward space, its physical location could be the problem. If you can't move it, try redecorating it. Use a small stereo so that you can play music that will raise your energy levels and even light aromatherapy candles if that will help—anything that will make you happy to be at your desk.

Try this antiprocrastination trick: Convince yourself to sit down and focus on the task for just fifteen minutes. That's all you're asking of yourself—just a quarter of an hour. You'll find that it gives you enough of a start on the project that you'll likely want to continue.

Dealing with Bad Days

Everyone and every business has bad days—they're inevitable. How you react to a bad day makes a huge difference, however. If you can keep the day in perspective, knowing that it'll pass and that things will improve, the bad days will be less likely to overwhelm you. Otherwise, you'll be left wondering if, perhaps, paid employment really is the answer.

One of the best ways to deal with bad days is to leave the office completely if you can or at least to take a break in some way even if it's ordering pizza for dinner or taking yourself out for a walk or a coffee. If you're losing your motivation, sense of humor, or coping strategies, it's a sure sign that sticking around the office is a bad idea and in fact might just make the problem worse.

Feeling Overwhelmed

You're producing the product, you're marketing it, you're selling it to the customer, and you're accounting for it. That's a lot to juggle at once. It's also easy to become a victim of your own success—being in demand is a compliment to the quality of your goods or services. But if you're running out of inventory or all of your clients are calling at once, the fast pace becomes increasingly stressful.

E ALERT!

> You need to recognize how you react to bad days. Do you become a workaholic, refusing to leave the office until the problem is solved? Or do you tend to "shut down" and become less efficient? Neither reaction is likely to be productive in the long run.

If you can feel the panic mounting, stop what you're doing. Sit down, make a list of everything that you need to do and when it needs to be done by and prioritize the list. If some of the projects are huge, and seem impossible, break them down into small, manageable chunks. If you're still left with a to-do list that outstrips the time you have available, call in help—maybe it's time to find a bookkeeper, for example, or an administrative assistant who can handle the filing.

Feeling Isolated

With all the motivation in the world, running a home-based business can still be a lonely endeavor. You might go days without leaving your property or seeing another person outside your immediate family, especially when you're in a busy period. Even if you're seeing employees or customers, the arm's-length relationship might not provide you with enough social interaction.

The solutions are fairly simple, but they take a conscious effort on your part to actually accomplish. If you're looking for solutions to feeling isolated, try these tips:

- Run errands to the bank, post office, or copy shop to get yourself out of the office.
- Attend business-oriented events locally or conferences farther afield.
- Improve your skills by taking workshops or courses at local educational institutions.
- Take courses or workshops just for fun.
- Go out for lunch or coffee with friends or business colleagues.
- Join a volunteer organization.

Struggling with Self-Esteem

Sometimes, trading a regular job for self-employment can trigger depression or self-esteem issues. Maybe you're no longer managing a team of people or enjoying the perks that come with a high-powered job title, and maybe you're missing that steady paycheck. Whatever the source of the problem is, identify it so that you can deal with it—quickly. You need to address self-esteem issues before you start feeling too negative about yourself and life in general.

Surrounding yourself with people who are positive influences and who believe in you can certainly help—as can staying away from people who don't support what you're doing. Recognizing the value in what you're doing now and the small achievements that you make every day can also help. However, don't hesitate to speak with a small business coach or even a therapist if you feel you're not dealing adequately with the problem on your own.

Stress Management Techniques

Being in business can be stressful—there's no way around it. You'll be faced with difficult customers, challenging deadlines, cash flow worries, suppliers who don't deliver, and a myriad of other problems. And to make it more stressful, you're the one who's in charge, and who's responsible for solving all of the problems.

FACT

Shake up your workday! Playing hooky for an afternoon is one of the benefits of a home-based business. Yes, you'll have to make up the hours at some other time, but if the sun's shining, and your clients don't need you, take a sanity break. If you're a retail outlet, pay someone (whom you trust) to watch the store for a couple of hours.

Stress management techniques can be helpful on an ongoing basis, but these techniques come in handy especially on days when the whole world insists on hassling you.

Because stress is a physical response, it makes sense to deal with it physically, at least in part. Your stress reaction can make your breathing shallow, so try taking three slow, deep, cleansing breaths—it's amazing how much better that can make you feel. Then focus on your posture to make sure that you're giving your lungs room to expand. Getting regular exercise can also help: Even a walk around the block gets the oxygen moving in your body. Plus, it gives you a mental break from the stress, which can be just as important.

If you need to vent, phone a friend: The buddy system works incredibly effectively to let you safely complain about whatever is causing you stress. Just make sure that it's a good time for the other person to chat for a few minutes and that you return the favor when it's his turn to need a release valve.

chapter 22

Moving On

It's wise to plan for the future of your business right from the beginning. If, as a sole proprietor, you decide to leave the business, it may simply disappear. Perhaps you're hoping that one or more of your children would want to take it over or that you could sell it. If you're involved in a partnership or corporation, on the other hand, the business may well continue on. However you choose to move on, there are key actions and decisions that you need to deal with first.

Making the Decision to Close or Sell the Business

Many people will assume that a business closure results from financial pressures, and in many cases they'll be right. Sales of certain products weren't as high as forecasted, perhaps, or an economic downturn put customers in a financial squeeze. Some business owners will change course within the business when this happens. Others—especially those who depend on the business for their family's living expenses—may choose to close or downscale while they head back to paid employment. There's certainly nothing wrong with either approach. In fact, closing the business before you incur serious debt might be the smartest thing you could do.

ESSENTIAL

> If you're planning to hand the business down to the next generation, ensure that you put a succession plan in place. This covers all of the details needed for an orderly transfer of business ownership and management between you and your child (or children). It may also include tax issues, timelines, or triggers (such as your illness or incapacitation).

However, business owners also close or sell their businesses for reasons other than financial. Some never find the elusive work-life balance, and they burn out. Others may be more interested in the start-up phase than the day-to-day operations of the business. Still others may be ready to retire completely to travel around the world or to start some equally new and exciting adventure. Entrepreneurs, after all, are hard to stereotype!

Of course, one of the best ways to wind up your involvement in a home-based business is to receive a great offer from someone who wants to buy all or part of it. The business has (hopefully) generated an income for you over the years; now it can provide a nest egg, as well.

Choosing Your Timing

Technically, closing or selling the business can be done whenever you make the decision to do it; however, there may be sound financial and professional reasons to choose your timing more carefully. For example, if you're a retail business and your best sales of the year are made during the run-up to the holiday season, you could consider closing the business in January. That would allow you to take advantage of increased sales in November and December to boost revenue and decrease inventory. The balance of your inventory can be sold in a January closing-out sale, when people tend to be on the hunt for bargains.

FACT

For tax purposes, you don't have to close the business down at the end of your fiscal year; you can close it any time. You'll need to note on your tax return that this is the business's final year, and you may need to file a "short" tax year form for the IRS.

If you're a service-oriented business owner, consider the natural peaks and valleys of your year. For many service providers, the summer months are slower paced than the seasons between September and May. Perhaps it makes sense to scale down and then close the business during the summer. You'll be inconveniencing fewer clients at that time, while giving them a chance to find someone to replace you before their own busy seasons start to pick up.

Understand, too, that closing or selling the business is not a single action where you lock the door and walk away. It's a process much like starting a business so it needs to be planned just as carefully. Give yourself the time you need to handle all of the tasks and paperwork involved and seek legal and tax advice from your advisors. Tax advice is particularly important when it comes to the timing of your closure: Depending on how much money you'll gain or lose on the sale or closure, you might want to choose the time of your fiscal year in which you leave the business.

Of course, if you're in dire financial straits and are facing bankruptcy, your best choice might be to close the business as quickly as possible to limit further debt. This might also give you more control over the sale of your assets, maximizing the amount that will be available to repay your debts. Again, legal and tax advice is essential.

Protecting Yourself

As mentioned above, legal and financial advice is essential when you're closing or selling a business. You don't want to be dealing with a massive tax bill, for example, that could have been avoided if you'd only done things differently. There are some additional measures that you need to take to protect your interests as well.

Dealing with Employees

Consider, for example, how much you want to tell your employees and when. You might need to be strategic about this. Perhaps you believe that your employees would be interested in buying the business. If that's the case, then talk to your legal advisor about how to approach them.

If that situation doesn't apply to your business, however, then consider how your employees might react to the news. Some employees will be entirely professional and will provide all of the help that you need as you close down operations. Others, however, might be tempted to skim cash from the till or even steal some of the merchandise.

ALERT!

> If you're already dealing with a problem employee, it might be better to let them go first and then handle the business closure on your own, even it means more work for you (consider asking for help from your spouse or children to take up the slack). Otherwise, you might be risking the employee sabotaging your closure or sales efforts.

Dealing with Customers

Similarly, consider when and how much to tell your customers, and keep in mind that you've generated significant goodwill with them over the years. If you're selling the business, you don't want to say anything to a customer that could devalue the goodwill portion of the sale price.

If you're closing the business, assess how much notice your customers will need and how crucial it will be to them. Service-oriented businesses might need to let customers know sooner than retail-oriented businesses; giving customers time to find replacement services might be an issue. If you provide professional services such as bookkeeping or writing, you may not be leaving the profession itself, but just the business. If you can't take your customers with you to your new business or employment, at least protect your professional reputation by not leaving them in a position that will hurt them in some way.

Selling the Business

Before you begin searching for a buyer for your business, you need to determine its value to someone else—and whether the business is so integrated with you as a person that it's not going to be an appealing sale for someone else.

For example, if you as a sole proprietor run an editing business in which you do all of the work, your clients are likely returning to you with work because they trust the revisions that you suggest to their printed material. It's going to be difficult to sell the business to someone else, because your clients won't necessarily transfer their trust in you to the new owner.

However, if you're selling a retail business, then your customers might be more interested in your merchandise than in you as the owner. Transferring the business to someone else might not be an issue at all in this case.

What You Can Sell

You can, of course, sell the entire business: name, customers, property, merchandise, accounts receivable—everything. However, you can also sell individual pieces of the business while keeping other pieces.

It's possible to sell a business without selling the business name or the property on which it's located, for example. If you've run an automotive repair business for years out of a building in your backyard, you can sell the tools, the contracts you have for ongoing work with other businesses, the client list, the receivables, and even the building itself if it can be moved.

If the location is critical to the success of the business, however—such as a country store in your barn along a busy road—selling the business may mean selling your home, too. Such a scenario might work out well for you between the appreciation of the real estate, and the added value of the business located on the property. But if you live in a homestead that's been in your family for generations, and you plan to live there through your retirement, and then pass it along to your heirs, you're not going to want to sell the business in its current location. In that case, consider including moving the business as a condition of sale. That way, you'll get the best possible value for the business without giving up your home.

What You Can Keep

When you sell the business, you can choose to retain whatever rights or elements of the business that you wish. However, you do have to balance this with the increased value of the business when you sell it as a unit rather than piecemeal.

If the business name is actually your name, for example, you might have a concern about losing control over how your name is used. In this case, it might make sense not to sell the name of the business along with all of the other items that go with it.

Also consider privacy issues and government rules. Seek legal advice whether you can sell your customer list, either on its own or as part of the business as a whole. Also consider how your customers will feel about having their names sold. If they've established a relationship with your retail business, and they want to know where it's moving to, perhaps it's not an issue—they'll welcome contact from the new owner. But you need to check first.

The Sale Process

While you could certainly place an ad in your newspaper classified section to advertise the business for sale, you shouldn't be doing anything along those lines before you speak with a lawyer who specializes in business sales. You're going to need advice on what you can sell and how best to go about it, and you're going to need a legal sales agreement drafted. This is not the time to be buying a forms kit from your local bookstore: the stakes are too high.

For example, your lawyer may be able to handle the noncompete issues that a potential buyer may insist on. If someone buys your business, she won't want you to set up a competing business six months later and steal back all of your customers. Your lawyer, however, will be able to phrase a noncompete clause that protects your ability to make a living. The lawyer will also be able to handle any intellectual property or copyright issues that come up (for example, if your business includes inventions or designs that you've created).

You should also consider placing the business for sale with a sales professional who deals in your trade or industry. They might have clients on the lookout for just your kind of business.

ESSENTIAL

You might run across "tire-kicker" customers when you're selling a business: They express interest, make an offer, look through your books, and then back away or even start their own competing business. Try to screen the people to whom you're giving access to proprietary information such as financial statements—and have each one sign a waiver acknowledging that intentional corporate espionage might be actionable in court.

The sales process (also described in Chapter 6) might be a long one, in which letters of intent are exchanged, and offers are made, accepted, rejected, or countered. Talking to your advisors ahead of time about the process and what to expect will reduce the frustration that you might otherwise feel.

Preparing the Business for Sale or Closure

The specific procedures that you'll need to follow in order to close or sell your business will vary depending on its structure and its products, but following a logical plan will help. You should consider each of the following steps:

- If you're not a sole proprietor, you need to come to a written agreement with your partners or corporation shareholders to either sell or close the business in part or in whole.
- Consult your legal, financial, and tax advisors to ensure that you receive the best and most timely advice possible on the process.
- Ensure that your financial records are completely up to date.
- If you're a retail or manufacturing operation, conduct an inventory of your merchandise.
- Ensure that your list of physical assets is accurate.
- Send letters to customers, suppliers, creditors, employees, and everyone else who might be affected by the business sale or closure, be clear about what's happening, and identify the timeline and whom they can contact if they have any questions.
- Conduct final sales of merchandise and assets as applicable.
- Settle accounts payable and hasten outstanding accounts receivable; pay off other business debts.
- File all necessary financial, tax, and corporate paperwork with federal and state agencies as necessary.
- Close bank accounts, and store business records (for seven years).

Document each of these steps thoroughly, even taking photos of assets to show their condition, for example. The closing or sale procedures will have tax implications for you so ensuring that you can back up the value of the assets that you've sold will assist you in dealing with any questions that arise later on.

Final Sales

Retail and manufacturing operations will likely benefit from holding a final "going out of business" sale to dispose of inventory—unless any of that inventory can be returned to your suppliers. Of course, when suppliers only offer you a credit with them rather than a refund, that won't do you much good: You'll still be looking at holding a sale. Hold the sale at your usual place of business unless renting a space to dispose of inventory and assets all at the same time makes economic sense. In general, it's more viable to hold the sale yourself rather than handing over everything to someone else (such as an auction service) on a consignment basis. However, that may be an option if you can't, or don't want to, shepherd the business through its final sale.

ALERT!

Before you set up your sale, be sure to check the consumer protection regulations in your state or province. Businesses that have abused the term "going out of business" in the past have resulted in many jurisdictions bringing in specific rules that govern advertising and holding these sales.

Consider advertising the sale in local papers or on your Web site and in flyers or e-mails sent to regular customers. You'll generate further goodwill if you give regular customers a chance to come in and shop the sale before the general public can—and you never know when you'll need that goodwill.

When it comes to pricing, you obviously want to bring in as much revenue as you can—hopefully avoiding any losses—but you also need to move the merchandise. Set the prices accordingly, perhaps pricing some items below or at cost in order to get people into the store. (These products are often referred to as "loss leaders.")

Disposing of Assets

You might also have considerable assets tied up in the business from vehicles to computers to office furniture. You need to convert these assets on your financial books from business to personal use (which will involve billing yourself for them) or sold off in some other way.

There are a variety of ways to do this including advertising in the classified sections of local newspapers, holding a public auction, and selling items over the Internet. Even a sign outside your premises might be enough to bring people into the store to look at its fixtures.

You should already have a thorough list of your assets as part of your financial records. Check that the list is up-to-date, that serial numbers are correct, and that the condition of the time is noted (photos or videos can help provide a record of this). Assess whether it's worthwhile to spend any time or money repairing or sprucing up assets before the sale. However, make sure that everything is clean, since this can make a big difference in their appeal.

FACT

> Consider donating assets to charity if they can't reasonably be sold for much monetary value but they could still be useful to someone else. The business will receive a tax deduction in return and, since many charities will pick up the items, you won't have to pay for someone to take them away.

Be sure to issue proper receipts for each sale and mark the paperwork "as is, where is" to protect yourself from having to deal with returns or liability issues. Also keep track of everything that it costs you to sell or dispose of your assets, because you'll be able to claim the costs as expenses when you're finalizing your accounting records.

Closing the Financial Books

Unless you have bookkeeping, accounting, or tax expertise, you should seek financial advice when it comes to making the final entries in your accounting records. You'll need to handle issues such as your physical asset disposal, for example, final pay and benefit payments to employees, and inventory write-offs for merchandise that you couldn't sell.

A mistake made during this process can come back to haunt you several years later in the form of a tax bill, possibly with interest and penalties applied.

Tax Issues

You'll need to tie up a variety of loose ends when it comes to tax issues. These include:

- Making your final federal tax payments.
- Issuing final wage, deduction, and benefit paperwork to employees and to the appropriate government offices.
- Reporting business gains or losses, including capital gains and losses.
- Marking your tax return for the business as "final" in the year of closure.

Other Government Issues

Whatever procedures you needed to follow to set up your business with your state, province or municipality, similarly ensure that you follow the required procedures to notify these government offices of the business sale or closure. This may include canceling or transferring business licenses, filing corporation dissolution paperwork, notifying and making final payments to sales tax offices, and handling any final employee paperwork issues.

chapter 23

Problem Solving

Running your own business will certainly be gratifying, but it will not be problem-free. There may be days, weeks, or even months when you seem to spend more time "fighting fires" than planning ahead and charting your course for success. Successful problem solving can, however, be a great source of a feeling of accomplishment. Greeting each problem as a challenge to rise to is essential—it really is all in the attitude and in recognizing that you have a problem while there's still time to solve it.

Recognizing Problems Early

Nearly any problem can be tackled effectively if you recognize it sooner rather than later. In fact, minor challenges often turn into major problems simply because the person in charge wasn't willing to face it down early enough. Of course, you may realize that there's a problem somewhere, but not be able to assess exactly where it is. In this case, it's a good idea to bring in some kind of expert.

Your accountant can be invaluable in this regard, especially if divining profit and loss statements is not your strong suit. An accountant should be able to explain the typical financial ratios for your particular industry, help you measure your own performance against them, and identify trouble spots such as accounts receivable on your financial statements.

FACT

Although an outside source of help can pinpoint a problem more accurately than you might be able to, you also need to trust your instincts. Listen to the experts, but if you don't believe they have a good "feel" for your business or if the advice doesn't suit your needs, then thank them sincerely and move on.

Other sources of help include small business development offices, colleges or universities (they often have mentoring or business analysis services), online Internet forums (as long as you know that you're dealing with a reputable Web site), and trade-based associations that you belong to. In the United States, there's also SCORE—the Service Corps of Retired Executives, who act as consultants to help you analyze your business and discuss problems and solutions.

Cash Flow Issues

With most home-based businesses, you'll be doing the work or creating the product before you get paid for it. This is especially true for service businesses—whether you're writing newspaper articles or landscaping gardens, customers will be used to paying either on completion or on being sent an invoice. This can create cash flow issues: You may not receive the money for a month or longer, but the bills for your expenses will already be arriving.

At the risk of stating the obvious, successful businesses have more dollars coming in than going out, and they carry a cash reserve to cover those temporary times when the opposite might be true. You need to maintain a sufficient reserve—which may mean having enough savings or financing availability on a line of credit to cover yourself during the tough times. But the key is to manage the cash flow as effectively as possible to avoid needing the reserve, especially if it would involve going into debt.

Credit Management

When you invoice your customers, ensure that you include payment terms on the invoice. Is the bill due in ten days, for example, or thirty? What are the interest penalties for late payment? Are there discounts for early payment? All terms should be clarified before the work is done, but make sure you remind the client of the terms by stating terms on the invoice. Also ensure that you send out invoices promptly—you don't want to slow up payment by delaying the invoice at your end.

ALERT!

Even the best of customers can experience financial problems: Beware of regular customers who are taking longer and longer to pay their invoices. Give him a friendly call to establish what the problem is—but be wary about continuing to provide credit in case the customer's problems become your disaster.

Reduce your risk with new clients by fully informing them about your rates or the cost of the job at hand, preferably in writing, before you start. It can be useful to have them sign a work order, agreeing to the work and the estimate and acknowledging that it's only an estimate. Let new clients know as the job progresses if it's going to cost more than your estimate. If your business involves purchasing parts or inventory for a specific job, ask for a deposit to cover the cost.

Collecting Accounts Receivable

It's a sad fact, however, that some customers simply won't be able to—or won't want to—pay the bill. Although it doesn't make sense to spend hundreds of hours and thousands of dollars to collect a $250 outstanding invoice, you can take some reasonable steps to collect what's owed. Start with a few phone calls—be pleasant and polite and ask for a specific date that you can expect payment. If you don't receive it then, contact the customer again by sending a letter, again pleasant and polite, insisting that you get paid—and set a specific date for payment.

ESSENTIAL

In some cases when customers won't pay the bill, it's because there's been a misunderstanding about the job or the invoice. Do your best to clarify the extent of the work and the payment terms ahead of time. When it's a large project, create a contract that outlines the obligations of both parties before starting to work on it.

If you still get nowhere, but you have some faith in your customer, you might offer to set up a payment plan—an amount paid weekly until the debt is fully extinguished. Regular payments are what you're looking for here—if the customer owes you $500 and can pay $25 a week, take it—as long as she continues to pay.

If you still have problems, you can turn the account over to a collection agency, which will take a percentage of what's collected. Depending on the nature of your business, you may also be able to place a lien on your customer's house (for your security system inside the house, for example) or vehicle (for your auto repairs)—this means that when the item is sold, part of the proceeds will go to you.

Or you can take the customer to small claims court, which is a court that you can use inexpensively, usually without the use of a lawyer, to make a small claim against another person or business (see Chapter 10). If you have the paperwork to back up your claim, you'll likely win—although that might not help you to actually collect if the customer simply has no money.

Dealing with the Big Guys

Larger companies sometimes take advantage of their size to delay paying their bills. If you're dealing with this, first make sure that your paperwork is in order. Send an invoice, whether or not they ask for one and ensure that you're sending it to the right person.

Second, ensure that your expectations are reasonable: Immediate payment is extremely unlikely; within approximately thirty days is probably the best you can hope for.

Third, do whatever you can to push the process along internally. Find out what their processes are and whether you can do anything to hasten them. If the check is overdue, follow up with the correct person in accounting, becoming a polite but persistent voice on the phone. Ask what you can do to improve the turnaround in the future. Sometimes, being a (polite) squeaky wheel can help; at other times, going up the hierarchy can help you get paid (especially if you're not worried about affecting your long-term relationship with the client). If it doesn't, and this is a perennial problem, assess whether this client is more trouble than it's worth—in particular, whether payment delays indicate a client who might be in financial trouble.

Inventory Overload

Managing inventory levels is a critical skill. Check with the trade organization covering your kind of retail business for the average "turn" rate—how often you can expect inventory to move in and out the door. If you have items for sale that are hanging around too long, then return them or put them on sale—move them off the shelves so that you can replace them with something else.

Watch and track sales: not everything will sell at the same rate, and some higher margin, high-priced items might take longer to turn and make a profit. But if you're stocking a particular item that's lingering on the shelves, it's time to exchange it for something new.

If you're trapped in an inventory deadlock—you can't sell the stuff you've got, can't return it, and don't have cash or credit to buy new inventory—then it's time to call your suppliers. They won't make more money from you until you reorder, so they have a vested interest in your inventory. Convince them to work with you—by sharing a markdown on the retail price so that you can put the item on sale or by allowing you to return items for credit on new inventory. Good distributors or vendors may listen if you're a good customer who pays your bills on time.

You can also try to unload the inventory you have to someone you know can use it. Call up the customers who bought some before, and offer them a deal on the rest. In the worst case scenario, when the goods aren't selling even if you cut the price, you might want to consider donating them to a charitable organization that can use them.

Funding Issues

So what happens if you run into a cash flow problem? Do you have the money to buffer you temporarily or will you have to go into debt to manage for the next few weeks? Do you have a loan source available, or do you already have so much debt that adding to it is only going to make the problem worse?

The future health of your home-based business depends in so many ways on money. If you're having problems in any area of your finances, talk to an expert such as your accountant or a business consultant who's familiar with your area of operations. You need to get a handle on it quickly—by securing a line of credit, for example, or by applying for a consolidation loan to get your credit cards paid off at a lower rate of interest.

ALERT!

> You may not want to ask your financial institution for advice if you're having funding trouble, especially if the bank has already loaned you money. Instead, do your research, identifying the problem and assessing various solutions. Then, if you need the financial institution's assistance, you'll be in a position to offer potential solutions.

Undercapitalization

In other words, you don't have enough money. It's one thing to cut back on personal expenses and live off a small salary temporarily as you start your business, but when your lack of capital seriously compromises the service you're able to provide your customers, you're headed in the wrong direction. For example, if your lawn care business is behind schedule because you don't have the money to buy and maintain the equipment you need, you're in trouble.

Too Much Debt

A problem related to undercapitalization is having more debt than the business can handle. If your debt repayments each month are becoming difficult to manage, again—you're in trouble. Some small businesses start out with a reasonable debt but continue to borrow during cash flow crunches and end up accumulating more debt than they can pay off. Even if the small business owner is able to manage the debt payments, she's not left with enough money to reinvest in inventory and other expenses needed for growth.

Competition Issues

One of the dangers of operating your own business is that daily operations keep you so busy that it's tough to keep track of what's happening with the competition. However, just as you needed to analyze your competition prior to opening your business, you need to monitor what the competition is doing so that you can respond effectively—before your customers start shopping elsewhere.

If, for example, a competing business launches a major online catalog for its products, you'll need to assess whether you should follow suit. Will the competition's catalog fulfill your customers' needs more efficiently than your bricks-and-mortar store, for example? Or are there ways to let your customers know that you can provide better service for them in the store than they'll get online?

The Big Picture

There's a bigger issue when it comes to competition, too: You need to monitor what's happening in your industry and in the local economy—the big picture. If a major employer is pulling out of your area and taking a significant number of jobs with it, the customer base might no longer be able to support all of the competing businesses. You need to take steps to ensure that yours is one of the businesses that survives.

Charge What You're Worth

Charging a rate for your goods or services is related to your competition. If you price yourself significantly lower than the competition, you may be sending the message that your products are lower in quality. Price them too much higher, and the competition will consistently gain the customers who are looking for better value. You need to find the middle ground where you're charging what you're worth but also keeping pace with the competition.

Customer Service Issues

You may be the greatest roofer, accountant, or resume writer in the county, but if you treat your customers with disrespect, you'll find it difficult to stay in business. Just as word-of-mouth can work for you, it can work against you. If your customers are saying that you do great work, but that you're difficult to work with, new customers may be reluctant to take a risk on you.

Yes, there are nightmare customers who push the limits. But you can be fair and direct without being unpleasant. Every customer deserves to have calls returned promptly, appointments kept in a timely fashion, and paperwork maintained in good order. That goes for potential customers too. Even when you're going through a busy period and you can't handle their project right now, you never know when you'll need the customer's business. Call her back to let her know that you can't take on the work and perhaps refer her to a colleague. Both your colleague and the customer will appreciate it, possibly returning the favor at a later date.

Management Issues

Yes, the buck now stops with you. Technically, everything from cash flow issues to customer service problems is an issue that management—that means you—needs to deal with. But you'll also find that there are some issues that deal specifically with your management style.

If any of the following problems sound familiar, it's certainly not the end of the world. Take a deep breath, assess how much of the problem starts with you and decide how you're going to fix it. And remember: Identifying the problem means that you're halfway to fixing it.

Unrealistic Expectations

Inadequate market research can lead to wildly optimistic sales goals or customer volume expectations. You need your research to lead you to accurate estimates, not ones that are overly rosy. You'll end up with too much inventory on hand or too much debt for your sales to handle. It's also possible to overestimate your own ability to turn work around, which may put you in the position of breaking your promises to customers. Either way, you can't sustain a business when your expectations aren't realistic.

Waiting Until It's Too Late

Facing problems can be tough—you may need to acknowledge a poor decision or an element of the business that you've overlooked. Not facing problems can be even tougher, because when you finally dig into the numbers to analyze the depth of the crisis, it could be too late to save yourself. Take responsibility for both the good and the bad.

Poor Planning

Even the most brilliant businessperson will have a tough time making the best decisions without a road map. A business plan focuses your efforts, helps you measure your progress, and keeps you on budget. Don't start a home-based business without it—and once you're into daily operations, make sure that you continue to compare your progress against the plan.

Looking Too Much Like a Home-Based Business

A customer phones, and the call is answered by one of your young children who hasn't yet mastered the art of taking the message. A client drops by, and you spread his project out on the kitchen table while dirty dishes sit in the sink. Your clients might not care if you're a home-based business or a multinational as long as you're providing the product or service that they need. But if you look unprofessional, new clients will likely take their business to someone they could take more seriously.

Poor Time Management

You're busy all the time, but most of your customers are still waiting. Maybe you have more customers than you can handle—or maybe it's not the customers that are the problem. You might not manage your available time as well as you could. Keep track of how you spend your day, noting down everything that you do, and how long you do it for. You might surprise yourself with the time-wasters.

Resistance to Change

One of the most important qualities of a home-based businessperson is flexibility. If something isn't working in the business or in your management, you need to change it. Investigate how other businesses handle challenges, read business advice books from successful entrepreneurs, and assess whether you're actually holding yourself back.

A Final Word

Running a home-based business isn't for the faint of heart. It takes courage, a willingness to accept risk, and more effort than you're ever likely to put into working for someone else. But the rewards—independence, greater control over your time, a better sense of balancing work and family life, the chance to give your creativity free rein—can far outweigh everything else.

If a home-based business is right for you, sit down and plan your way through the opening and operation of the business, and then go for it. Sure, there'll be a few rough patches along the way, and you may even decide in the end that this is a temporary or part-time venture for you. That's absolutely fine—but you'll never know how successful you can be until you try.

appendix a

Glossary of Basic Business Terms

Account balance
The amount of a particular account at a given time.

Accounts payable
Amounts you owe vendors for supplies or services already provided.

Accounts receivable
Amounts that clients or customers owe you for products or services that you've provided.

Administrative expenses
Expenses related to managing the business rather than to sales or cost-of-goods-sold.

Aging
Tracking the time between now and when payment was due on an invoice (generally described in terms such as thirty days, sixty days, and ninety days overdue).

Amortization
The length of time over which the repayment of a debt is calculated.

Annual report
A yearly summary of the finances and general situation of a business.

Appraisal
An estimate of an asset's value.

Appreciation
The increase in an asset's value over time.

Arrears
An amount that's overdue, often used in relation to taxes.

Asset
Something of long-lasting value that is owned by you or the business.

Bad debts
Amounts owed to you that are uncollectible.

Balance sheet
A summary of the business's assets, liabilities, and equity.

Bill of sale
A receipt stating what was sold, to whom, when, and for how much.

Bottom line
Net profits, which is what's left over after all expenses are deducted from income.

Break-even analysis
A calculation of prices and costs that projects the point at which a business will make as much as it spends.

Budget
Projected income and expenses.

Business plan
A document that describes your business and its projected growth, including goals, strategies, and financial information such as revenues, expenses, and profits.

Capital
Money invested in a business.

Capital equipment
Assets such as vehicles that generally depreciate, or lose value over time.

Cash discount
A discount offered to a customer in exchange for paying immediately.

Cash flow
Tracking money as it flows into and out of a business.

Collateral
Something of value, such as a vehicle, that's pledged to a lender in order to secure a loan.

Commission
A percentage of the sales price paid to a salesperson.

Consignment
Placing products for sale with another business, which takes a percentage of the sales price in return.

Corporation
An incorporated business and a separate legal entity from its owners.

Cost of goods sold
The expenses that are directly related to the production or purchase of the products that you sell.

Current assets
Items such as cash or inventory that are assets of value, but which will be used up or converted to cash in the short term (within a year).

Current liabilities
Amounts due (payable) by a business in the short term (within a year), including outstanding bills, loan payments, taxes, etc.

Current ratio
The comparison of current assets and current liabilities.

Debt
Borrowed money that you or the business owe.

Depreciation
The decline in value of a capital asset over time.

Direct mail
Selling products or services by mail.

Distributor
A business that buys products from manufacturers for resale to retailers.

Entrepreneur
Someone who starts and runs his or her own business; often considered a positive risk-taker.

Equity
The value of a business after liabilities are subtracted from assets. This reflects the business's earnings over time and the start-up funding that the owners or investors contributed.

FIFO
Accounting for inventory on the basis of "first in; first out."

Franchise
A business that involves an ongoing relationship with a parent company, usually including a shared trade name and a franchise fee.

Gross profit
Sales revenues minus the cost of goods sold.

Income
Money that flows into a business.

Income statement
A summary of income and expenses for the business.

Interest
A percentage that you pay in return for borrowing money.

Inventory
Goods purchased for resale but not yet sold or raw materials to be used for making a product for sale.

Investment
Money (or other assets) put into the business.

Liability
Any debt or unpaid bill that the business owes.

Liquidity
How easily a business can convert assets to cash.

LIFO
Accounting for inventory on the basis of "last in; first out."

Limited liability company
An LLC, a type of business organization similar to an S corporation, in which the business exists separately from its owners, limiting their liability for the corporate debts.

Limited partnership
A type of business organization in which one or more of the partners is solely an investor and whose liability is limited to the amount invested.

Line of credit
An open source of funds up to a maximum, such as $10,000, that you can borrow as needed and pay back when possible with certain conditions.

Loan
A lump sum of money that is borrowed and then paid back with fixed payments over time.

Loan agreement
The written terms of a loan including the amount, term, and interest rate.

Market niche
A small part of a customer base that a business could target.

Market research
Finding out how big the market is for your business—how many potential customers there are, how much they spend, and what your competition is.

Marketing plan
A plan that identifies the market for a product or service and the methods by which the business will approach and sell to that market.

Merchandise
Product for sale.

Net sales
Sales revenue minus discounts and returns.

Net worth
What's left over when you subtract your liabilities from your assets (what you owe from what you own).

Operating costs
What it costs you to run the business on a day-to-day basis.

Overhead
Ongoing administrative costs that typically need to be paid no matter how much or how little you sell.

Partnership
A type of business organization that involves two or more people who are owners (not employees) and who are fully liable for the debts of the business.

Payables
Money due to suppliers of products or services.

Principal
The amount of money that's borrowed.

Profit and Loss statement
A financial statement, also known as a P&L or an Income Statement, which shows a business's income and expenses.

Pro forma
A projected estimate, as in a pro forma income statement.

Projections
Estimates of future sales, expenses, or profits.

Publicity
News stories in the media that you haven't paid for. They're considered editorial, not advertising.

Receivables
Amounts that clients or customers owe you for products or services that you've provided.

Residential zone
An area of a community set aside for homes.

Retail sales
Sales to the public.

Retailing
Selling to the public.

Revenue
Money coming into a business.

S Corporation
Also known as an S Corp, a form of incorporation providing tax and liability benefits, often used for small businesses.

Sales lead
A potential customer.

Sole proprietorship
The simplest form of business organization, in which there is only one owner and that owner is personally liable for the debts of the business.

Target market
The specific group of customers to which a business expects to sell.

Telemarketing
Selling by telephone.

Trade association
A group dedicated to serving a particular trade or kind of business.

Turnover
The frequency with which inventory sells, or "turns over" during the year.

Venture capital
Outside investment in a business.

Wholesale
Selling (or buying) items that are destined for resale to the public.

Working capital
The money needed to operate the business on a day-to-day basis—usually the difference between current assets and current liabilities.

Zoning
The division of a community into zones set aside for specific uses, including residential, commercial, or industrial.

appendix b

Sample Business Plan: Gift Baskets Galore

This sample (and briefer than usual) business plan is intended to show a start-up business as the owner moves from conceptualizing the business into operating it on a day-to-day basis. A business plan provides a "road map" for the first year of operation that will help the owner establish who the customers are, how best to reach them, and how sales should flow throughout the year.

Executive Summary

The mission of Gift Baskets Galore (GBG) is to bring joy, comfort, and inspiration into the lives of its customers by delivering affordable, imaginative gift baskets that connect the giver and the recipient at key moments in time.

Customers can be divided into several categories based on who they're giving the baskets to: businesspeople, friends, family, and networking acquaintances. Gift Baskets Galore reaches its customers primarily through its Web site, which allows visitors to preview standard gift baskets by "occasion" category in a range of price points or to request custom-designed baskets. Visitors can select, order, and pay for their baskets on the Web site or by calling the phone number that's prominently displayed on the site.

The business operates in a marketplace that has other gift basket competitors including florist shops and supermarkets. However, GBG sets itself apart by focusing solely on gift baskets, by pricing them affordably, and by providing services for both buyers and recipients that have a uniquely personal touch, thus encouraging repeat business and referrals.

GBG is a sole proprietorship that's owned and operated by a college-trained floral designer with seven years of experience in the industry, primarily spent in supermarket floral/accessory sales departments. It is a recently launched home-based business located just outside the downtown core of a city with a population of 10,000. GBG's goal is to generate $15,500 in sales in its first year, increasing to $20,000 in year two, and $30,000 in year three. The owner is running the business part-time while also caring for their own pre-school children. Long-term plans include switching to full-time business operation when the children enter school full-time. If the business begins to exceed its sales targets, and thus the time available from the owner, contingency plans include hiring an employee to handle the work overflow.

Marketing Plan

In terms of its overall market, GBG operates in a community that is well diversified in its economic base with businesses in the manufacturing, resource, information technology, and health sectors. The regulatory framework for home-based businesses here is not burdensome: The state has no sales tax, and the home-based business permit for GBG was approved without difficulty. In summary, the economic climate is healthy, with no immediate threats to it.

Target Market and Customer Characteristics

GBG's customer purchases are occasion-driven and include birthdays, anniversaries, thank-yous, get well wishes, congratulations, and employee recognition. Customers tend to be those without the time or desire to assemble their own gift baskets. Part of the purchase process is therefore a need for convenience and for imaginative baskets/contents that make people say, "I wouldn't have thought of that."

Customers can be found across demographic categories, but individual repeat clients tend to be men and women with incomes of more than $50,000 a year, indicating that they have busy lives and need gift solutions that are meaningful and yet convenient to purchase. Repeat business clients are often in service businesses, such as real estate agents. Late November through December is expected to be one of the busiest times of the year for GBG, because businesses purchase holiday gifts at that time. GBG's location near downtown, where many business offices are located, makes quick deliveries possible.

GBG's greatest potential for increasing its client base is the business sector, where it can be promoted as a convenient, personal (yet appropriate), and high-quality tool for customer care, and employee/supplier recognition. GBG will not overlook the potential of its individual clients, however, promoting itself as a solution for those gift-giving times that require a personal touch.

Competitive Analysis

GBG's primary competitors include supermarket floral departments and stand-alone florist/gift shops. Supermarket gift basket prices tend to be slightly lower than GBG prices, but they draw their products from within their own store: Customers may view them as somewhat limited in scope and personal touch as a result. Florist/gift shops are comparable in price to GBG, but because baskets are a secondary product line, they have a more limited range of gift baskets than GBG.

GBG's SWOT analysis includes:

- **Strengths:** the personal and creative touches that it provides to its customers, including thank-you notes that are sent to basket buyers along with order delivery confirmation.
- **Weaknesses:** the lack of a physical location for customers to drop by and select gift basket products.
- **Opportunities:** GBG does not currently have a presence in local hospital gift shops, and could pursue this as a revenue stream.
- **Threats:** the potential for competitors to recognize GBG's strengths, such as its personal touches and its extensive Web site resources, and copy them.

Marketing Strategies

To make up for the lack of a physical location, GBG needs to focus on attracting customers to its Web site. Because the business does not have a significant advertising budget, GBG will focus on attracting positive publicity through local newspapers and magazines. A publicity plan targeting specific publications with story ideas will be developed. In addition, GBG's Web site address and phone number will be prominently displayed on all communication materials. The Web site will also be assessed for its search engine rating so that key words can be increased if necessary.

In addition, GBG will contact local hospital gift shops to offer its services as a value-added product line. Although the gift shop will likely require a portion of the sales price, the advantage for GBG is that select baskets can be displayed within the gift shop and available for immediate purchase, This should increase sales and will reach a currently under-served customer niche market. It will have the added benefit of providing a public display space for select gift baskets.

GBG will also assess marketing tools such as discount programs for repeat customers and for customer referrals. It will also research local service-oriented businesses to determine which ones to target with personalized letters of introduction and follow-up with free sample baskets during a personal interview.

Financial Data

GBG operates from a dedicated room in the owner's home, where baskets and contents are stored and assembled. Furnishing requirements are minimal: a large folding table and a comfortable office chair. The owner's personal computer has now been transferred to use as a business asset. The owner also uses a personal vehicle for gift basket delivery, entering business usage in a mileage register.

As a result of this reduced requirement for capital equipment, funding has not been sought from outside sources. The owner relies on an unsecured personal line of credit with a maximum of $10,000, but follows a policy of never using more than $5,000 of the available credit at any one time. This limits the owner's exposure to too much debt, while also providing a ready source of funding if personal or business emergencies arise.

Financial Statements and Ratios

Sample financial statements can be found in Chapter 5, on page 62 (income statement) and 63 (cash flow projection) and 64 (balance sheet).

The income statement shows that in the first year of operation, cost of goods sold is 51 percent of gross sales and that operating expenses are 29 percent of gross sales, leaving room for a net profit for the owner of 20 percent of gross sales at year's end. Finding a cheaper source of supplies for the gift baskets is essential in order to bring down the cost of goods sold. The owner needs to manage operating expenses to reduce them as much as possible. Sales need to be increased if the business is to be sustainable—if it is to provide a reasonable return on the owner's time and funds for payment of the owner's income taxes.

From the cash flow projections, it can easily be seen that the owner will be forced to use the line of credit funding to support the business for the first two months that the business is operating. The owner will only start to see positive cash flow balances, and the possibility of beginning to repay the line of credit from the business in the third month.

From the balance sheet, the debt-to-assets ratio at March 31 is $3,085 divided by $8,085, which equals 38 percent. This means that 38 percent of the business's assets are currently financed by debt. As the business begins to make money and the debt begins to be repaid, this ratio will decrease.

Financial Targets

To reach the sales target of $15,500 in the first year, assuming an average price of a basket at $60, sales targets for the year are 259 baskets, basically the sale of five baskets per week. Realistically, however, some weeks (prior to Valentine's Day, possibly, and during late November/December) will be much busier than others.

Based on the percentages from the above analysis, the break-even point in terms of number of baskets can be determined. The calculation is as follows: the year's operating costs ($4,500) divided by (the unit selling price [assume an average of $60] minus the unit cost of goods sold [51 percent or $30.60]). This equals $4,500 divided by $29.40, just over 153 baskets. This means that GBG will need to sell 154 baskets to cover the business's costs and that each sale after the sale of the 154th basket will increase the business's profit.

Sales Plan

Based on the target markets and the marketing plans, the following sales targets have been set for the first year:

- Business sales: 144
- Individual consumer sales: 75
- Hospital sales: 40

Marketing Plan

The business owner, who has sole responsibility for owning and operating the business, has a college certificate in floral design, which included course material that dealt with gift basket design. She gained experience by working as a paid employee in the floral departments of major supermarkets for seven years.

The owner's experience and education mean that she is well versed in the creation of new and innovative gift baskets for GBG's product line; however, the administrative and strategic tasks involved in running a small business are less familiar to her. In order to improve this situation, professional development over the coming year will include four weekend workshops (one per quarter), dealing with bookkeeping, tax issues for small businesses, inventory control, and marketing.

In addition, the owner is working on an ongoing basis with a volunteer coach at the local small business development center to identify and solve problems for the business.

In terms of daily business operations, the owner is currently able to manage gift basket order taking and creation and delivery of gift baskets on her own. However, busy periods such as Valentine's Day and pre-holiday November/December sales could increase volume to the point where she can only handle two of those three tasks. Strategically, the owner has decided that she needs to handle order taking and basket creation to retain control over the creative side of the business.

Delivery, however, is something that can be delegated to someone else. The owner will investigate, prior to the onset of the busy periods, whether a local courier company would be willing to partner with GBG to deliver the gift baskets at a discounted price. If this price is out of reach of GBG's resources, then the owner will hire an independent contractor to handle basket delivery in their own vehicle.

In the longer term, GBG will grow, as the owner's time and resources allow, from a part-time operation to a full-time operation. As time progresses, the owner will determine whether employees will need to be hired and business space expanded.

appendix c

Home-Based Business Resources

Business.gov
www.business.gov

Federal Trade Commission
www.ftc.gov

Internal Revenue Service
www.irs.gov

U.S. Census Bureau
www.census.gov

U.S. Department of Commerce
www.commerce.gov

U.S. Department of Labor
www.dol.gov

U.S. Small Business Administration
www.sba.gov
1-202-205-6600

U.S. Social Security Administration
www.ssa.gov

Canada Revenue Agency
www.cra.gc.ca

Industry Canada
www.ic.gc.ca

Personal Information Protection and Electronic Documents Act (Canada)
www.privcom.gc.ca

Statistics Canada
www.statcan.ca

appendix d

Supporting Associations and Organizations

American Bar Association
www.abanet.org

American Home Business Association
www.homebusiness.com

Canadian Bar Association
www.cba.org

Home Office Association of America
www.hoaa.com

International Franchise Association
www.franchise.org

Internet Business Standards Association
www.internetstandards.org

National Association of the Self-Employed
www.nase.org

National Association of Professional Organizers
www.napo.net

PC World
www.pcworld.com

Professional Organizers in Canada
www.organizersincanada.com

Service Corps of Retired Executives
www.score.org

Index

A

B

C

D

E

F